AF593526

the GUINNESS guide to freshwater angling

the GUINNESS guide to freshwater angling

PAUL BOYER - BRIAN HARRIS

illustrations
henri deuil

guinness superlatives ltd.

contents

introduction 10

the fish's world 17

the salmonids
salmon 28
trout 70
charr 102
grayling 106

predators
pike 124
perch 142
zander 148
black bass 154

cyprinids
carp 164
chub 176
roach 186
other cyprinids 190

other fish 207

tackle 218

the future 224

glossary 232

The original text of this beautifully illustrated book was in French and when I was first asked to read some of the translated text for an English edition I was frankly a little dubious.

Although fishing is truly global in its popularity, there are many different trends, fashions if you like, concerning how it should be done. And besides the more practical aspects of the sport, there are diverse opinions concerning the ethics.

For example, many French coarse-fish anglers take fish such as pike, carp, tench and gudgeon to eat; a British coarse fisher scorns such a practice and returns 99 per cent of his captures to the water alive.

British coarse fishers use rods of between 10 and 13 ft (3–4 m) long, in general, the rods equipped with rings and with modern reels that permit a baited hook and terminal tackle to be cast 40 yards (36·50 m) or more with ease. The rods are so well made, the reels so beautifully engineered, that in the hands of a competent angler even fish of 20 lb (9 kg) or so may be subdued on line of, perhaps, only 5 lb (2·26 kg) test. The French coarse fisher, and trout bait-fisher however, favour a very long rod, often more than 16 ft (5 m) long, maybe 25 ft (8 m), and many of these rods are used without a reel, the line being fixed to the slim rod tip by a rubber attachment which acts as a shock absorber to protect the delicate line used. Also, many of these rods used by French anglers—and by those in Germany, the Low Countries and Italy, for example—are of the telescopic type. And as I have said, these very long rods without reels, specially telescopic ones, are not favoured by most British coarse anglers.

Having pointed out some of the reasons for my initial misgivings about this book being produced in an English version, I can now say how it was I came to change my mind.

My sudden change of attitude occurred when I was shown the actual book, the French version, and flipped the pages of superb colour and monochrome photographs, of fine drawings which very clearly explain what the written word cannot do alone.

I began to see that here was a book from which we British anglers could benefit.

Rumanian fisherman fly-fishing in a small tributary of the Danube. ▶

Continental anglers may not be superior to British anglers in all spheres—it would be very strange if total superiority could be proved on either side—but in recent years French and other European anglers have taught our British match anglers a thing or two and caused not a little consternation in the camp. But—and this is an important point—British anglers are beginning to adopt French competition tactics and more of the French tackle that was once thought to be "no good for our sort of fishing".

If further justification for this English version of the book is necessary, then look for it in the number of French artificial lures which for many years have been so popular with British anglers.

So far I have talked of the differences between freshwater angling in France and in Britain; but there are many similarities, too; much common ground. In fly-fishing, for example, there is perhaps more standardisation, both of technique and ethics, than in any other branch of angling.

There has been much exchanging of ideas, on tackle and techniques, between British and French fly-fishers. Charles Ritz (actually Swiss), Tony Burnand and the great caster Pierre Creusevaut are Frenchmen who have been appreciated in Britain for many years. Frank Sawyer, the famous Hampshire angler and riverkeeper, Geoffrey Bucknall and the late Oliver Kite have similarly earned reputations in France. Firms like Pezon et Michel, Mitchell, Lerc, Mauborgne in France and Hardy, Farlow, Sharpes and Veniards in Britain have sold their wares both ways to further the cause of continuous progress in fly-fishing.

Reading this book, looking at the illustrations, one has to admit that the popular idea in most British anglers' minds, of all French coarse-fish anglers sitting side by side along scummy canals or rivers and "tiddler-snatching" with their roachpoles, is far from accurate.

I have attempted to retain as much of the original material and thought in this version as is reasonably possible, at the same time introducing new material I felt to be essential to avoid a unilateral aspect—and to avoid the publishers being inundated with letters from British anglers who might have felt a completely straight translation of the original text a trifle confusing.

Brian Harris

introduction

fishing: mystery, cunning, duels

From time immemorial men have occupied themselves with fishing; prehistoric man had to catch fish to eat and twentieth-century man fishes both for food and amusement. Is fishing more of an art than a sport? It seems difficult to answer this question categorically: on the one hand there are various ways of fishing; on the other, art may be a sport and vice versa.

The practice of fishing will always be characterised by the unexpected and the mystery existing under the mirror-like surface of the water, because to us the world of the fish is totally alien, and herein lies the difference between hunting and fishing. Without wishing to belittle the art and the sport of hunting, a different, but complementary parallel to the art of fishing can be traced. These two factors have always been closely linked: early man had no other means of sustaining life and he was totally dependent on these two activities for his survival.

In hunting, the dog detects the game, stops it or springs it and what follows is only a question of weapons and skill. In fishing everything is different; man cannot catch a fish without deceiving it, so it becomes a question of permanent cunning. Fishing is dependent on a large number of favourable or unfavourable factors, the obvious one being the presence of the fish.

Feeding the fish to attract them, or to keep them where they are, even the use of the correct bait and tackle, will not necessarily ensure that the fish will bite.

To make the fish bite is a problem which mathematicians could not solve, so variable are the data—atmospheric pressure, air temperature, water temperature, state of the water, water level, prevailing wind in relation to the course of the river, and many others.

And what about the bait? And the tackle? What size hook should be used to catch bleak on paste: 18, 20, 22? And the line: $\frac{3}{4}$ lb b.s. or $1\frac{1}{4}$ lb b.s. (340 g–570 g)? Such choices have a considerable bearing on the success of the catch.

In game fishing skill is also important and if added to the other qualities of a good fisherman make him an ace with fly or spinner. However, fishing is above all a duel between man and fish, because for most people the pleasure of fishing lies half in getting a bite and half in overcoming a vigorous adversary fighting to avoid death in an alien element.

fishermen back in favour

Alphonse Allais poked savage fun at the angler when he wrote: "Fishing is a line with a worm at one end and a fool at the other." In those days such remarks might have been harmful, but now the image of angling and the people who practise it has changed a great deal. Today more than 8 million fishermen in Great Britain and France can be said to constitute a modern social phenomenon. Who are these fishermen? Recent surveys have provided these surprising percentages: management 34 per cent; office workers 19 per cent; manual workers 15 per cent; students 15 per cent; others 17 per cent. Therefore a general social rehabilitation of angling seems to have taken place. The sport has for too long been a victim of class distinctions in which, for example, the fly-fisherman tended to scorn the coarse fishermen, dressed in overalls, sitting on their fishing baskets. On some rivers spinning experts even looked down condescendingly at the "peasants" fishing with long bamboo rods and worms.

Today, happily, the old senseless rivalries between the practitioners of various types of fishing have virtually disappeared, and modern anglers feel free to indulge in the type of sport they most enjoy, whether it be coarse or game fishing—or both.

the sport of fishing

Fishing, an art and a science under Izaak Walton, became a popular sport under Michel Duborgel, which does not exclude it from being both an art and a science today. Some fishing techniques are more athletic than others. In coarse fishing, for example, the fisherman baits up a swim and may fish for hours without moving. In contrast fly-fishing or spinning imply much more frequent movement. All these types of fishing will be discussed. The sport which fishing provides varies not only according to the different methods, but also according to the fish. The salmon, the trout and in general all the salmonids and carnivores can be classed as sporting fish. There are also fish, such as the chub, which can be classed as game or coarse fish according to the method by which they are caught—by dry fly, for example, or by stalking with natural or even live-bait, or by spinning.

The angler casting a line from a canal bank will not have much in common with his fellow sportsman wading in a fast-flowing mountain river or among the slippery rocks of a torrent. Therefore it is possible to define the sport of fishing as depending not only on the venue but also on the fish and the tackle. Generally the mountain fisherman is ignorant of the techniques of the match or coarse fisherman in still water or in a slow river. Conversely, the latter will know little of fishing methods in a torrent or broken water. However, the movement of population and the ubiquitousness of the car have tended to modify this. While on holiday or spending the week-end in the country numerous city dwellers have discovered the joys of fishing in trout streams, while many country dwellers moving into the big urban centres have learned the techniques and subtleties of bait fishing in rivers or ponds. It is becoming increasingly clear that fishermen are willing to enlarge their knowledge and their experience.

The number of anglers is increasing yearly throughout the world. Similarly, fishing tackle is improving and techniques are evolving very rapidly.

At a time when we are being promised more leisure time in the future, it is noticeable that fishing is the pastime which attracts the largest number of newcomers, whether they are only summertime freshwater fishermen or sea fishermen. Fishing answers a need for escape, a need for the overworked man to soak himself in the calm of nature, without remaining inactive.

The practice of fishing is closely linked with the knowledge of the medium: the water. It is necessary to study its composition, its flora and fauna—and above all its fish.

Naturalists very often make the mistake of not being fishermen, so that in the world which surrounds us the fish seems to play the part of the poor relation to the bird. It is high time that the fish took its rightful place in the animal world, at a more honourable level.

a leisure pursuit

The phenomenon of angling may be a surprise from various points of view, particularly in its economic importance. In 1936 in Great Britain the turnover in fishing was £23 million. Nowadays, according to certain calculations, this figure has risen to £40 million. Half of the fishermen in Europe are said to spend more than £40 a year per head on tackle and equipment. In the economic context of fishing "tourist fishing" and the effect of fishing on the promotion of the hotel industry and its subsidiaries must be mentioned. Fishing must also have a considerable bearing on the development of camping and caravaning.

What importance can fishing have for the man of the 1970s? How would the Marcuses, the Galbraiths, or the Khans answer this question? What philosopher or sociologist will one day make up his mind to produce an exhaustive study on the modern phenomenon of fishing?

In this age of extreme materialism in which man is becoming more and more a slave to his insatiable appetite for the luxuries of modern life, what can fishing bring to him? Jean Lestrade, translator and adapter of the writings of Izaak Walton, has written these words: "Free from vain cares this life glides on its way; a beautiful river full of sunshine; an exemplary life. And to our age, prone to foolish and inhuman fears, he is an example worth thinking about." Fishing is a school, a school for patience, moderation, sang-froid and tenacity. Man needs his intelligence to deceive the fish, to catch it, and also in certain circumstances to protect it and ensure its reproduction.

The fisherman must accept defeat, must not resent returning home empty-handed, and he must accept the moods of the fish or the ever unpredictable whims of nature. He must master his own failings, and always act calmly and precisely however he is fishing.

All arts and sports improve the individual and fishing is no exception to this rule. Maurice Genevoix, one of the most illustrious enthusiasts of nature, insists that fishing is one of the keys to happiness when he writes: "One more fisherman, in fact, another, and yet another. What happy men! What poets!" Jean Venesmes, Tony Burnand, Maurice Toesca, Louis de Boisset and many others have shown that fishing is quite simply a philosophy, and that is a great deal.

literature

Although more restrained than the literature on hunting, the literature on fishing is an interesting collection of works. Numerous books have appeared since those of the fisherman and poet Izaak Walton, who was one of the leading lights in English letters in the seventeenth century. Guyonnet, Rouquet, Walker, Skues, Marsvallet, Sawyer, Lacouche, Ivens, Barbellion, Bourgeois, Biguet, Righyni, Helluin, Ritz, are only a few of the best known. One might think that they and others must have written everything about fishing. This is why certain critics of fishing write regularly: "After this book we cannot see the possibility of another, so exhaustive was this one about . . . fishing, a fish or a region."

Yet other books still appear. They do not necessarily claim to create a sensation in an area in which the sensational scarcely exists. The present age of change produces numerous books on the different types of fishing, the varieties of fish and on different countries. They are certainly all interesting, because progress makes a book a kind of guide and guides inevitably become out of date.

So twenty years or more ago the appearance on the scene of the fixed-spool reel, the light rod and nylon lines were to revolutionise fishing methods. A few years later fibreglass was to completely alter fishing, or rather angling. Similarly with baits—plastic materials, their pliability, their resemblance to the real thing means that certain artificial baits are as readily taken as natural ones. Fishing is bound to progress and therefore several books appear as landmarks at each stage.

The acclimatisation of new species means that new books may be needed to provide original material on the subject; for example, forty or fifty years ago little was known about the *hotu* (nase) which today has invaded numerous waters. The rainbow trout which many fishing societies are now stocking—and in some cases overstocking—was hardly known. The zander, a fish which until recently was virtually unknown, has now replaced the pike in the catch of numerous fishermen. A magazine of about fifty years ago features an article in favour of the catfish and its acclimatisation in European waters and rivers; different reviews are just as ecstatic about the qualities of the sun-perch or rainbow-perch.

In the landing-net . . . the decisive moment of capture. ▶

Time has shown that these two introductions were mistakes, but today they exist and must be taken into account.

All this explains the evolution of fishing, of fish, and also of the literature on fishing.

In the following pages fishing and fish in general, or at least the principal sorts of fishing and the principal fish caught on rod and line in Europe, will be discussed. Of course, in order to understand fishing better it would be necessary to start with the local conditions prevailing in each region, each river, and on certain typical beats, taking into account the nature of the water in relation to the surrounding land, the natural features, surrounding vegetation, the river-bed growth and obstacles.

Therefore references will be in conditional rather than absolute terms, in order to allow the reader the chance of examining for himself a river, its biotope and the methods of fishing which are suitable to each particular case.

brief history

One may safely assume that the origin of fishing is closely linked with that of the human race. Having been drawn by hunger to the edges of lakes or rivers prehistoric man rapidly developed ways of catching fish.

The results of archaeological excavations support these claims as fish bones and shells have been discovered on many prehistoric sites. Some archaeologists believe that before the Paleolithic Age man lived principally on fish and only later ventured into the hostile forests to hunt for the mammals which became his staple diet. The use of boats and hooks probably goes back as far as the beginning of the Neolithic Age, a period which saw the advent of fishing in its true sense.

Harpoons, gorges and then hooks were man's first fishing tools and whether they were fashioned from stone, bone, shells or thorns were equally effective for catching adequate supplies of fish. The revolutionary discovery and use of the first practical fishing net completely changed early man's fishing habits. For the first time he was able to catch more than he and his family required and so inevitably a crude form of trade and barter evolved.

However, man's inventive mind was continually working to ensure his food and survival, and about 2,000 years ago the bronze hook with barb appeared. Archaeological discoveries have enabled historians to compile a chronology of fishing in ancient times.

The Assyrians, Egyptians, Greeks, Romans and Chinese all appreciated the importance of fishing. The Bible contains numerous references to fishing, such as the miraculous catch on Lake Tiberius and the miracle of the five loaves and two fishes. Several of the apostles were involved in the flourishing fishing industry and it is not surprising that St. Peter has become the patron saint of all fishermen.

A capitulary of Charlemagne made in 800 was probably the first law concerning fishing. Later, in the year 1280, a statute of Philippe III prescribed rules for the mesh of nets and the size of fish, particularly pike and chub. Colbert, more than three centuries ago, forsaw and feared pollution, and in 1669 his statute on waters and forests contains the first anti-pollution law and its consequent penalties. "No throwing of lime, nux vomica, Indian berry, tar and other drugs or bait into rivers on pain of corporal punishment."

The importance of fishing has thus grown and developed over millions of years to the industry, art and sport that it is today.

◂ *Fishermen from Central Europe and Brittany. Both inspired by the same passion.*

The Rio Narcea, a magnificent Spanish coastal river (Asturias). ▶

The Driva, a Norwegian torrent pouring into a Sunndalsora fjord.

▼

the fish's world

▲ *Winter on the Loire near its confluence with the Allier.*

◄ *Lake Aureilhant. A peaceful waterway in the flat Landes region.*

the river basin

The fishing area of the continent of Europe is extremely varied. On the one hand it is made up of scores of large rivers and their tributaries, smaller rivers, streams, torrents and dykes, and on the other by the still waters, lakes, ponds, reservoirs and canals. Each river basin is demarcated by mountains or hills which cause the direction of flow of the water, their valleys giving birth to the streams and small rivers which feed the main river. This great collector flows towards the sea, either directly when the descent is steep like the course of the Rhône, or slowly with numerous bends, when more gentle, like that of the Seine.

M. Charpy, the engineer-in-chief of Waters and Forests, and Secretary of the Fishing Council, has recorded 169,105 miles (272,150 kilometres) of river water and about 580,000 square miles (150,000 hectares) of still water in France alone. These figures speak for themselves and indicate that the waters available for fishing are far from being overloaded in spite of the continual increase in the number of anglers. Pascal said: "Rivers are moving roads", and it could be added that water is the source of life and therefore no one has the right to pollute it. The great evil of this age, pollution, ruins the water, kills the flora and fauna and renders it lifeless. Fishermen were the first, more than fifty years ago, to denounce both the industrial pollution and organic pollution caused by urban centres pumping sewage directly into a river.

The flora and fauna and the mixing of the water absorb and decompose the organic refuse to a certain extent and in most cases it is an efficient sort of self-purification. However, there are such concentrations of polluted water that some large rivers and certain stretches of European watercourses have been rendered useless as far as fishing is concerned.

More than thirty years ago, speaking about the harm done to fishing, Louis de Boisset wrote: "Desperate ills call for desperate remedies." He was referring to the great evils that progress can bring out, hoping at the same time that progress could manage to control the harm it produced. But this was not the case then and it is still not the case today. However, a great step forward has been taken, as, thanks in large measure to the efforts of fishermen, public opinion and the powers that be, all nations have at last become conscious of the imminent and very grave dangers presented by all types of water pollution.

A river basin constitutes a biological unity and the numerous manifestations of life can be studied in different ways for the whole length of a river, starting from its source. It is a question of this biological whole coming under the influence of different factors, which may be geological, physical or chemical. Great ichthyologists like Leger, Kreitmann and many others have recognised that each river basin is divided into zones each possessing a predominating fish. These zones are delineated by the nature of the water, its temperature and altitude, the nature of the river bed and all other relevant conditions.

The source might be glacier water, which is practically sterile. This is followed by the trout zone, a mountain beat with highly oxygenated water in a relatively poor biotope. Then comes the home of the barbel and the grayling with well oxygenated water of a slightly higher temperature and more hospitable river bed. This stretch of the river may be very long and is characterised by a fine silt bottom and is not so fast flowing but has deep undercurrents.

Further on is the haunt of other coarse fish, mostly cyprinids which proliferate according to temperature and food. These include chub, bream, tench and carp with their normal predators, the carnivores: pike, perch, black bass, zander, eels, etc. In Europe this is without doubt the most extensive stretch of most waterways.

Finally there is the mixed environment of the deltas or estuaries. As the river approaches the sea the salt content of the water increases and the biotope varies. Apart from the migratory fish such as salmon, shad, eels and lampreys there are also lesser travellers which live periodically in both salt and fresh water: notably the mullet and the flounder. Next we come to the lakes.

Rivers sometimes flow into lakes which have differing zones: the clear shallow regions near the bank, and areas of deep green and blue water along the edge of a steep shelf, called a "mont"

An artificial fly hooked in the jaw of a brown trout. The symbol of angling.

in the sub-alpine lakes.

Oxygen content varies with depth and temperature. As well as these factors pressure or lack of light create the particular conditions which, in a lake, help to support an enormous variety of freshwater fish.

In general, then, it can be said that trout are found at the sources of such rivers as the Rhine, the Seine, the Loire, the Garonne, the Avon and Wye. The middle courses of these rivers provide the home of the coarse fish and their habitual predators, whilst in the lower reaches are to be found both sea and freshwater fish. There are special cases, particularly in coastal rivers. Thus in Norway or Ireland, for example, a relatively short, highly oxygenated coastal river flowing from the mountains may contain only trout.

On the other hand, some lowland rivers exist which, theoretically, are not suitable for game fish, although occasionally chub may be found in stretches which would seem eminently suitable for trout.

diagram of a river system showing the typical fish species in their zones

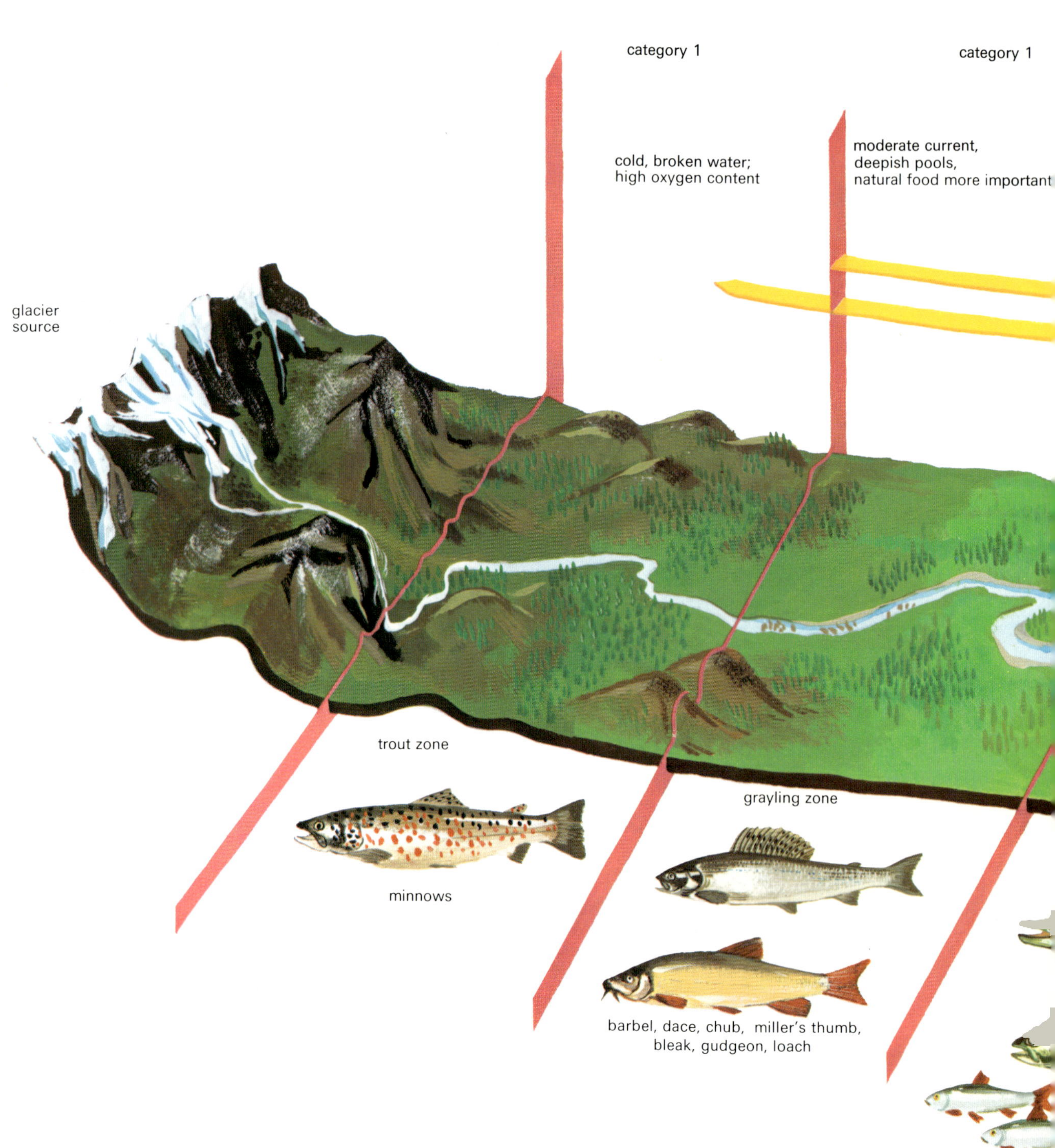

Shown in this diagram are: the main species found in the various stretches; the arrows indicate the stretches frequented by most freshwater fish, including migratory species.

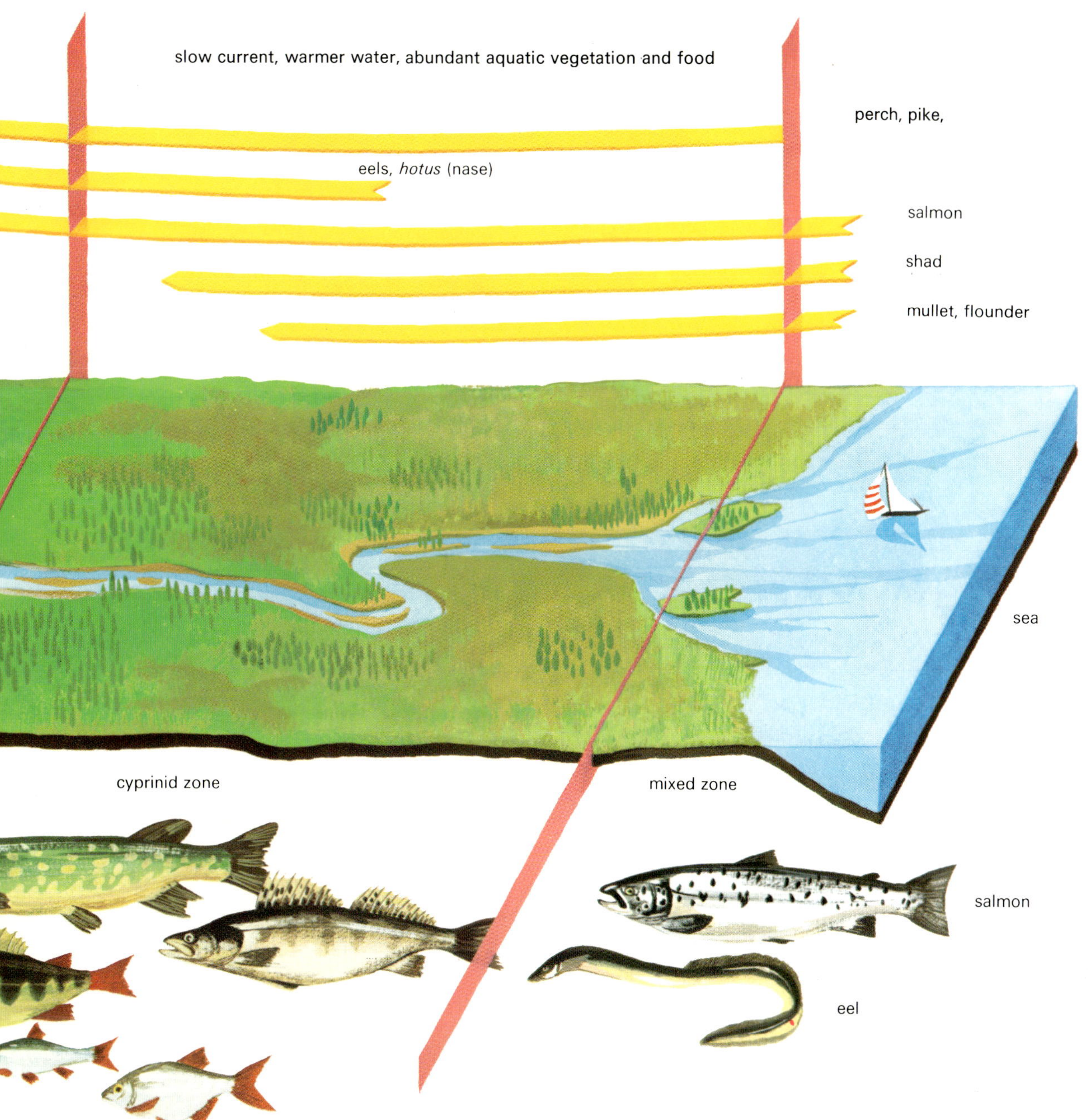
category 2
estuary
slow current, warmer water, abundant aquatic vegetation and food
perch, pike,
eels, *hotus* (nase)
salmon
shad
mullet, flounder
sea
cyprinid zone
mixed zone
salmon
eel
bleak, bream, tench, carp, pike, perch, zander

biological balance

Each stretch in a watercourse possesses a different biotope which determines both the quality and quantity of fish to be found. A carp will not survive in a mountain stream: on the one hand because the current and the cold water do not suit it and on the other because it will not be able to find food. Put a trout in a sluggish river and it will be able to find food far superior to that of its original habitat—but the high temperature and low oxygen content of the water may either kill it or cause it to flee upstream.

Ecological factors such as current, temperature and chemical composition mean that it is impossible to be specific in the classification of rivers and their fish populations. There are so many variables that only generalisations are possible, even though most eminent ichthyologists have made definite statements concerning the biological balance of a particular stretch of river, a lake or a pond. Without wishing to deny the existence of this balance, it is wiser to say, paradoxically enough, that there is a dynamic equilibrium controlled by a series of variables.

If this balance is upset nature can usually manage to correct it without man's intervention. In this domain the part played by the predators is crucial. When one species proliferates too quickly the number of predators increases in proportion. However, if they in turn become too numerous their numbers are quickly reduced by the shortage of food. Every year fishing clubs carry out massive restocking, believing that in this way they can satisfy the demands of the growing numbers of fishermen. These efforts are usually doomed to failure because each stretch, each sector, even each square yard of river bed and cubic yard of water will feed only a certain quantity of fish, and when they become overpopulated it means that the fish will either migrate, or die, or cannibalism will increase, even among those of the same species. The fish that survive suffer from disease and become stunted.

Thus the number of fish in a river can only be increased if the capacity of the river to feed them is also increased. For example, the creation of artificial waterfalls to produce more oxygen, the growing of aquatic plants, and the addition of lime to the water to enrich the bottom and aid the production of nymphs and crustacea and other small sub-aquatic animals can be successfully carried out in trout streams.

predators

In their own habitat the role of pike and other carnivores which limit the stock of coarse fish is well known, as is that of eels and crayfish, the freshwater scavengers. However, too often little or nothing is known of the effective role of certain birds such as the heron, the kingfisher and the gull, which the fisherman often detests. The presence of these birds in certain waters is in a way a proof of their rich fish population.

Unfortunately previous generations had the habit of regarding too many predators as harmful. Nowadays, when more than mere lip-service is paid to ecology by the experts, the problem of vermin has been reconsidered and it is realised that all these predators are not in fact harmful. They play a very important role in limiting certain over-prolific species and in eliminating sick and feeble stocks.

However, in all natural environments the deadliest predator is man himself, as it is he who blindly destroys the balance of nature by his excessive demands on it. It might seem rather paradoxical to stress the need for conservation in a work like this, in which the aim is to teach the reader more about fish and how to catch them. However, this conservation is essential. Make no mistake, it is the fundamental basis of all our future fishing. Conservation means firstly a sensible adult approach to fishing; and secondly, the rearing of fish in fish farms to replenish and maintain stocks.

Trout hatchery on the Hampshire Avon at Charlton Mill, Wiltshire. ▶

fish breeding

It is not without reason that the association of French fishing clubs is called the A.P.P.: Association de Pêche et de Pisciculture (Association of Fishing and Fish Culture).

It seems that pisciculture is an inseparable part of both professional still-water fishing and its amateur freshwater counterpart. Artificial fertilisation, the installation of Vibert boxes in the water, a natural method of restocking trout, pike culture and all forms of fish breeding contribute to the success of the breeder's world and help to maintain the biological balance already mentioned.

Certainly fish can and do reproduce freely and prolifically, but reproduction and spawning are affected by a variety of factors. Drought, violent floods and too low a water temperature can prevent these functions.

The fecundity of fish varies considerably, e.g.: trout, 2,000 eggs per kg of weight; salmon, 1,500–2,000; pike, 30,000; perch 100,000; bream, 40,000; carp, 140,000; tench, 600,000; burbot, 1,000,000.

So it is evident that extremely fertile fish such as tench or burbot would quickly overrun a stretch of water without the presence of predators.

However, it is necessary to qualify this. Not all the eggs laid are necessarily fertilised, the level of fertility varying according to the conditions at the time of laying. Sometimes more than 50 per cent are lost after fertilisation, and there are large losses, particularly amongst the salmonids, when the young fish face the almost hopeless task of survival among the hazards of life in stream or river.

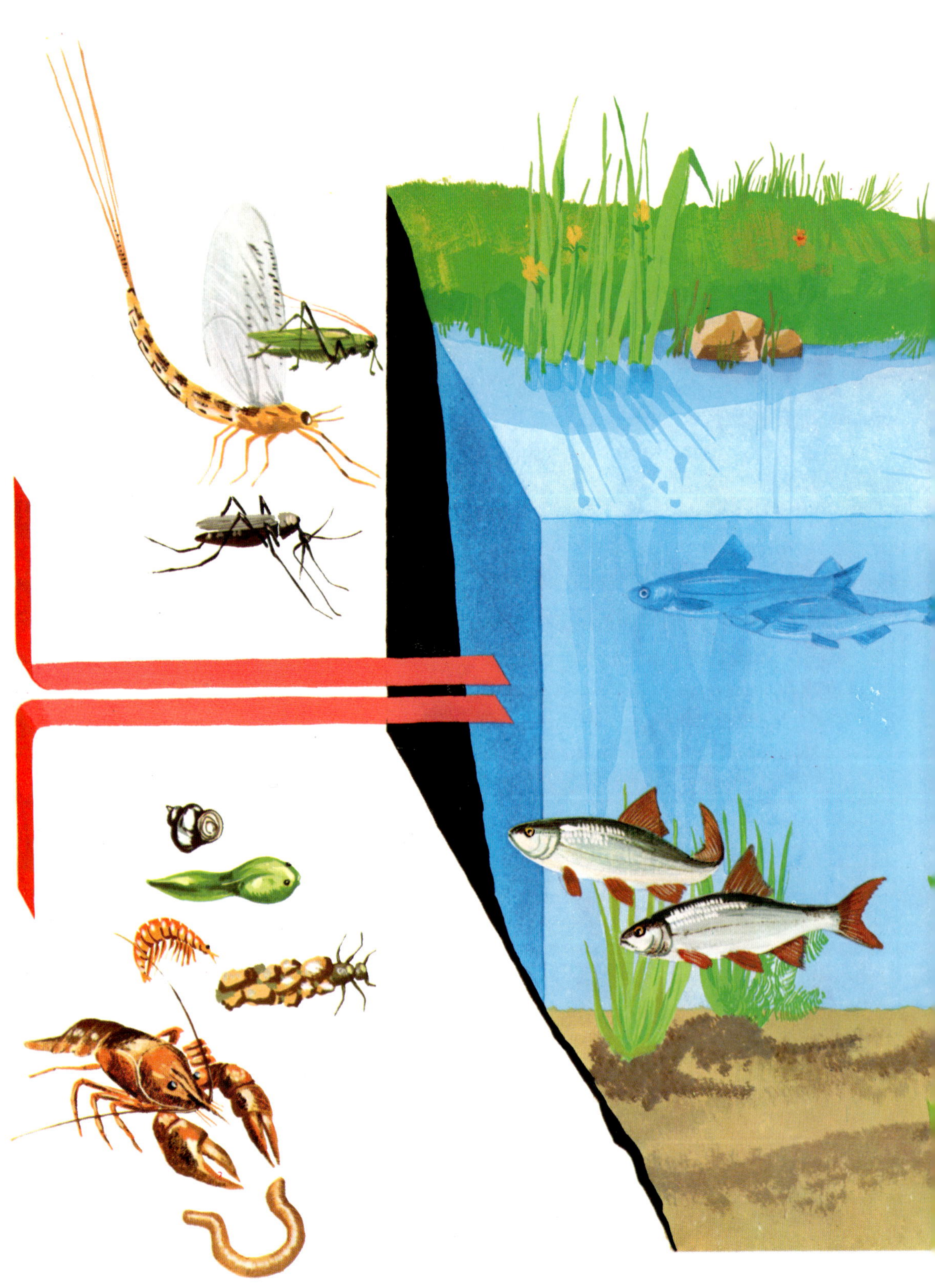

This diagram shows the essentials of the fish environment: the river bed and water plants sheltering and nourishing the fauna of molluscs, larvae and crustacea eaten by the coarse fish (cyprinids); finally the predator appears, the pike, which feeds primarily on coarse fish; the kingfisher, like the heron, plays its part in maintaining the biological balance of the water.

salmonids

What tremendous power and nervous energy is expended by a rainbow trout as it leaps to try and escape from the fisherman.

salmon

At the age of fifteen the author watched a fisherman of eighty land his hundredth salmon. The fisherman was Louis Sauvant, doyen of salmon fishermen on the Allier and, in spite of his age and experience, he stood there beaming with satisfaction as he regarded his victim. It was a magnificent specimen: silvery sides, slate-grey back, pure white belly, perfectly tapered body ending in a broad, powerful caudal fin. It was lying inert on a bed of greenery and only a slight quiver of the gill-cover indicated that the great salmon had just passed from life to death on Auvergne soil only a few miles from the spawning-ground where it had been born five years earlier.

A drop of blood level with the dorsal fin seeped from a thin wound as pink as its flesh, the inevitable mark of the sharp gaff. The vigorous migrant had met its match in the no less vigorous old man and the activity of the struggle now gave place to a sort of homage to nature. Both of us were fascinated by the magnificent fish, this "respected adversary which one loves and admires", as Tony Burnand puts it.

No true salmon fisherman is blasé. This wild, capricious, even magical fish quickens the pulse of all who seek it. These fanatics invariably gather each winter, spring and summer in sacred places with names such as Navarrenx, Hereford, Châteauneuf-du-Faou, Perth, Panes, Niceria, Grantown or Sunndalsora. Neither the fish nor its would-be captor pays any attention to frontiers. It is commonplace to see on the banks of the Rio Narcéa (in the Asturias) a French car carrying a battery of salmon rods on its roof. A few days earlier it had parked regularly on the edge of the Massey Pool on the Oloron torrent, and a month or two later, covered in dust or mud, it may well be found in the arctic regions on the banks of the Alta or the Tana.

The exclusive world of salmon fishermen is rather like a masonic lodge. Entry is restricted and an apprenticeship is indispensable. The experts, however, are usually approachable and friendly but it is a gifted fisherman indeed who is worthy of the advice of the great masters.

the mystery of the salmon

Twentieth-century humanity has evolved in such a way that progress is reckoned only in such developments as rockets or reactors. The man who steps on to the moon, however, need know little or nothing about the fauna of his own planet. There are few unsolved mysteries about most mammals or birds because they exist in man's own environment, which facilitates their study. However, much less is known about the alien environment of the water and about its inhabitants, the fish.

The Atlantic salmon is an example of the problems of study. It is impossible to follow it from the sea into the coastal rivers and streams. Some experiments have been tried—the Japanese, for instance, made salmon tags with tiny trans-

The enormous hooked jaws of a 30 lb (13·60 kg) cock salmon. ►

mitters to trace their journeyings in the open sea, but the results were not conclusive.

The salmon can be observed in many habitats, at sea where trawlers often massacre large numbers, and at the mouths of rivers trying to avoid the nets that await them. Then they can be observed upstream in a river leaping the dams or natural obstructions. There are salmon gauges with automatic counting systems. In Canada counting stations permit the size of these runs to be evaluated. Two platforms are placed on the banks and watchers working in shifts observe and count the salmon as they pass over sheets of metal installed right across the river bed.

Finally the salmon can be observed leaping in pools while waiting for a spate in order to continue the long journey upstream to the redds, but the easiest time to approach the mysterious Atlantic salmon is during the spawning period.

The author has spent hour after hour watching or trying to catch this beautiful fish, and the more he thinks he understands it the more inaccessible it turns out to be.

Thanks to parr markings some experts think they know the meeting places at sea for salmon coming from the same spawning grounds. This cannot be conclusively proved because everything in this domain is hypothetical, and the assertions of ichthyologists are not sufficiently supported by concrete proof. The mystery of the salmon is undeniable. Many questions must be asked about the great Atlantic salmon, among them:

1. What happens to the smolt when it reaches the sea? Does it stay in the region of the continental shelf or does it seek deeper waters? Does it re-emerge in the "growth areas" of Greenland or in the Arctic seas under the ice cap?

2. Does it smell its way back to its native river?

3. Why does it not feed in fresh water?

To the fisherman the unsolved mystery of the salmon is continued in these three questions. There are many excellent books on this fish, among them, *The Salmon*, by W. L. Calderwood, Inspector of Salmon Fishery in Scotland; *The Salmon in the Upper Allier*, by H. Boyer; *The Salmon*, by Dr. Tixier; *The Salmon, Royal Fish*, by Louis Carrère and *The Salmon*, by Pierre Bertin. The scientific works of professors Roule and Fontaine, in particular, are respected as authoritative throughout the world. M. Guyard, the famous breeder, has also made a close study of the salmon; and M. Guy Thioulouse is preparing a thesis on the salmon, which will probably make him the first true "fisherman-doctor of science and salmon".

Some specialists will say: "We now know everything about the salmon; your so-called mysterious fish has revealed all to the march of progress and science." Hypotheses and exceptions to the rule notwithstanding, the salmon is still the fish of mystery *par excellence*.

Fifty years ago Le Clerc, Chief Inspector of Waters and Forests, wrote about the salmon: "The true story of the salmon is a gigantic edifice on which many generations of students have already worked, hampered in their efforts by the myths which have become entangled with the inevitable problems and have succeeded in obscuring and delaying their solution.

"At present the edifice has assumed grandiose proportions. Its outlines have been drawn by artistic and scholarly experts such as Professor Roule, who has shed light on the mystery surrounding the habits of this fish, and has shown us the harmonious process which is responsible for the phases of this life, regulated for all time by the great Artist who created it. But many details are still in the rough, and the patient chisel of numerous craftsmen is needed to give them shape."

This last sentence remains true and full of good sense fifty years after it was written, and these still unexplained details are of vital importance.

Pierre Bertin is both modest and honest in his book, *Salmon and How to Catch Them*. "I am afraid", he writes, "of putting too many errors on paper. I am also afraid of contradicting myself too often on points which find experts still at the stage of pure conjecture."

Following his wise example the author will confine himself to most of the arguments and adding a few observations of his own on the life of the salmon in the river.

the life cycle

the descent of the parr

It is known that the parr lives in the fresh, oxygenated water of the spawning grounds, that it tends to live in shoals (between five and ten parr have been caught in one spot, without moving, by using a wet fly downstream), that it is extremely voracious and almost omnivorous, that its growth depends on the richness of the environment and that it grows more quickly than indigenous trout during its stay in fresh water.

At two years old the parr measures between 7 and 10 in. (18 and 25 cm) and then, as a smolt, begins its long, often slow journey to the ocean. With their heads facing upstream the smolts allow themselves to be borne along in shoals by the current, and numerous observers have seen thousands of smolts milling in front of dams and sluice-gates in spring, searching for a safe passage. (At some obstructions, such as hydro-electric power stations, many infant salmon are killed or injured, and in the past poachers wreaked havoc with fine-meshed nets.)

This descent to the ocean may last several months for the Allier salmon which has a journey of 560 miles (900 km), a few weeks for those of the Gave, and only a few days for those of the coastal rivers of Asturias, Brittany or Norway.

The journey can be delayed by all sorts of obstacles as well as by violent floods. The little salmon is battling against heavy odds to reach the end of this journey, little suspecting that the return one, at a weight of anything from 10 to 25 lb (5 to 12 kg), may be even more hazardous.

There are various theories about the journey of the smolt from fresh to salt water.

Professor Dottrens maintains that, "the transformation of the parr to the smolt stage is also the result of new hormonal activity accompanied by an urge which results in the journey downstream". He adds: "A more detailed study on the interaction of hormones will probably enlighten us as to the internal, physiological causes of migration."

Some experts believe that the parr start their journey when their numbers become too high and they have difficulty in satisfying their appetite.

The years pass, but the understanding of the migratory instincts of salmon is still lacking. The mystery remains concerning the smolts' journey downstream, the length of their stay in fresh water, the areas where they grow and the return of the adult salmon, because conclusive proof is lacking.

Having made observations in the Allier, Henri Boyer claims that the females go down to the sea at 15 months, but that the 15-month-old males remain another year in the river.

Recent examinations of salmon scales in Brittany, carried out by the biologists MM. Boulineau and Arrache, of the C.N.E.X.O.[1] with the help of the A.P.P.S.B.[2], revealed however that most of the salmon had spent only a year in fresh water. This would indicate that the stay of the parr in rivers is proportional to the length of the particular river and to the number of obstacles encountered.

When does the early life of the future salmon reach completion? When does it enter the estuarial waters of a river? Here again theories conflict; some maintain that it waits for a spate or a high tide where fresh and salt water meet, while others say that it moves straight into the salt water, preoccupied only with finding more food.

the salmon at sea

For years ichthyologists believed that salmon migration was limited, that the fish usually remained in the estuaries or along the coasts, and never went further than the continental shelf.

Markings and commercial sea-fishing have disproved the theory and today it is known that *Salmo salar* travels a long way. Scottish salmon have been caught near Norway, Norwegian salmon in the U.S.S.R. and French salmon in the Davis Strait between Canada and Greenland.

The salmon, however, does not wander at will. Like migratory birds, it has established migration

[1]See Glossary. [2]See Glossary.

the life cycle

*The life cycle of the salmon from the egg to the mature fish. The different stages of the growth of the magnificent fish (*top section, green arrow)*, its young life in the river; the egg, the alevin with its as yet unabsorbed yolk-sac, the perfect fry, the parr, the smolt.* (Bottom, red arrow) *the period of growth at sea during which time it feeds on herring and prawns (hence the pigmentation of its skin). Finally the return to the river* (green arrow)*, and the run up to the spawning grounds.*

The great Salmo salar *leaps again and again to clear the hazards on its way to the spawning grounds.*

1

4

3

The amazing, magical, salmon which is so beautiful and fights so hard that it deserves to be taken only by sporting methods such as spinning (4), or with the fly (3 and 5). When finally gaffed (1), the salmon is revealed in all its glory (2 and 6), a magnificent catch.

5

6

routes converging on particularly rich oceanic zones. Several specialists have agreed on the existence of deep "holes", immense reserves of natural food, areas which the salmon head for in order to attain their remarkable growth. There are also vast zones under the arctic ice-cap which are rich in shrimps.

From the enormous catches made by trawlers off Greenland during the last ten years it can be deduced that there are varying concentrations of salmon in the triangle formed by Ireland, Greenland and Iceland. No one has yet been able to tell whether salmon from the same rivers travel together or whether they mix with their fellows from different areas. The enigmas of nature are not logical, but it seems unlikely that the most southerly salmon, such as those from the river Minho in Portugal meet those from, say, the river Tana, near the North Cape.

There are several theories concerning the method by which the salmon from the rivers of Britain, Ireland and Continental Europe find their way to the feeding grounds of southern Greenland and to the north of Norway—where, incidentally, overfishing by commercial fleets, notably the Danes, has reduced the runs back to our rivers to an extremely dangerous low. What is sure is that the fish smell their way into the rivers of their birth, this having recently been proved by an American scientific investigation. One recent suggestion by an angling writer is that the smolts follow the kelts to the feeding grounds, also by smell.

A few years ago the author of a magazine article claimed to have found the key to the mystery of migration. He put forward the theory that the salmon is a surface fish, a night fish navigating by sight and the position of the stars. ... Evidence and proof were predictably missing.

The growth of the salmon at sea is almost miraculous. In a year a 7 oz (200 g) smolt may increase in weight by 6½ lb (3 kg) and in two years by 22 lb (10 kg). This tiny fish, measuring 7 or 8 in. (18 or 20 cm) long on its journey downstream, may return two or three years later measuring between 2½ and 3½ ft (80 cm and 1·10 m). Quantity and quality of food must be equally important in producing such growth.

These great fish, some of which come to die in the upper reaches of the Allier, are a valuable factor in our diet. One of their most important attributes is that they grow fat feeding on the free riches of the ocean, eventually to become themselves the food of land dwellers. This was especially true in the Middle Ages. Three hundred miles (500 km) inland from the coast the salmon was the fish *par excellence* as far as food was concerned, but at the time when Pliny wrote: "How plentiful salmon were in the rivers of Gaul", nothing was known of their long foraging journeys.

This has digressed from the subject of the growth of salmon. Rapid growth means wealth but in 1971 fewer than 3,000 salmon were landed on rod and line in France. Yet just one river like the Oloron or the Allier might have 20,000 salmon working upstream, of an approximate gross value of £480,000 (about £2 a pound).

However, unfortunately, France has no official policy on salmon (see Anthony Netboy's book: *How France Has Wasted its Salmon Wealth*).

the return of the salmon to its birthplace

From the parr and smolt the salmon develops into the mature fish ready to reproduce ... the fish which interests the freshwater angler.

For the grown salmon returning to its native river after two or three years in the sea the period of growth was not an end in itself. At this point in its life cycle the sole aim of the salmon is reproduction; it ensures the continuity of the species and then many die.

In order to achieve this goal the salmon makes a long trek to its birthplace and the eggs are hatched at roughly the same spot as their parents. This often very long journey, in which they are menaced with traps and harassed by floods and droughts, can bear comparison with the great migration of birds and mammals.

The salmon has been known to cover more than 3,000 miles (5,000 km) at sea and 500 miles (800 km) in fresh water to reach the spawning area, which truly earns this royal fish the description of migrator extraordinary.

Theories put forward by specialists about the

run from the sea to fresh water and the probable motives behind the continuing journey back to the spawning ground have already been examined.

It is obvious that the salmon from Brittany or Ireland will have less trouble than the Allier salmon, for example, in reaching their reproduction area because the coastal rivers are shorter in length.

The routes taken by the Atlantic salmon in Europe contain many deadly obstacles. Firstly in the estuaries it has to avoid the seines and drag-nets, then in some main rivers it needs stamina and cunning to get past the fixed barrier-nets of the commercial fisheries. Finally there are stretches of water used either for industrial (hydro-electric dams) or for tourist purposes. In certain particularly hilly regions this valiant fish has only to struggle against such natural obstacles as waterfalls and strong currents.

Man has tried to lessen not so much the physical weakness of the fish as the abuses of a progress which is blind to the needs of nature, by constructing salmon passes, which also aid other migratory fish. They are called "ladders" and in theory they help the fish to negotiate most of the man-made obstacles, "in theory", because reservations must be made concerning the efficiency of these ladders, as the designers are too often ignorant of the behaviour of the salmon when faced with obstacles.

One such obstacle has caused the salmon to disappear from the Dordogne, another for it to vanish from the Garonne; the same applies to the upper reaches of the mountain streams in the Pyrenees, the upper Allier and the Rio Narcéa.

For the sake of a few hundred thousand kilowatts of electrical power a far more precious wealth has been destroyed. This destruction has taken place in Brittany as well, where a rash of small mill dams have appeared, equipped with turbines and providing a tiny amount of power, bought at a ransom price by the French electricity network.

There are also hazards which are very different and just as dangerous: polluted tributaries. In industrialised countries where sewage is being carelessly disposed of, the waterways are gradually becoming open sewers. Fortunately the migratory salmon, which usually travels at times of spate, is not permanently submitted to this hazard. It is thought that salmon moving in the almost pure water of a river and arriving at a confluence with a polluted stream, wait for the right moment to proceed. A succession of polluted streams can form a kind of chemical barrier which must delay the salmon's journey upstream considerably.

These obstacles are not the only ones. For example, owners of riverside estates in Norway quite legally use salmon traps consisting of gigantic bow nets made with wooden stakes which are extremely deadly when the river is in spate.

The salmon has always been coveted by both men and animals. At the turn of the century poachers caught it with such devices as harpoons or tridents, and in some rivers in North America the bears wait at the foot of waterfalls to gorge themselves when the salmon are running. The otter, which until recently was fairly plentiful in Europe, also caught large quantities of salmon.

The powerful salmon is a stubborn fighter but he needs all his reserves of energy to fight the

An angler with a salmon from Ireland's River Suir. ▶

A salmon ladder with staggered pools on the Rio Cares (Spain). ▶

▲
Some men do everything they can to protect salmon, while others do all in their power to catch them. Here is a trap in a Scandinavian river: it is a gigantic wooden bow-net, very deadly at high water. Centre, foreground: The salmon ladder of the Bajasse dam on the River Allier (France).

A salmon ladder of the modified Lachadenède type. In the foreground note the trap for the adult fish; further back the deflectors are designed to check the current. ▶

hazards of nets, dams, pollution and predators (of which man is not the least).

Whether it is British, Spanish, French, or Scandinavian, its strength and courage are the same. Once hooked it fights with desperation to the last second; attacked by a lamprey the fish will leap and get rid of its tormentor with a short aerial somersault. When the eggs are threatened on the redds by intruders the salmon will at once drive them away. Thus the salmon earns respect, and truly justifies its title of the king of fish.

The times of the salmon's run upstream in fresh water vary considerably as they depend on the condition of the river, the weather and also the hazards mentioned above. Usually the first move occurs in the autumn. Choosing a favourable tide the salmon manage to move into the estuaries, and an autumn flood tide helps them to reach pools, where they can rest until conditions encourage them to continue their migration.

This was once known as the run of the great winter salmon as most of the fish weighed between 18 and 25 lb (8 and 11 kg). In the spring came the medium-sized 10–18 pounders (4·50–8 kg) with their silver livery, and finally in early summer it was the turn of the small, Sainte-Madeleine salmon, popularly known as "Madeleineaux", to work upstream to their native headwaters. Nowadays these divisions scarcely exist, and the medium-sized and small salmon often reach the end of their journey before the large winter fish. Many fishermen have observed this and blame it on the increasing number of obstacles which slow the larger fish considerably. All the experts say that the majority of the larger fish beginning the run are females, and it appears that the males tend to move into the river later. An old theory that, having completed a common growth at sea, all the fish move in family groups, has still not been disproved. As it is possible to trap 20 pounders (10 kg), medium-sized and small salmon in the same nets it seems probable that, if conditions are unfavourable, the fish gather in large numbers before venturing into the estuaries, and move upstream in their own time.

In some rivers with very clear water, particularly in Spain, it is possible to watch from the banks and bridges the salmon move upstream. They rarely travel alone, usually moving in groups of three, four or five and swimming quite quickly to reach more oxygenated water. They progress swiftly and powerfully in the currents and much more slowly in the pools. Sometimes a salmon leaves the group, rises to the surface, rolling and greeting the fisherman with an auspicious splash of its tail. During these runs, which are popular sights, large concentrations of salmon—sometimes twenty, sometimes more than fifty—can be seen waiting in neighbouring pools. What causes this halt? Is it due to a sudden lowering of water and atmospheric pressure, or to the cold, or to a manifestation of their mysterious natural instincts? The largest concentrations of the migrants usually gather at the foot of dams and rapids. Here their progress stops and with the arrival of each new group, the number of fish below these obstacles increases. The smaller salmon, which are lighter and very strong, usually use the ladders, but the others are unwilling. The sloping sides of the dams provide a relatively easy passage, but here again favourable conditions are needed for the salmon to leap. A little spate, a slight increase in temperature and the barometer climbing to fair, are all that is needed for fish to suddenly hurl themselves at the dam.

A few trial leaps are made as if to size up the obstacle and then the fish launches itself into the milky torrent. Finding holds on stone or cement, it propels itself rapidly upwards by means of its powerful caudal fin. However, it rarely reaches the top of the dam at its first attempt and usually falls back into the pool. Eventually it succeeds and rolls or leaps to show its satisfaction before resting for a time in the more hospitable waters.

life in the river

reproduction

What does the salmon do when it reaches waters which are suitable for reproduction? It does not climb indefinitely, otherwise one would observe enormous concentrations near the source or below the last obstacle. When it has found water favourable to its survival during the summer it steadies itself and prepares for a stay until spawning. These protected stretches of river where the salmon remain for a long time may be deep pools or holes, salmon lies where the fish feels safe and where the temperature is fairly steady even during heat waves. In flood conditions it is possible to see the salmon romping in the shallows in less than three feet of water; when low water comes they withdraw to the deepest parts. The water temperature and the river-bed are of vital importance. The salmon loves holes strewn with stones and boulders where it can hide, shelter from the light and avoid the fishermen's bait or the poachers' nets. If it runs short of oxygen it can leave its deep lie and swim into a current; then it looks for the shelter of a rock which serves to deflect the violent current, allowing it to remain without effort in this fast-flowing and highly oxygenated water. Thus the life of the salmon depends on climatic conditions; as for the impulses these are dealt with in the chapter on catching salmon. First the life cycle of this valiant migrator must be completed; after its journey down to the sea, its growth at sea, its return to the river and its life in fresh water, the most important stage is reproduction.

Summer ends and some salmon have died, victims of pollution, sometimes of drought and, since 1964, many more from the terrible disease of ulcerative dermal necrosis. The supreme goal approaches: the sexual urge quickens, and the fish move up to headwaters and tributaries with stony shallows. The salmon, which may have been in fresh water for six months or more, changes livery. As spawning approaches, its silvery sides turn pink and then red. The gill-covers take on a marvellous copper hue and the back darkens under green or brown patches and red spots.

Diagrammatic plan of a salmon river. The fresh-run salmon (top) travels upstream to the headwaters where the eggs are deposited on gravelly shallows. The kelt, below, is dropping downstream, via the lake, to see the sea again, where it may feed in the Arctic waters and return to spawn again.

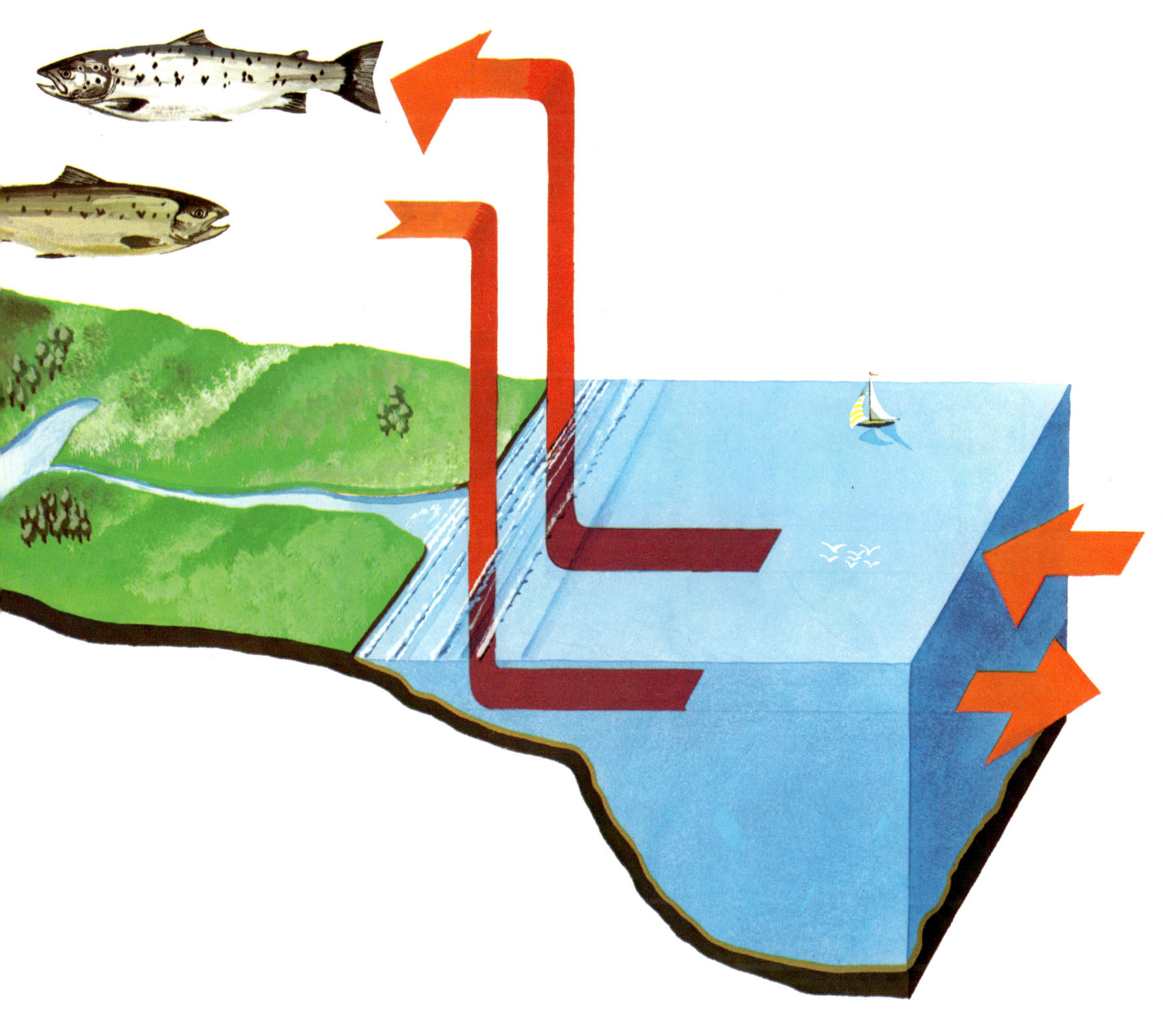

Now the male is easily distinguishable from the female. Apart from its longer head and the position of the eye in relation to the mouth, the lower jaw lengthens into a sort of hook, known as a kype.

With the first October frosts the water is much cooler and normally at the beginning of November it is really cold (4–8 °C) (39–46 °F). This is the time for spawning.

This period is ideal for observing salmon closely. Before spawning there takes place a sort of wedding procession in very shallow water, usually at the tail of a pool. The males swim side by side, suddenly accelerating or turning back, then they rush downstream into the lower pool; the females do not waste time; they nuzzle the bed (quite violently), testing the density and quality of the gravel—they are looking for the best place to establish the spawning trough called a redd. Then the salmon start their excavations; by causing turbulence with tail movements, each digs a hole between 5 in. and a foot deep (13–30 cm), in which she will deposit some of her eggs.

The spawning takes several days, during which time the fish sometimes rest or make new redds. The female rubs her belly on the largest pebbles to strip clutches of eggs, which the male, at her side and slightly to the rear, fertilises by shedding his milt simultaneously. As she deposits her eggs the female appears to be convulsed, and the male shivers frantically. One can also see the simultaneous gaping of the jaws as the effort is made; but the reproduction instinct does not stop there; the fertilised eggs, denser than water, drift downstream and stop in the lower gravel of the redd. The hen fish then digs a new redd upstream, covering the eggs as she does so with gravel; protected from the light and from predators the incubation of the eggs continues. In spring the tiny alevins or baby salmon are hatched and the unchanging life cycle begins again.

after spawning

What do the parents do after spawning? One cannot answer in general terms or categorically; everything depends on the length of the river, its winter floods and on obstacles; these exhausted salmon (called kelts) should drift downstream to the sea, but have they the strength? In the event of a flood they let themselves be carried down by the currents, otherwise they wedge themselves in a hole under the bank, under a stump, a dead tree or some other temporary refuge. These kelts present a sad spectacle—skinny, emaciated and livid. Many of them—specially the cock fish—die a few weeks after spawning.

Cock and hen salmon on the redd, dug out by the hen in the gravel. The cock fish sheds milt which fertilises the eggs simultaneously being shed by the hen fish.

Ripe cock and hen salmon, showing the different shapes of their heads: on top the lower jaw of the cock is hooked into a kype.

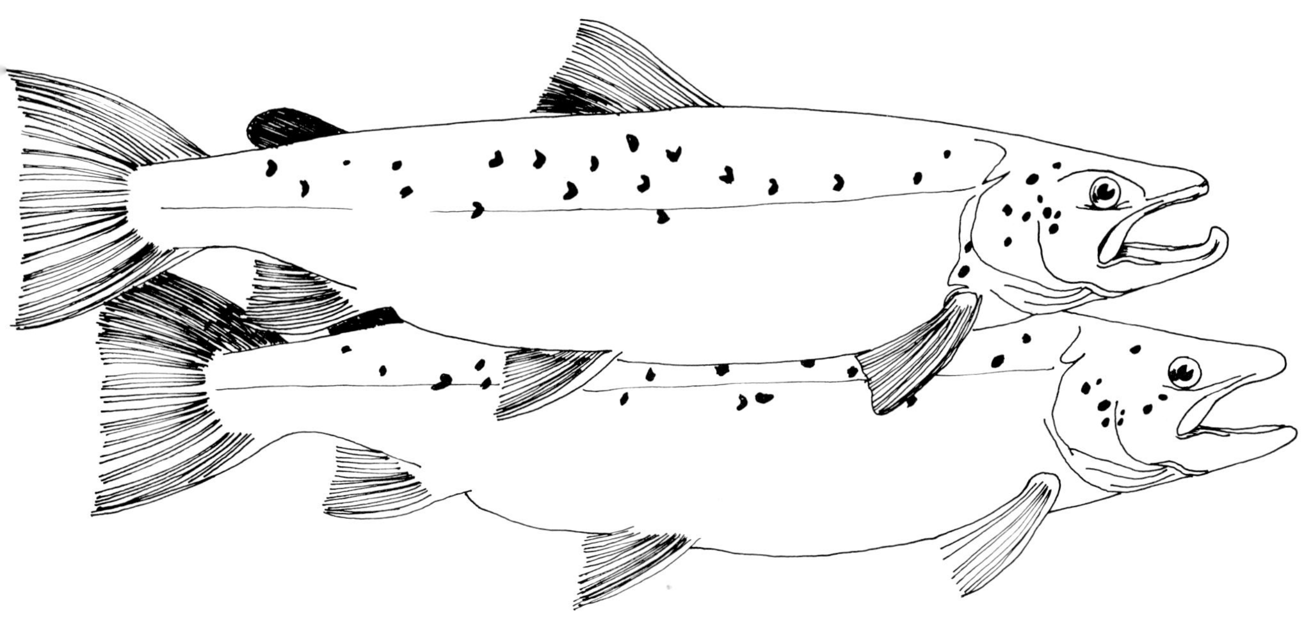

But some hen kelts, and a smaller number of cocks which have suffered less, manage to reach the sea again and regain their strength after an indeterminate lapse of time. It is quite probable that these worn old salmon meet their offspring on the way to the feeding-grounds.

There are two main conflicting theories about the weight of the salmon returning to the river a second time. Most experts say that a salmon grows in proportion to the number of journeys it makes, which would explain the unusual size of some Norwegian salmon which spawn a few miles from the fjords and can therefore move up and downstream without difficulty. Others maintain that a salmon which is large on its first journey will not change size or weight much more on its second return; they say simply that a new stay at sea allows the weakened fish to regain weight and the necessary strength to complete a second cycle.

does the salmon feed in the river?

The river life of the salmon has one more mystery: does it feed in fresh water? The best study of this aspect, simple and concise, is by the late Henri Boyer. He was clever and courageous enough fifty years ago to say that the salmon does not feed for almost a year: "After a stay in fresh water the migrator is physically incapable of digesting food . . . the digestive organs gradually become so atrophied that on the eve of spawning they have almost completely wasted away." This is confirmed by thousands of examinations of salmon viscera.

Why are salmon caught with shrimps, earthworms and even artificial flies? This is the eternal question from those who do not believe in this theory. The author, having fished for salmon near the sea, notably on the Sélune and in Ireland, believes that the salmon still feeds in the lower reaches of rivers; it takes the worm quite easily and one often finds the hook in the belly, but its appetite must decrease as it moves upstream, so that only the habit of feeding remains; in other words the appetite is transformed into a sort of aggressive instinct.

Several times in summer during the hatching of the May-fly the author has seen salmon rise and take them. An angler's salmon fly hardly looks like an insect, yet the salmon sees it, rises to the surface and seizes it. For sport? Curiosity? Aggression? No one knows.

salmon fishing

We anglers believe that when they return to the rivers salmon should be caught only by rod and line. This would permit a reasonable number to be taken, but in fact the fish are seriously endangered by the nets, traps and other gear used by the professionals, which take so many fish we consider it to be no more than legalised poaching. French salmon in particular are being exploited and between 60 and 75 per cent of the adult fish running back to their rivers are caught by the coastal nets and by poachers, etc. before they have completed their first spawning journey.

The present useless legislation must be changed if the French salmon is not to disappear entirely.

Coastal and estuarial netting, poaching and the disease apart, the greatest threat of all to the Atlantic salmon is the massive commercial netting and line fishing carried out in recent years since the Greenland feeding grounds and routes to the grounds were discovered. In spite of a number of international conferences, which tried to limit and phase out this sheer massacre of salmon on their feeding grounds, no real success has come about, and some anglers feel that the species is doomed to extinction due to man's greed. In the past few years up to 1974 the number of salmon in the rivers of north-west Europe has dwindled to a shameful total and angling has been done only as a token operation.

True, there are still salmon, from the North Cape to Spain, but their numbers are a fraction of the potential.

Isaak Walton, the first notable angling writer, wrote: "Fishing is an art . . .". He was, of course, referring to angling with rod and line; and unlike the science of catching roach with wheat and carp with potatoes, salmon fishing *is* an art.

Important though endurance and patience are in salmon angling, other qualities are indispensable. Some people maintain that luck plays a big part in successful salmon fishing—and it is true that the unpredictable and sometimes bizarre behaviour of the fish produces pleasant surprises to those who believe only in luck.

While accepting that luck can play its part, there are too many nonsensical tales of the tyro who lands a salmon after a few casts, under the noses of the experts, or of hooked fish so big that some anglers carry a knife with which to cut the line should the need occur . . .

People who talk like that know nothing.

A little luck and much skill is needed to be a successful salmon angler—unless all the top European anglers have had inordinate luck for years. On every river one finds exceptionally gifted anglers who possess a sixth sense, a feeling for the water and the fish, and who manage to attract salmon that ignore all the baits offered by others. At first others say they are lucky, then that they are extremely expert, then that they have a knack, and if they catch too many fish they are cursed by the many anglers who lack the ability and are jealous of success.

This all adds up to the fact that salmon fishing, indeed all fishing, is full of subtleties and finesse, little details that matter, both in the tackle and in the way it is used. And all of this is subordinate to a complete knowledge of the river, its bed, its water and its fish.

1. A salmon running a river leaps to pass a waterfall.
2. A 17 lb (7·70 kg) salmon from the Allier, caught spinning a devon.
3. Seconds before the gaff or tailer is used, a played-out salmon is drawn towards the angler.
4. A cock salmon's head and the comparatively small Orkla spoon on which it was caught.

1

2

3

the first salmon anglers

England was the real birthplace of the sport of angling and with the early stumbling into the techniques came the written word—books on the fish, the waters and methods. Even in the 1600s writers mentioned angling for salmon, but it was early in the 1900s when a French army captain succeeded in landing a salmon after a long fight when he hooked it on a minnow while trout fishing in the Allier at Brioude.

Local anglers followed his example and salmon angling in France was on the way up. The sport has progressed considerably in the seventy years since, having acquired a nobility, and many thousands have derived immense pleasure from hooking, playing and landing (for subsequent admiration) a salmon on a spinner or a fly.

Tackle was improved as knowledge of salmon and salmon fishing grew. After the last war many new materials were used to produce lighter and better rods and lines, more mechanically perfect reels. Heavy wooden rods of bamboo and greenheart, among other materials, were replaced by fibre-glass and tubular steel; lines were of nylon, and thinner, and the reels permitted longer casts with ease.

Anglers no longer needed herculean strength to fish for salmon.

The multiplying casting reel at first gave way to the fixed-spool reel, but now many experienced salmon spinners use the modern free-spool multiplier because it is better for playing strong fish which drag many yards of line from the reel (which can cause tangles on a fixed-spool reel), and also casts heavy baits further.

Fly-fishing, and the tackle, tended to remain more traditional: while some anglers are very happy with the lighter hollow-glass rods, many others prefer the slower, more sympathetic action of a good split-cane rod of 12–14 ft (3·60–4·20 m), even 16 ft (4·90 m). The most popular—and certainly the best—of these cane rods are the work of makers such as Hardy and Sharpes and Johnsons of Britain and Pezon et Michel of France.

Some of the older patterns of salmon flies—like Jock Scott, Silver Doctor, Mar Lodge and many others—built from feathers, silks, wools and tinsels are still in use, but salmon flies are also of the present, and many anglers use tube-flies (on which the body and hackle/wings are tied on a tube of plastic, brass or aluminium, which is then threaded on the leader, a treble hook tied on and pushed into a plastic or rubber socket at the tail end). There is also an increasing use of hair and fur in the flies, with the dressings much simplified, because many of the exotic birds from which plumage was used are now either extinct or, happily, prevented from becoming so by protection. Hair flies seem to be even more effective than the traditional originals.

Early salmon spinning was done with small dead fish mounted on a "flight" of hooks with small vanes set at the head end. When drawn through the water or held in a fast current, the vanes made the fish spin. Mounting natural baits is (and of course was) a fiddly business and they are seldom used today, most anglers favouring metal, plastic or wooden devon minnows, or the Continental bar-spoons, or Swedish wobbling spoons, and wriggling plug-baits.

Most anglers who fish for salmon in Europe do so by spinning, often exclusively, not appreciating the art of the fly rod. Rods for salmon spinning, and reels too, must be chosen according to the river being fished: heavy lures, strong lines, powerful rods and reels big enough to hold some 200 yards (180 m) of the line on, for example, the fast-flowing Norwegian rivers with their massive fish; lines of perhaps 25 lb (11 kg) test. Yet, on a west of Scotland spate stream in summer a slim, supple rod of 7 ft (2 m), used with perhaps 8 lb (3·50 kg) test on a fixed-spool reel would replace the 10 ft (3 m) double-handed rod and multiplier used with the heavy line on the Norwegian river.

In fishing for the big spring-run salmon in the February to April period when rivers tend to run high, in France, England, Scotland or Ireland, for example, a double-handed rod and 15–20 lb (6·80–9 kg) test line would be standard; the main difference would be that the French angler would be most likely to load his line on a fair-size fixed-spool reel, while the British anglers in spring have a preference for the multiplier.

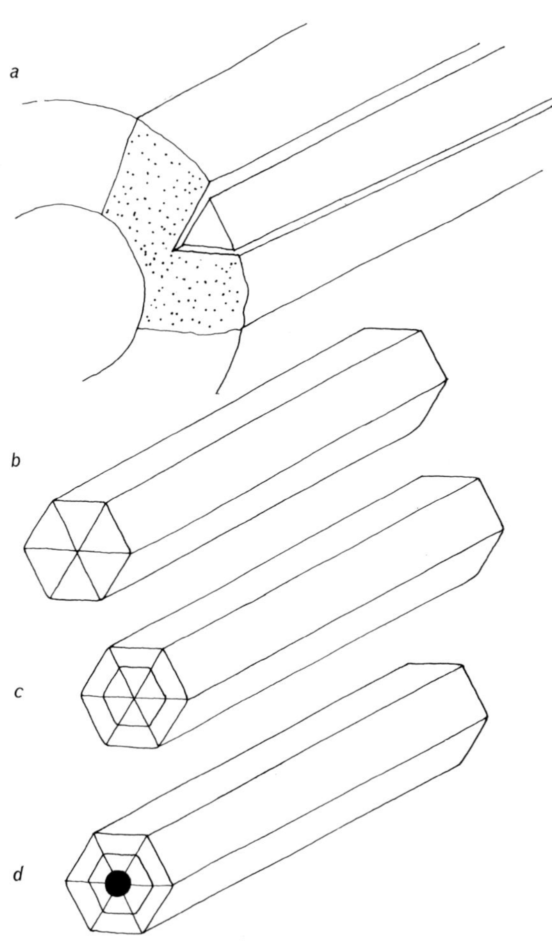

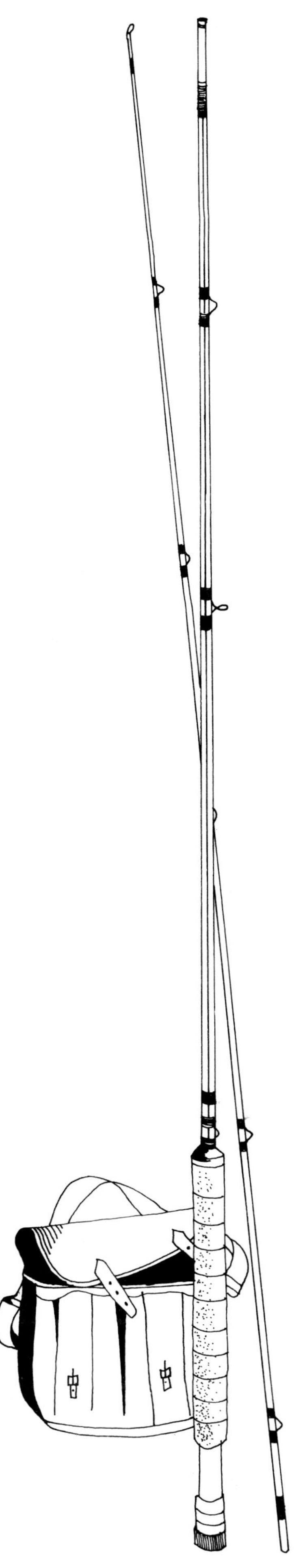

Split-bamboo cane fishing-rod construction:
*A whole cane is split into triangular sections and each is then planed accurately so that six sections fit together (*a*).*
*The six sections glued together (*b*).*
*This is a double-built rod, the inner six glued-up sections in turn covered with six more (*c*). This system has largely been abandoned today.*
*And this (*d*) is a double-built rod with a thin spring-steel wire through its centre. This, too, is little used today, since the wire not only rusts and becomes useless, but is heavy.*

spinning

Spinning lures for salmon rarely weigh much less than $\frac{1}{4}$ oz. (7 g), including any necessary weight on the trace, and so it is untrue to say (as so many anglers unthinkingly repeat, like parrots) that multipliers cannot cast light baits but the fixed-spool reels will. In salmon fishing, even in high summer when using $1\frac{1}{2}$ inch (3·80 cm) devons or $\frac{3}{4}$ inch (2·80 cm) bar-spoons, the small multiplier *will* cast them; however, the fixed-spool reel is generally faster on the retrieve, which is necessary when casting a little lure upstream and bringing it back at a speed a little more than the current.

The angler must think about the task he has to perform, then select his tackle to permit him to do it most successfully. At all times, however, the angler should have at least 150 yards (140 m) of line on his reel, preferably 200 yards (180 m), since there is always the chance, on any river, of a very big fish—bigger than the average—and it is mortifying to hook one of these monsters, only to lose it because the reel ran out of line.

the behaviour of spinning lures

It is well to understand the various types of behaviour of spinning lures in the water so that one may select an appropriate lure to meet the conditions. For example, if the aim is to fish the lure very near to the bed of the river in an area where the flow is very fast, then the lure must be streamlined, and some form of devon minnow is usually the choice of experienced anglers. A heavy metal devon will do, or the alternative is a light devon with a heavy lead on

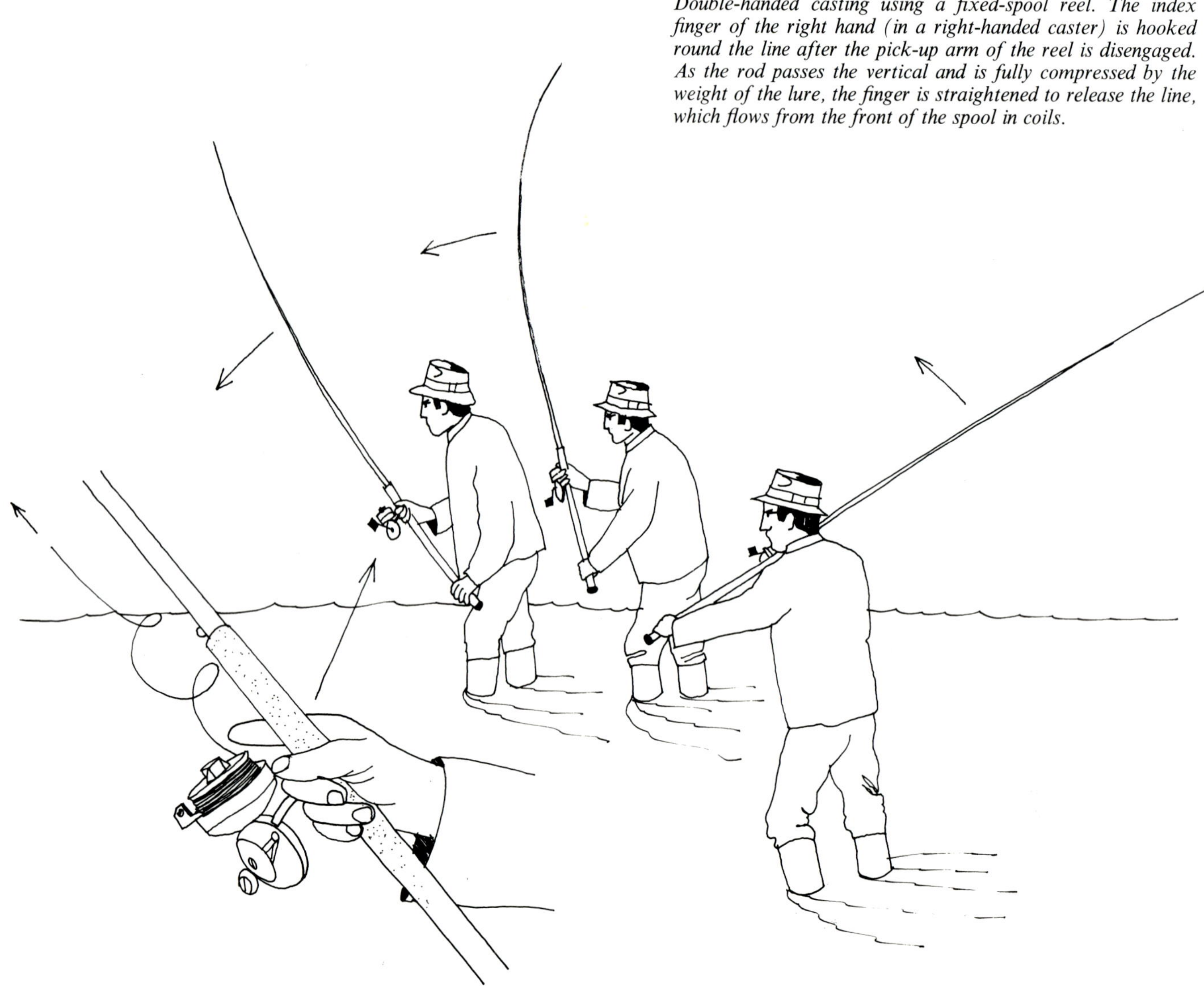

Double-handed casting using a fixed-spool reel. The index finger of the right hand (in a right-handed caster) is hooked round the line after the pick-up arm of the reel is disengaged. As the rod passes the vertical and is fully compressed by the weight of the lure, the finger is straightened to release the line, which flows from the front of the spool in coils.

Brian Harris spinning for spring salmon on the River Lune below Kirkby Lonsdale.

Angling magazine writer Dave Steuart with three fine south of England salmon.

Brian Harris holds a 15 lb (6·80 kg) spring salmon, caught spinning on the Hampshire Avon. ▼

the trace some 2 ft (60 cm) ahead of the lure. This is normal practice in early spring with rivers full and with strong currents.

It is possible to fish fairly deeply with a lead-headed bar-spoon, such as the Voblex; but other bar-spoons, even those with very heavily weighted bars, such as the ABU Droppen, tend to fish high in the water owing to their water resistance. An uptrace lead can help to get them down, but the fishing is unpleasant because of the enormous pull of water pressure on the tip of the rod.

Some heavy elongated wobbling (as opposed to spinning) spoons will fish deeply, again with a lead 2 or 3 ft (60 or 90 cm) ahead on the trace, but beware of attempting to fish Toby spoons in such a way. The Toby is a special spoon, often used either in smooth flows at times when the fish are running, or to hang over a known lie at about 1 ft (30 cm) below the surface to mid-water. The Toby does not spin but wobbles while lying on an even plane with the concave side down. It will fish beautifully when cast across and downstream, then allowed to swing round with the pull of the stream, rod held high out over the river and without any line being recovered on the reel.

Bar-spoons may also be used in this way, as may a lightweight wooden devon minnow without any lead—or just a tiny one—on the trace.

Bar-spoons for salmon really come into their own: (*a*) when the water is coloured and a big flash is necessary to make an impact on the fish—but they cannot even then be fished deeply in strong water; (*b*) when fishing low, clear water in late spring and summer. Then it is necessary to cast upstream and wind the lure back at a speed faster than the current to create the illusion of a small creature in flight suddenly appearing in the fish's sight, then trying to pass by. The fish tend to make a sudden attack. Also, in such conditions the angler remains below the fish and therefore unseen.

Plugs, like wooden devons, fish well in slow water and floating types can be held almost stationary over known salmon lies, especially useful in cold-water conditions. But they are no good in very fast water.

fishing with lures

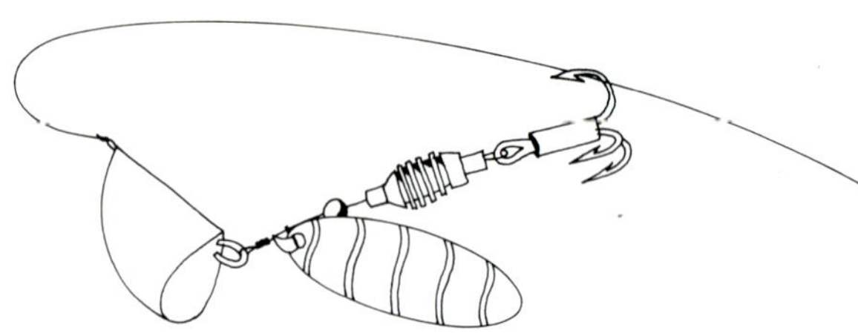

The lure can tangle with the line when casting, if it is not checked before it starts to fall.

Voblex spoon: the hook is fitted with a small piece of rubber tube, which holds it rigid in order to avoid tangling.

Choose an appropriate lure according to conditions and tackle. Carry out across-and-downstream casts of increasing length so as to cover all the available water in successive sweeps.

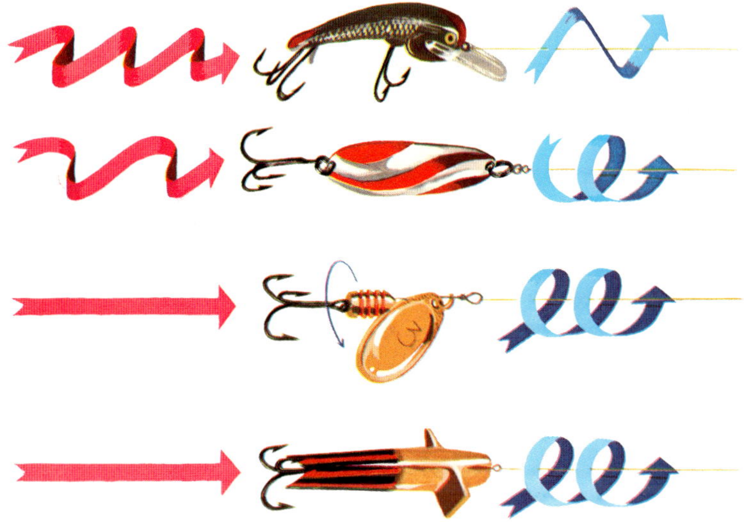

The red arrows show the side to side movements, the blue arrows the up and down or rotating movements of the Flopy, the Orlac spoon, the Mepps spoon and the reflex devon (from top to bottom).

Three useful knots for attaching spoons or swivels to medium-strength lines (9–20 lb b.s. (4–9 kg)).

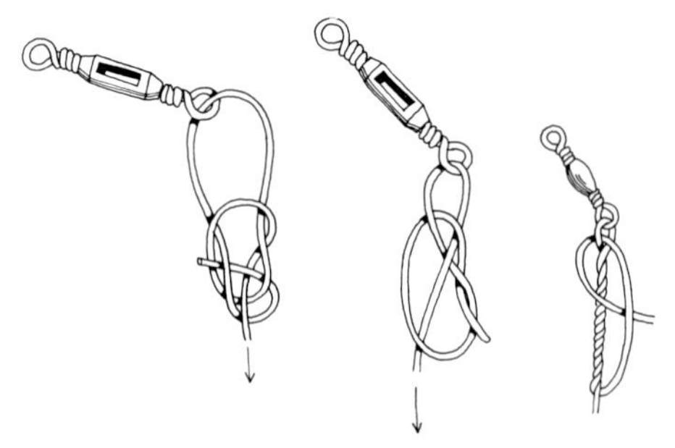

devon minnows

The devon minnow is the most popular spinning lure for salmon. Originally made only of metal, it is now made of plastics or wood, which makes the lure more adaptable because of the buoyancy of these materials. Some anglers use no other lures when spinning for salmon.

Devons attract salmon—and other species—as the contrasting dark back and bright belly of the lure "flashes" as it turns in the running water. Popular colour combinations are blue and silver, brown and gold, red and gold and green and yellow.

Most devons have round bodies, but for very strong deep currents the flat-bodied reflex model of metal is useful. The rate of spin of a devon depends on its weight, shape and the size and angle of the fins, set about one-third of the way back from the head.

Some anglers believe that the spinning devon attracts fish not only because of its flash in the water but because of vibrations it sets up; and so they add to such effects, often putting on gadgets to create sound or vibrations.

It is necessary to use a ball-bearing swivel with devon minnows to avoid kinks being put in the line by the spinning lure, which does not always revolve round the wire or nylon axis of the mount which carries hook, swivel and bead. Ordinary swivels are seldom free-turning enough to prevent kinks, in which case an anti-kink vane of celluloid may help (*see sketch*). Devons ride up the trace when a fish is hooked and help prevent the hook being levered out.

When fishing in deep water with a devon, the angle of the line, even if the rod is low, makes it difficult for the lure to rotate. It is therefore advisable to replace the anti-kink device with a small lead of about $\frac{1}{3}$ to $\frac{1}{2}$ oz. (10 to 15 g) with a double swivel and spring clip which considerably improves the lie of the devon and makes it attractive (*see sketch*).

Plugs are not specifically designed for salmon fishing but there is nothing to stop them being

Anti-kink devices:
1. *Lead on fine nylon dropper attached to three-way swivel (for fishing with shrimp or worm).*
2. *Loop of line at swivel on which to hang lead as an anti-kink device.*
3. *Anti-kink device consisting of a small, rigid plastic vane connected to a box swivel.*

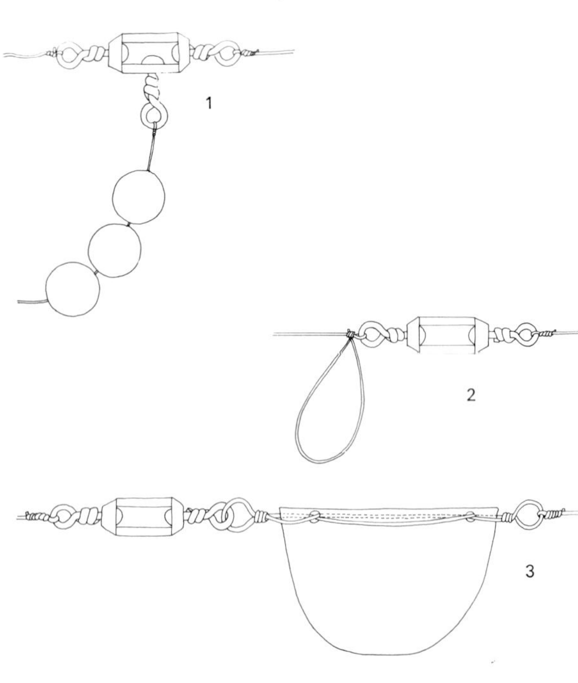

Lead weight with swivel and link; small lead with simple clip; drilled bullet with copper wire clip; quick-release spiral lead (left); three-way box swivel; box swivel with link; diamond eye swivel; barrel swivel; three-way barrel swivel, fold-over lead.

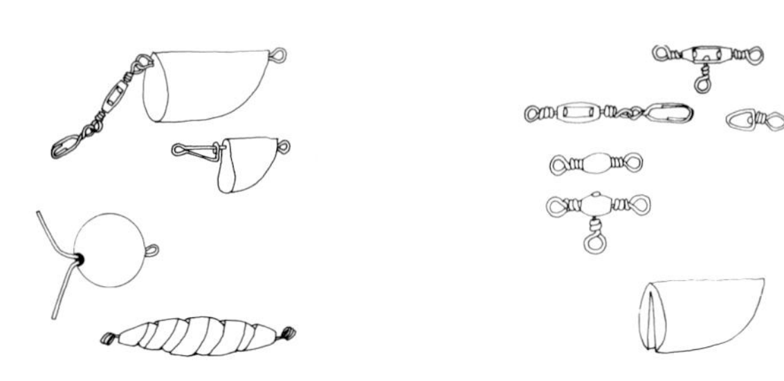

The use of an uptrace lead helps to keep the lure (in this case a devon minnow) on an even keel.

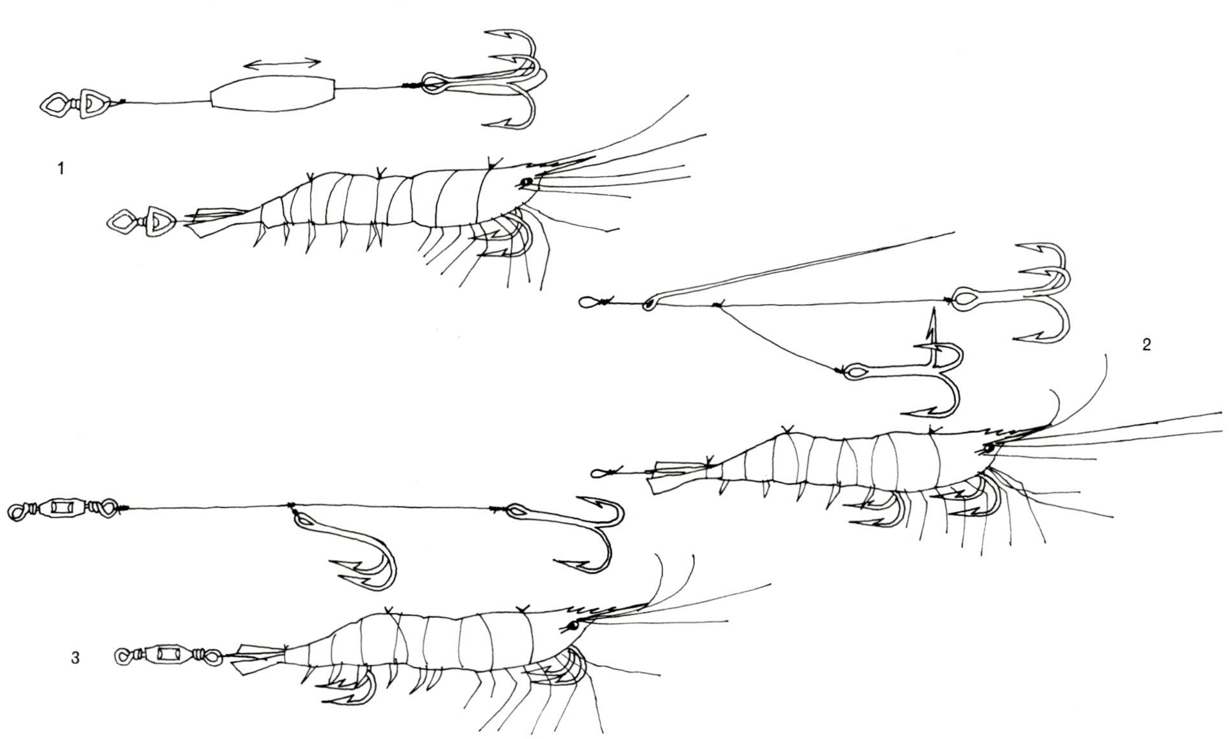

Some shrimp mountings:
1. Rigid mounting weighted with a barrel lead.
2. Flexible Norwegian mounting with fixing needle.
3. Flexible mounting armed with two double hooks.

The decisive moment of gaffing, certainly more cruel than the tailer for getting the fish out of the water. The point of the gaff, turning downwards, has to penetrate the back of the fish. This photograph shows the wrong way: gaff should be pulled in across fish's back. ▶

◀ *Wobbling spoons for salmon fishing.*

◀ *A selection of bar-spoons, some with leaded heads.*

▼ *Fishermen spinning for salmon at Brioude on the Allier in April.*

used to tempt the appetite or to excite the aggressive instincts of a lazy fish. Which is the best—Plucky, Sosy, Flopy, Spiky or Vivif? Will the Scandinavian Rapala give better results than the ABU Killer or the Stingsilda? It is all a question of personal preference; the most important thing is to fish with a bait in which you have confidence.

natural bait

shrimps

Shrimps are used in most areas, varying from region to region. In the Allier the pink shrimp or prawn is used (*see sketch of mountings*), preserved in glycerine. In Norway they use big red prawns, while in Spain small, live, grey shrimps, mounted on a single hook, are used.

Fishing with shrimps is different from fishing with metal lures: shrimps should be fished slowly with numerous checks which bring them to life. The long rods (12½–14 ft) (3·80–4·20 m) are very suitable for this type of fishing which is similar to fishing with worm.

The sketches of shrimp mounts will be clearer than any description, but it is important to mention the lead. Apart from a few experts who manage to weight the shrimp itself without changing its outward appearance, the most common leads are made of drilled or split bullets threaded on a weaker line (6–9 lb b.s, 2·70–4 kg) (*see sketch*), attached to a three-way swivel placed about 3 ft (1 m) from the shrimp. This mounting is advisable for rocky or congested pools where snags are frequent, as nine times out of ten the leads snag, the weaker nylon gives way and the leads are lost, but the shrimp and its mountings are saved.

worms

As has been shown, worming for salmon is almost identical to fishing with shrimps, with similar techniques, similar tackle, similar leads, only a different mounting. However, it is a much simpler method as it consists merely of a hook attached direct to the line.

Although the author has rarely used this method himself, there are several ways of baiting a hook with a worm or worms. Good lob-worms are needed which have been dug previously and put in moss in a well-ventilated box. They will attain the consistency of rubber and be far tougher than freshly found ones.

In the same way that a small hook is baited with worm for trout fishing, for salmon a larger worm is mounted on a stronger hook (1/0 to No. 3). However, two or more worms are better, one completely covering the hook and the others hooked through the middle. A bunch of worms with no life in them is useless; it is essential that the worms wriggle at each check.

Worming for salmon, which is sometimes banned in Great Britain, is certainly the most deadly method, and is less onerous and tiring than fishing with lures.

One of the many mountings used for salmon fishing with worm: a large hook whipped to nylon, the barbs helping to hold the worm.

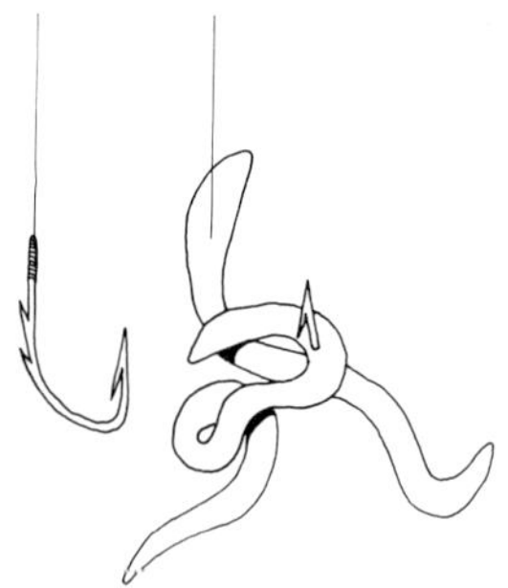

fly-fishing

Fly-fishing for salmon is the supreme art in fishing. The British experts left a large legacy of flies and works on salmon fishing at the end of the last century. The choice of salmon flies was and still is a Chinese puzzle compared with the choice of trout flies.

Let us continue with a description of tackle and techniques. There is no standard fly-fishing tackle, it must be chosen according to the width and depth of the river, the current and the fish to be taken.

rods

For fly-fishing in most rivers in Brittany, Normandy, England, Ireland and Scotland a 12 ft (3·50 m) medium-strength rod is suitable, made either of split cane or tubular glass and capable of casting a fly about 30 yards (27 m) and powerful enough to land 8–12 lb (3·50–5·50 kg) salmon. In certain narrow, shallow waters some fishermen prefer to use a light single-handed rod of 10 or 10½ ft (3 or 3·20 m) and line to match.

For fly-fishing in large rivers like the Gave, the Allier, the Spey, the Tay, the Sella, the Narcéa, the Eo, the Driva and others, 14 and 14½ ft (4 and 4·50 m) rods are common, but some anglers needing to make very long casts to fish lies which would otherwise be inaccessible, use rods as long as 18 ft (5·50 m). In this way they are able to cast more than 40 yards (40 m) of line without danger of snagging on the back-cast.

flies

Wet flies are unlike any insect. The most common artificial salmon flies go in size from No. 8 to 5/0. The illustration on page 96 shows the colours of some of the best known flies.

There are several shapes and mountings, such as the classic flies on a single hook; the longer streamer types; low-water flies mounted on large hooks which have the advantage of small flies without the disadvantage of the small hook; the ABU Optic-Salmos with their protuberant eyes; and the original tube-flies, which have given way to the weighted variety armed with a treble (*see sketch* on page 58).

Finally there are the spoon-flies designed for light spinning in low water.

lines

A fly line has to be heavy so that it may be cast by the flex of the rod and the angler's forward and backward movements, much in the same way that a stock-whip is used. The fly is linked to the heavy and very visible line by a nylon leader which not only permits the fly to enter the water quietly but separates it from the line.

So, the heavy fly line is cast in forward and backward loops in the air, the fly on its nylon leader following it and finally turning over to touch the water. Flies are too light to be cast in any other way.

Today fly lines are usually made from man-made fibres coated with plastics: floating lines from a braided level nylon core over which a smooth coat of plastic filled with bubbles of air is arranged, tapered so that the tip of the line can alight on the water gently; and sinking lines from Terylene and Dacron cores with heavy plastic coatings.

The old type of fly line, made from silk plaited into a taper and then soaked and polished with linseed oil, is largely falling into disuse and only one company is now producing it: the line is the English Kingfisher brand, and its main advantage is that its diameter for weight is less than plastic lines and its slow-sinking qualities make it superb for some salmon fishing techniques.

Fly lines are made in three profiles for salmon fishing: level throughout; double tapered (level for perhaps 98 ft (29·80 m) on the middle, with each end tapered for some 12 ft (3·50 m) to a fine tip), and weight-forward taper, on which the first 35 ft (10·50 m) or so is tapered, slowly like the double taper at the front, then quickly at the back down to a thin level line, which permits the angler to make long casts by shooting the slim line after he has cast the heavy forward part out over the river. The heavy front part pulls the thin line, which is coiled in front of the angler's feet, or in a line basket round his hips, through the rod rings and gives great distances.

The disadvantages of the weight-forward line for floating-line fishing for salmon include the fact that any manipulation of the line while the fly is being fished is much more difficult to do than with a double-tapered line, though not altogether impossible, though some types of casting are impossible.

The weight of the fly line has to match the action of the rod, but the matching is far less critical with hollow glass rods than with split-cane or greenheart rods, and a size up or down on the maker's recommendation will generally be perfectly in order.

Fly lines are described in both their weight and profile characteristics by an international code, first used by the American Fishing Tackle Manufacturers' Association (the AFTM code). The code states the weight in grains of the first 30 ft (9 m) of the line, excluding the level foot or so at the extremity (see table).

Sizes for most salmon fishing go from 6 for low water in summer to the heavy size 12 for deep, powerful spring water when the line has to be sunk deeply. For example, a double-tapered floating size 8 line would be described thus: DT8F—the F signifying floating. If sinking, the letter would have been S. A line that will sink if ungreased but float when greased (silk) is described as an intermediate line by the letter I.

DT: Double Taper
L : Level
S : Sinking (wet fly)
I : Intermediate (must be greased to float)
WF: Weight Forward
F : Floating

The numbers and corresponding weights:

No.	1	2	3	4	5	6	7	8	9	10
g	3·9	5·2	6·5	7·8	9·1	10·4	12	13·6	15·6	18·2

Most 12 ft (3·50 m) salmon fly rods will cast size 8 or 9 lines, some even size 7; 14 ft (4 m) rods for big fish and big rivers, specially in spring, will cast size 10 or upwards.

Leaders for salmon may be tapered or level lengths of nylon, as light as 8 lb (3 kg) test for use in low summer water, as strong as 25 lb (11 kg) in a Norwegian torrent, and between 6 ft (2 m) long for sunk-line fishing to 12 ft (3·50 m) or more for low-water fishing. Nylon is best joined by blood-knots.

A final word on rods, since they are so much a part of the act of casting and fighting a salmon: although there are several types of action—tip action, middle to tip action, and all-through action—most of the really experienced fly-fishermen choose an action which comes well down towards the handle, which not only makes all-day casting, including some of the specialised casts, less tiring, but makes for safer playing of fish as the rod absorbs shocks better.

In a general book it is not possible to discuss this in any depth, but the basic intent is to cast the line across and down the river so that the fly travels across and down the current, behaving like a live thing. In water temperatures of late spring to early autumn the floating line is often used, the fly fishing from midwater to only an inch (2·54 cm) beneath the surface. In the February to April period, in general, the fly must be fished close to the bottom, slowly on a sinking line.

Three fly rods with different actions. Left to right: fast or American action; soft or English action; parabolic action (French). ▶

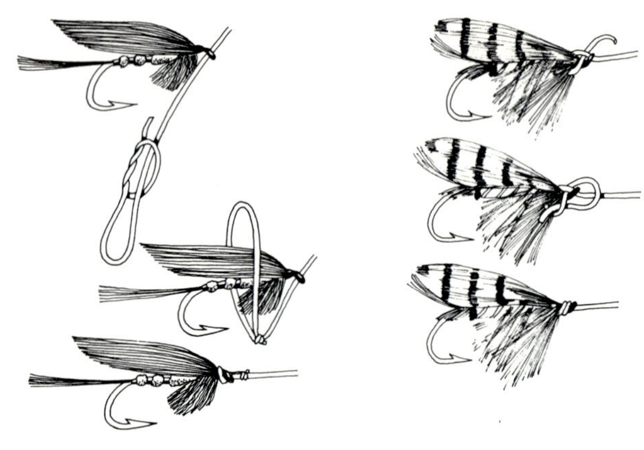

Two knots for attaching the fly to the point.

Four artificial flies. (Fully dressed salmon fly, top left; top right, a streamer; bottom left. low-water fly and tube-fly.)

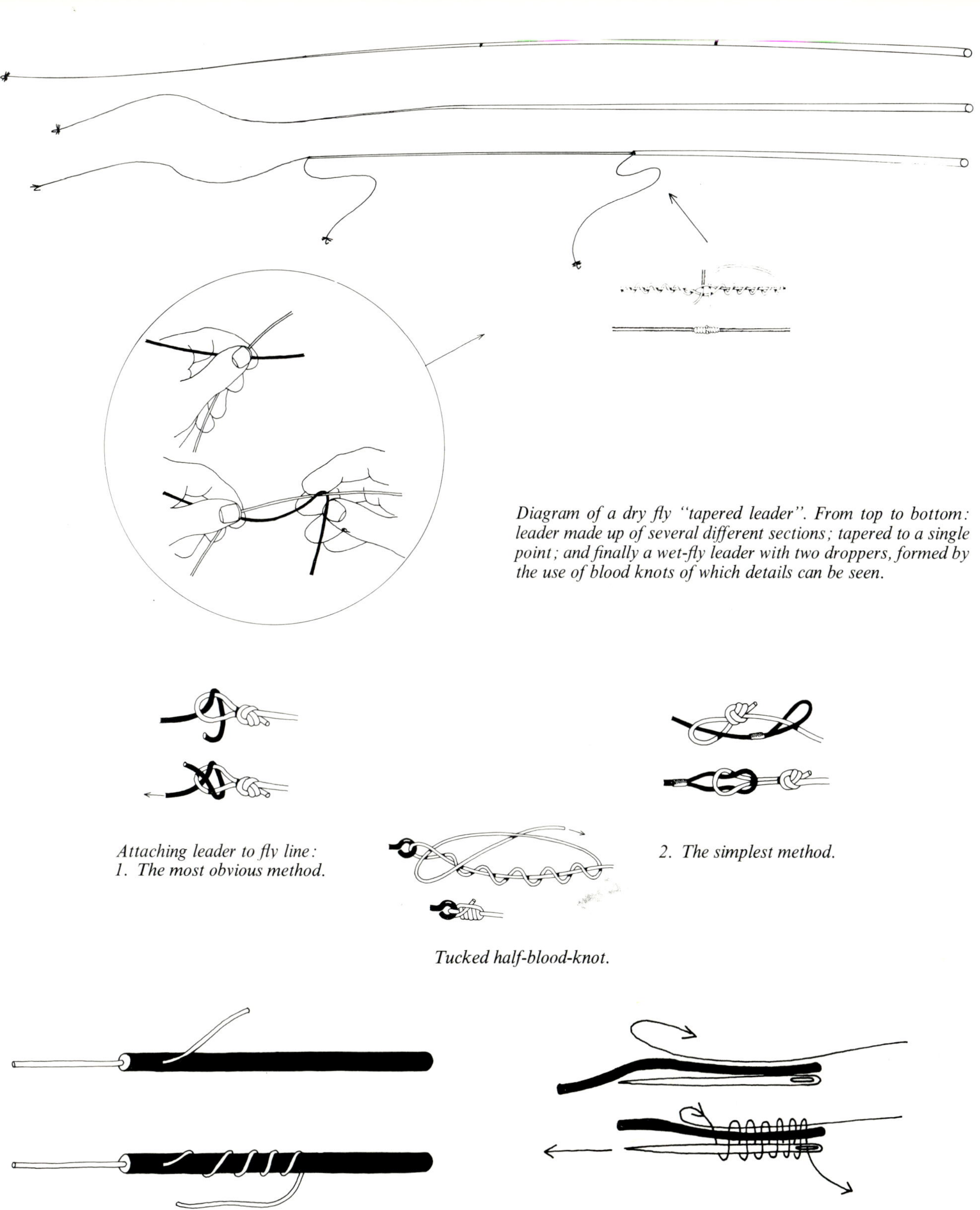

Diagram of a dry fly "tapered leader". From top to bottom: leader made up of several different sections; tapered to a single point; and finally a wet-fly leader with two droppers, formed by the use of blood knots of which details can be seen.

Attaching leader to fly line:
1. The most obvious method.

2. The simplest method.

Tucked half-blood-knot.

3. The most secure method.

4. A needle-knot, which forms a whipping over the fly-line.

fishing technique

The sketch opposite shows some of the normal overhead casting technique. It is important to let the line extend fully, back and front, before pushing the line (and rod) into the opposite direction. Spare line is held in the fingers of the lower hand on the rod butt, and is shot into the cast as the line is projected forward.

The progress of the fly through the water is controlled by the angler, who must be aware of his line, especially if it is floating. He can prevent the line being drawn by fast currents into a downstream bow, thus dragging the fly too quickly down and across the salmon lies. He is unable to manipulate a sinking line, unless he does it by throwing an upstream bow in the line at the moment it alights on the water, so he usually makes his cast at an angle of about 45 degrees downstream and across, so that the fly fishes deep and slow.

It is very important to do nothing when a fly is taken by a salmon, for the fish takes it in a slow and deliberate manner and returns to its lie holding the fly firmly in its mouth. One of the maxims is to count to five, then, as the line tightens and the rod tip is felt to become heavy, to give a firm pull. Never tighten when you see a salmon rise to the fly.

When fighting a salmon try to keep either on a level with the fish or slightly downstream of it; if the fish runs down a rapid, do not try to pull it back but follow it down, if possible. It is essential to have plenty of backing (100 yards (90 m) at least) of 20 lb (9 kg) braided line on one's fly reel and attached to the fly line. In strong water a big fish will often run out all the line and backing. A good reel with an exposed drum rim for manual braking is a great advantage for salmon.

Previous pages:
This angler gaffed his salmon too far back and in the belly: he was lucky to land it.

presenting the fly

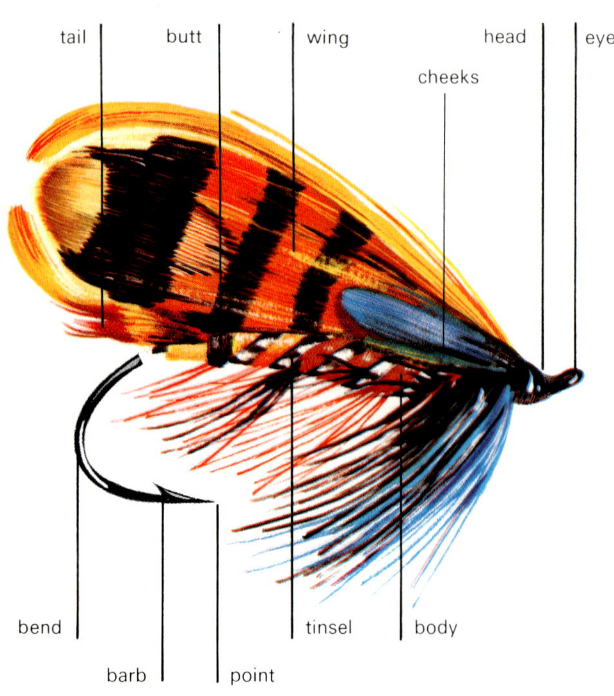

Salmon fly (Durham Ranger) from collection of Hardy Bros. of Alnwick.

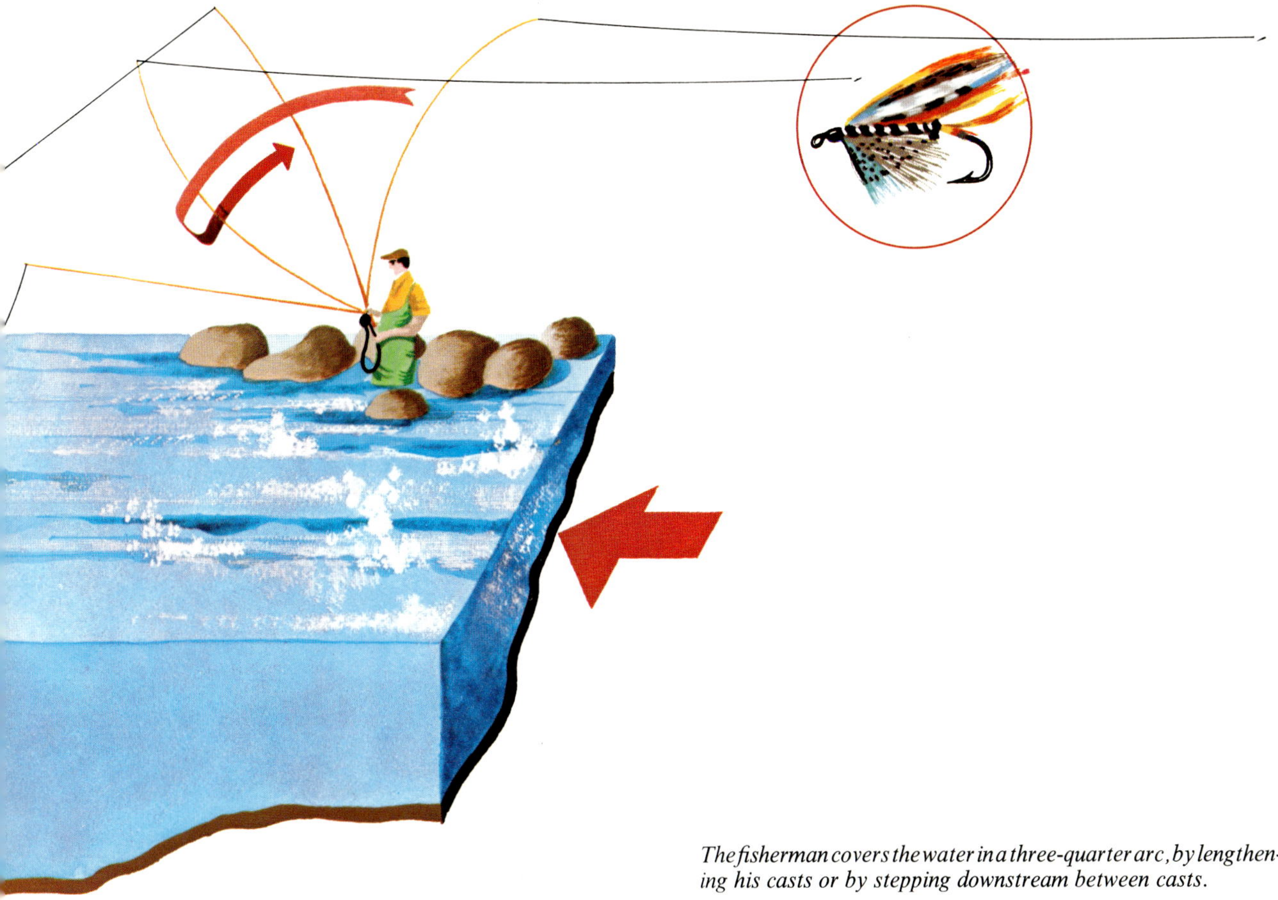

The fisherman covers the water in a three-quarter arc, by lengthening his casts or by stepping downstream between casts.

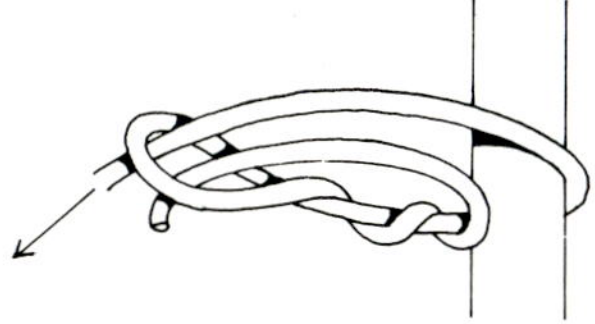

Special knot for fixing backing on to the reel.

Movement of fly tackle in the water on a slack cast:
1. *Line being recovered.*
2. *Line becoming slack.*
3. *Slackened line, the fly seems to grow in size.*

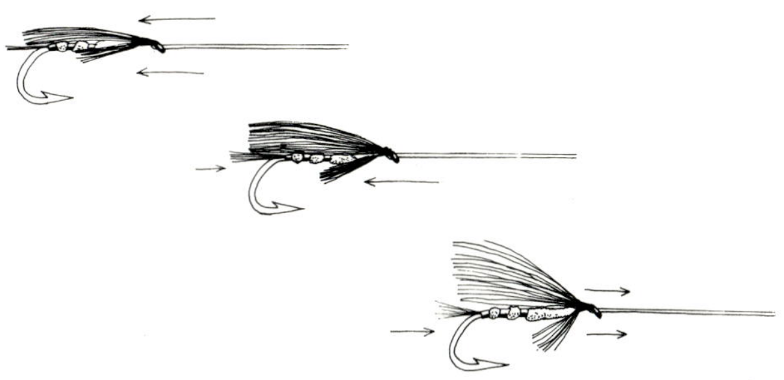

These three movements together give an impression of the fly being alive.

From the Davis Strait to the arctic ice of the sea around Greenland, the adult salmon make their mysterious way back to the mouths of the rivers of their birth.

salmon rivers of Europe

Most of the rivers of Europe, from the North Cape to the northern part of the Iberian Peninsula, flowing into the Atlantic, Baltic, North Sea, English Channel and Irish Sea, should hold Atlantic salmon. Hundreds of years ago they did, but with the Industrial Revolution came a mad get-rich-quick race and filthy wastes polluted the rivers, and water was abstracted from them so that they were unable to dilute the pollutants and cleanse themselves. Farmers have added to the killing of salmon rivers by not only abstracting water for irrigation but by allowing chemical fertilisers and crop sprays to poison them. Dams blocked the rivers.

Over-population brought additional pressures on water supplies, and the need to dispose of more human waste into rivers. Local authorities tried to reduce costs to ratepayers by not improving sewage disposal as populations grew.

And the disease of salmon has also cut down stocks.

Some of these ills are still with us: the main cause of environmental pollution is probably too far advanced ever to be overcome: there are too many people on this earth and the resources are not being properly used, nor fairly shared.

The Thames, the Medway, the Rhine, the Seine and many other big rivers once held great salmon stocks: now they are polluted, probably beyond all redress. With the high-seas netting and the inshore coastal and estuary netting and poaching that goes on, it is a terrible fact that the Atlantic salmon is becoming extinct and there seems little "man the killer" can do about it, even if all nations involved could agree to try.

In 1974 salmon fishing on most European rivers has been the worst for years, and when in 1975 the full effects of the heavy Danish catches off Greenland made in 1969 are felt, it is conceivable that many rivers will have so few salmon as to be not worth fishing.

France

Normandy

The Sélune, Sée and Sienne are the three main salmon rivers, the first being the best. Fewer fish have been seen in the rivers Vire, Saire and Couesnon.

Ducey on the Sélune is the main centre for salmon fishing; the river being dammed above the town.

The three rivers in upper Normandy, Picardy and Boulonnais that once held good runs, the Risle, Bresle and the Canche, produced only 13 fish to anglers in 1970–71 and are of little use now for salmon fishing.

Brittany

This is France's best salmon-fishing area and the rivers of the three *départements*, Côtes-du-Nord, Finistère and Morbihan, annually yield rod catches of between 2,000 and 3,000. The fish average only about 8 lb (3 kg), however.

The best known and most popular rivers are the Aulne, the Laïta and Ellé.

The Loire basin

The Allier is the only salmon-fishing river in the Loire basin today and fish only use the river for access to the spawning grounds of the upper Allier, which river gives about 200 miles (300 km) of salmon fishing. Vichy, Pont de Crevant, Issoire Brioude, Langeac and Monistrol d'Allier are the main centres.

The Adour basin

Salmon can run only one river, the Oloron, in this basin. Compared with the Allier this water is much shorter, but it does not necessarily hold fewer fish. Main fishing centres are Sauveterre de Béarn, Navarrenx and Oloron-Sainte-Marie.

In most of the French rivers both spinning,

with lines of about 15 lb (6 kg) test, and fly-fishing are used. For most waters fly rods of between 10½ and 12 ft will be found suitable, but on the Allier and Oloron stronger spinning lines are used due to the rapids down which strong fish will run. And on the Allier fly rods of more than 14 ft (4 m) are often used.

Spain

The Atlantic coast of Spain has several salmon rivers which flow down from the Cantabrian mountains. The most notable are the Rios Anson, Navia, Deva-Cares, Sella and Narcéa in the Asturias. Principal fishing centres: Panés on the Deva-Cares and Corneliana on the Rio Narcéa. Each year this picturesque Asturian city holds an "International Festival", a fishing tournament which brings together fly-fishermen, not just from Spain, but from the whole of Europe.

In Galicia there is just one notable river, the Eo, which has some very beautiful stretches for fly-fishing.

Tackle: it is difficult to advise on tackle for every river; an all-purpose rod of 9 ft (2·80 m) is probably best. However, in view of the crystal-clear water in some rivers, fishing must be relatively fine, but sometimes it would be taking a chance to use 9 lb b.s. (4 kg) line.

the British Isles

Compared with what has happened in France and in neighbouring European countries on the subject of pollution, abstraction, dams and overfishing devastating salmon rivers and salmon stocks, the British Isles, though suffering from many of the ills of Continental Europe, still has the finest salmon fishing of all.

The cream of the salmon fishing is in Scotland, but Ireland, both the North and the Republic, can boast superb fishing, although the inshore and estuary netting needs proper control.

Wales has some fine rivers, and even England has rivers like the Wye and the Hampshire Avon, both of which have salmon averaging nearly 18 lb (8 kg), although big spring fish have been rarer in the past few years. There are well over 100 salmon rivers in the British Isles, including Ireland, and those on the east coasts tend to produce spring runs while those on the west have summer runs, being smaller rivers in general and dependent on rainfall for their fish.

Among the best known rivers are:

England and Wales: Hampshire Avon Wye, Eden, Lune, Esk, Towy, Cothi, Teifi, Ithon, Ribble, Hodder, Irt, Exe, Torridge, Tamar, Test, Itchen, Severn, Dart, Camel, Aln, Coquet, Taw, Tavy, Teign, Tyne, Conway, Clwyd, Dee, Glaslyn, Mawddach, Usk, Cleddau, Dovey.

Scotland: Tweed, Tay, Awe, Border Esk, Nith, Stinchar, Findhorn, Annan, Kirkaig, Lochy, Alness, Beauly, Conon, Aberdeenshire Dee, Deveron, Don, Ness, Spey, Lossie, Thurso, Ythan, Earn, Lyon, Conon, Fyne, Carradale, Helmsdale, Brora.

Ireland: Blackwater, Shannon, Barrow, Bann, Suir, Slaney, Bandon, Boyne, Lee, Nore, Feale, Ilen, Inny, Laune, Maine, Maigue, Mulcaire, Owenmore, Corrib, Erriff, Bundrowes, Moy, Owenea, and the Northern Ireland rivers such as the Mourne, Foyle, Finn, Faughan, Roe, Bush, Main.

Scandinavia

Norway

Norway's salmon, too, are fewer in numbers than the halcyon days of the past, but it is still a wonderful country with immense fish to attract the salmon angler, plus superb water in which to fish—steep, short rocky rivers that roar and crash their way to the fjords.

Alta, Driva, Aaro, Laerdal, Nea, Vosso, Jolstra, Namsen, Mals are some of the main rivers, and the season usually begins in June when the waters clear from melting snows. Some of the rougher rivers demand heavy tackle, since a fish once hooked must be retained in the gentler flows or once it gets into the main flow it is certain to go downstream and be lost.

Unfortunately, due to the astronomical cost of salmon fishing in Norway, only a very few people get the opportunity to fish there, which is why the British Isles attracts so many anglers.

1

2

An English fly rod of split cane, made specially for Lucien Bonnenfant (1).

An early-morning fishing expedition on the Rio Narcea in Spain (2).

The smolt, young two year-old salmon in juvenile livery. As its tail is spread out it is not possible to see the characteristic fork (3).

Fishermen with their first Icelandic salmon (4).

Fishing for salmon with ultra-light tackle (5).

Three salmon from the Rio Cares weighing 12, 14 and 16 lb (5·40, 6·30 and 7·20 kg) (6).

4

3

5

6

Sweden

There are some salmon rivers in Sweden, but they are not famous and are not comparable to the Norwegian rivers.

Finland

In the extreme north of Scandinavia, Lapland is a super-paradise for fishermen, and the river Tana is regarded by many as the best in the world. The Tornio is also excellent and the minor salmon rivers are too numerous to mention. In this region, which is extremely rich in salmonids, it is possible to fish by the light of the midnight sun, the only one disadvantage being the thousands of mosquitoes.

Tackle: the same as the standard tackle for the Allier or the Gave. Apart from the breaking strain of the line, hooks must be checked as, if possible, only the strongest hooks, capable of holding the large fish, should be used.

a great fisherman

Salmon fishing has its artists, and pre-eminent among these, its geniuses. For thirty-five years this difficult art has been dominated in France by a man who has acquired a reputation to match his size: Lucien Bonnenfant, the doyen of European salmon fishing.

Since catching his first salmon in the Allier in 1934, he cannot count the number of great fish which he has brought to the gaff. He remembers the best years, and does not forget the worst; for example in 1945 he took 132 salmon on the Allier, 67 of these on the fly. That same year he took 42 on the fly in the rough waters of the Oloron. In this golden age he might take eleven salmon in one day, a record which seems like a dream today. Times have changed and the decrease in salmon runs has made such catches impossible, but Lucien Bonnenfant is still the grand master.

The author often meets Lucien Bonnenfant while in search of the adversary which attracts them both. For about twenty years the author has been privileged to watch this champion in action and to observe the application that he brings to his art. There is no improvisation; all his actions are calculated to be effective and to tempt even the most wary salmon. Starting with short casts and then increasing his distance the angler moves forward to concentrate on lies which the salmon are known to favour and wasting no time with those pools where only luck could bring him a fish. "Chuck-and-chance-it" fishing does not interest him, except in times of spates when he admits that fishing becomes something of a lottery; indeed at such times the salmon cruise a great deal and even good anglers are forced to improvise.

For spinning Lucien Bonnenfant prefers two lures above all: a wobbling spoon and the devon. For fly-fishing he has no preference, although he has caught twenty-eight salmon on the same fly. He makes his selection according to the state of the weather and the water. For him the size of a fly is as important as its colour but the main factor is its presentation. An excellent fly poorly presented will be refused, whereas an unsuitable fly well presented may tempt a fish. Lucien Bonnenfant's advice for successful fishing is:

1. Work hard. Don't give up even though conditions seem all against you. This is a question of character as much as of physical strength.
2. Have confidence in your lure or bait.
3. Cultivate a "feeling" for the water.
4. Know your salmon lies.

Having seen Lucien Bonnenfant fishing, the author would add one more point: Learn to fish well: in a way a *sine qua non* of success. How should one present a devon to a salmon rising 50 yards (50 m) away at the tail of a pool? Why should it be fished from the other bank, and if it does not take the devon, why should it be offered a Jock Scott or a Lemon Grey?

As soon as he has spotted the fish, Lucien Bonnenfant knows what to do. He knows the best way of making the most wary fish take.

It is difficult to describe this champion's fishing

Lucien Bonnenfant.

action. It has a mysterious perfection which stems from his physical fitness. Near the Aren bridge, up to his waist in a strong current, he fought for hours to lure a recalcitrant Béarnais salmon. His flowing action, the perfect curve of his long 18 ft (5 m) rod, the great arabesques of the line and the delicate presentation of the fly, 40 yards (36 m) away on the other bank of the river, provoked admiration. After three hours the salmon rose, took the fly, broke the surface and the fight was on. It weighed 18 lb (8 kg), to the satisfaction of its captor.

trout

The first fly did not appeal to it. It had a close look without taking it. The last fly was more successful.

the classic fish

The legend of the cunning, furtive, suspicious yet intelligent trout is confirmed by experts each time they return from the river bank. Yet the legend is only half true; this fish's vulnerability lies in its appetite, and it is more difficult to take a chub than a trout in a trout stream.

Before starting to fish, find out what the trout are feeding on. The trout's diet varies from shrimps to worms and flies so, depending on the season, it should be offered its favourite food.

At the start of the season worms should be used, or dead (or live) minnows after a storm, when the water is coloured. In spring, fish the wet fly and at the end of spring the dry fly. During the summer, when the water warms up, use lures, spoons, devons or nymphs, not forgetting natural baits at the beginning of June. Beware, though, of using bait and spinners on "fly-only" fisheries!

worm fishing

In order to conform to the fisherman's calendar, drawn up by many generations of experts, the standard worming method will be discussed first. This is the early-season method when the fine spotted fish have a good appetite because of the scarcity of food, which in turn is due to the low air and water temperature.

Everyone knows the common earthworm, although there are several species. In general, for trout fishing use a good sized worm; the "black-headed" one is as good as any.

Before describing the tackle and fishing methods, a word on the way of preserving this relatively delicate bait. Worms may be obtained by the classic methods, i.e. at night on lawns, armed with a torch, when a surprising number of them are visible; or they may be dug up with a fork. Whichever method is used, the worms are put in a well-ventilated box lined with bog moss. The box should be stored in a cool place such as a cellar and left for a week. In this way the worms take on the consistency of rubber; they become harder, easier to put on the hook and also more lively in the water.

tackle

The tackle for worming, for trout as well as other fish, depends on the width and depth of the river and on the size of the fish which are to be found there.

For worming, an all-purpose three-piece rod of 10–15 ft (3–4·50 m) in hollow fibreglass is recommended. An Avon or light "roach" rod with stand-off rings works well. This rod can be fitted with a light centrepin reel or an ultra-light fixed-spool reel. For the main line 6 lb b.s. (3 kg) nylon is good, but the hook link must be finer, 3–4 lb (1·40–1·80 kg). The most difficult part is selecting the weight and the hook.

The choice of weight in a slow-flowing plains river will differ from the choice in a fast-running mountain stream. The rougher the water, the heavier the lead will be.

Many excellent French fishermen adopt the following tackle: a double No. 6 hook to 5 lb (2 kg) nylon; 10–12 in. (25–30 cm) from the hook two split-shot are pinched on to the hook link which is attached to the main line. No float is used, just a piece of red or white wool knotted to the line 5 or 6 ft (1·50–1·80 m) from the hook, to act as an indicator. Such a mounting is suitable for fishing in very strong currents, in fast runs where one is searching for trout lies and where the current on the bottom varies in speed from the one on the surface, thus making the use of a float impossible because it would spoil the natural presentation.

So look for the trout lies, in the shelter of rock cavities under which the fish seeks refuge, and also at the bottom in holes or even the calm parts of a pool where it frequently wanders in search of food.

technique

In rivers with particularly clear water much finer tackle is suggested, with hook links of $2\frac{1}{4}$ or $3\frac{1}{2}$ lb b.s. (1–1·50 kg) nylon, No. 8 or 9 hook, single or double, and more lightly leaded with dust shot. If the river is calm enough, a Toulouse-style float or a well-cocked quill is sufficient. In this case be careful when a fish takes; while worm-fishing for trout one should wait a few moments before striking. This fish generally likes to chew the worm before swallowing it, and an immediate strike causes many misses.

Another way of worming is rolling the bait along the bottom. For this a fixed-spool reel is essential as each swim must be searched by letting the bait drift on the bottom. In small streams this method can have one drawback. It causes frequent snagging and the weight has to be constantly modified according to the current and the depth. However, it is a good method in that it is possible to take big fish from a distance; fish which might have hesitated to bite if the fisherman had not been fishing fine and far off.

In many parts of Britain, worm fishing for trout is frowned upon, or banned completely. However, even where fly-fishing is the normal accepted way of catching trout, a worm is sometimes considered acceptable, ethically, in the very low clear conditions of summer.

Then, with a slim roach or bottom rod, 3–5 lb (1·40–2 kg) line on a fixed-spool or centrepin reel, the angler wades cautiously upstream, swinging the hook, normally a No. 12, or one size up or down on that, baited with one or two tiny redworms (dug from old manure heaps or leaf-mould mounds) upstream. He may have only the weight of the bait to help him, or he may squeeze on a shot or two. As the stream brings the bait back towards him he raises the rod and gathers line to keep in touch. If the bait stops, or the line twitches, he tightens into the fish. By casting upstream, he remains unseen and the hook usually pulls neatly back into the corner of the fish's mouth.

The Stewart tackle (three hooks) or Pennell tackle (two hooks) are old rigs sometimes still used for worming. Their main function was to permit a quick strike directly the worm was taken.

caddis

From spring onwards, caddis-grub fishing brings good results. Late spring and summer are the best, as the caddis matures late in spring, but all depends on the weather conditions and the region.

The trout adores this tasty morsel, which is its staple food in many rivers. The stomach contents of many trout which have been examined prove how much they enjoy gorging themselves on caddis. They enjoy them so much that the tube in which the caddis lives, a mixture of twigs and gravel, is no deterrent.

So, always interested in possible food, the trout must be particularly attracted by a caddis grub out of its case which passes in front of its nose.

The best rod for this method is a hollow fibreglass one of 10–16 ft (3–5 m) length, never longer as its unmanageability in medium-size rivers would counteract the advantage of its length; add to this a centrepin reel or make do with a line attached to the tip, again depending on the area.

Remember that it is important to fish much finer with a caddis than with a worm. Therefore, a line of 3 or 5 lb b.s. (1·40–2 kg), a link of 2–3 lb (900 g–1·30 kg), a No. 9 or 10 hook and a much lighter lead than would be used for worming, such as a little split-shot or one bullet, is recommended.

In water deeper than 5 ft (1·50 m) a small float will be useful, but is not necessary in broken water, in eddies, and while searching for individual lies.

As with worming, the fisherman feels the bite as the trout takes the bait and chews it before swallowing; but strike fairly quickly, for it is often impossible to conceal the hook point in the soft body of the caddis, thus making the trout more suspicious.

water shrimps

This method is one of the most difficult and deadly. If they are available, collect the shrimps in the stream you are fishing. They are usually found under rocks or in tangles of water weed and once caught they should be kept in a large, well-ventilated box lined with weed.

The rod and line may be the same as those used for caddis fishing, but for mounting the shrimp the hook should be much smaller. One frequently hears of good fishermen landing 1 lb (450 g) trout on No. 12 hooks, so a small No. 12 or 14 is probably the best for this type of fishing. The shrimp can be mounted in two ways, either by threading one shrimp on the hook by its tail, or by using two shrimps, one completely covering and masking the bend of the hook and the other hooked lightly at the caudal end. The latter mounting is particularly effective.

With this method of fishing, practised mainly at low water and in summer, the lead may seem to be out of proportion in relation to the breaking strain of the line and the size of the hook. However, in this type of fishing, the trout will be found in the roughest water, where comparatively heavy leads will be needed to keep the bait at the correct depth.

A fixed or roving leger may be used, or alternatively, a length of nylon finer than the hook link weighted with a small bullet or split-shot, and attached to a three-way swivel. A float is quite unnecessary and might even be a handicap.

Baits like maggot, cheese, offal or salmon roe are all tempting, but all are forbidden in trout fishing in many countries. In fact, fishing with such baits is considered as poaching, because it enables too many trout to be taken too easily and is too effective to be considered sporting.

natural insects

There are an infinite variety of natural insects, which provide a host of equally delicious snacks for the trout. With such a variety to choose from, we will pick three: the grasshopper, the cricket and a natural fly—the mayfly.

the grasshopper

At harvest time the fields are full of grasshoppers, green, yellow, winged and wingless. The trout take them all, but they seem to have a preference for a particularly fine green specimen with a yellow body.

Remember, grasshoppers will not keep for much longer than a day, and then only in a well-ventilated box.

To bait up with a grasshopper, please refer to the diagram opposite.

Tackle: in clear, wide rivers a fairly long rod, say 16 or 18 ft (5–5·50 m), is used in France. It should be stiff-actioned for a quick strike.

The rod can be equipped with a reel, or the line tied directly to the rod tip. The latter method is probably preferable. Ten feet of 5 lb b.s. (2 kg) nylon, a link of 3 or 4 lb (1·40–2 kg), a No. 8 or 9 hook, which must be sharp, completes the outfit.

Before we go on to fishing technique, it should be emphasised that trout will take a grasshopper on or below the surface. The latter method is effective in sultry weather with a storm gathering as the trout then seems to find attractive all insects reaching its lie from upstream.

When fishing a sunken grasshopper, the insect can be lightly weighted. An excellent way of doing this, learned from Michel Duborgel, is to take a long-shanked hook and bait it up with a dead grasshopper, replacing the head with a split-shot of the same size, which one pinches on to the far end of the shank just below the eye.

This method is very suitable for an ultra-light line, with a grasshopper mounted on a very fine link not exceeding 1½ lb b.s. (680 g). In this way it is possible to dangle the grasshopper in the eddies, at the edge of holes and below falls, or let it drift to the bottom of pools.

The only problem of using the grasshopper on the ultra-light line is the take, or rather in feeling the take, and the strike. It is a question of instinct and a sharp eye.

Now, a more usual method when using a long rod. It is important that the grasshopper appears to be alive so that the fish is deceived into mistaking it for an insect that has fallen naturally into the water. It is therefore better to put the grasshopper on the hook without killing it, so that the insect is still able to move its legs and give some semblance of life. The hook should, therefore, be inserted just behind the head of the grasshopper so that the barb emerges at the bottom of the abdomen, and the eye lies under the grasshopper's head.

Thus only the line emerges from the insect's body and that is almost invisible to the fish.

It is essential that this appearance of life continues in the water. Obviously the best way would be to let the grasshopper drift downstream, but then it would be lost to sight very quickly.

Therefore the best method is to check the line from time to time, so making the sunken insect more appetisingly lifelike as it passes a trout lie, over-hanging banks, rocks, stumps and other haunts.

When using a floating grasshopper a different technique is needed, compared with, say, fishing for chub. It is better to let the grasshopper drift down several times over a swim containing a trout rather than hold it in the current, for the wily trout would think the latter unusual.

If the grasshopper should sink, leave it; just try not to lose sight of it in the shallow water. Wherever it is the trout will have seen it fall and if it wants it the take will be immediate.

The strike must be quick but not brutal, and unless the fish is very large it can be landed almost immediately without using the net.

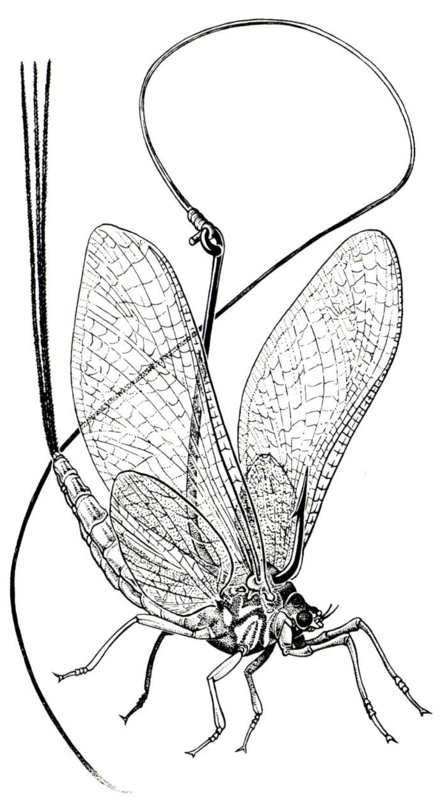

An adult mayfly hooked as for the dapping technique.

1. Grasshopper on a long-shank hook. Above: no weight needed for surface fishing. Below: position of lead for sunken grasshopper.

2. Two methods of baiting with insects or shrimps. Left: a single insect hooked through the end of the tail. Right: two insects, one of them hooked through the body, and the other one alive, with the hook through the end of its tail. This method is particularly recommended.

the cricket

Trout fishing with a cricket for bait is perfectly acceptable but they are difficult to obtain.

The best time to collect them is at the end of August and beginning of September in meadows and fields. It is a fragile bait but very attractive to trout, chub, dace and barbel. This mode of fishing uses the same rod, terminal tackle and technique as employed with the grasshopper.

the natural fly

A natural fly is any winged insect of relatively small size.

Anglers have caught trout on house flies while fishing for dace in small brooks. However, one of the flies the trout particularly likes is the mayfly. It must be said straight away that it is more difficult to catch mayflies than it is to catch trout on mayflies.

During the evening hatch it is possible to go to reservoirs or very calm waters and catch flies with a fine butterfly net as they go downstream. Perhaps even better, at the riverside at dusk on a very warm summer day a sort of manna falls from the sky as hundreds of hatchings take place, and there is no difficulty in obtaining flies.

Mayfly fishing is certainly more wearing on the patience than the wrist because, owing to the fragility of the bait, only a few casts are possible before it has to be renewed.

For fly-fishing with the standard fly rod, line, leader and relatively small hook (No. 12 or 14), with the fly lightly mounted, patience and delicate casting action are needed so that the fly is not thrown off the hook. The natural fly is immeasurably superior to the artificial fly. There is plenty of proof of this on rivers like the Loue and the Doubs, where the locals grass well-nigh miraculous bags.

It is with the natural fly that the Irish catch their beautiful lake trout, by the method known as dapping. The gypsies are the masters of this style, but they also have another less sporting one using a rod at least 18 ft (5·50 m) long, with a short line of 5 ft (1·50 m) at the most, a hook tied directly to the line, and of course no reel. They dap a fly along the surface of the ripples and take large numbers of trout, especially in the evening rise during the massive fly-hatchings.

spinning

This method is becoming increasingly popular. Popular as it is, however, it should be realised that it is not responsible for the biggest bags.

lures

The simplest and best known lure is the spoon. Firstly, there are the revolving bar-spoons, and whether they are called Mepps, Celta, Veltic or something else, they always look the same although each is marginally different from the others. Good trout fishermen always seem to favour the same ones.

There is also the little Colorado, which is not quite as popular as formerly. This is more suitable for catching large trout, which are prepared to attack a larger lure.

Then there is the devon, a very efficient lure even if it does not hold pride of place at the moment.

Plugs do not seem to find much favour with fishermen who spin for trout. These ingenious, richly coloured lures are used principally for pike fishing.

The quill minnow, made from the thick end of a bird quill and fitted with vanes, has caught lots of trout, and still does.

There are plastic minnows which bear an astonishing resemblance to the real thing and fine trout are caught on them.

Finally the Mepps tandem spoons and the Mitchell spoons with vanes turning in opposite directions must be mentioned.

the dead minnow

Where spinning for trout is concerned the dead minnow is without doubt the delicacy most appreciated by the fish. However, it is absolutely vital that it is presented correctly.

There are numerous classic methods of fishing with the minnow and numerous mounts. The mount opposite is most effective (*see diagram*); but there are many others such as the "cap" mount, the Maurice Laurens, the Donzettes etc.

technique

Firstly, what spinning tackle should be used? Which river is going to be fished and how deep and wide is it? Rough water or a chalk stream? Does it hold monsters or just average trout?

It is unnecessary to go to extremes, and a two-piece rod of 5–6 ft (1·50–1·90 m) is suitable in

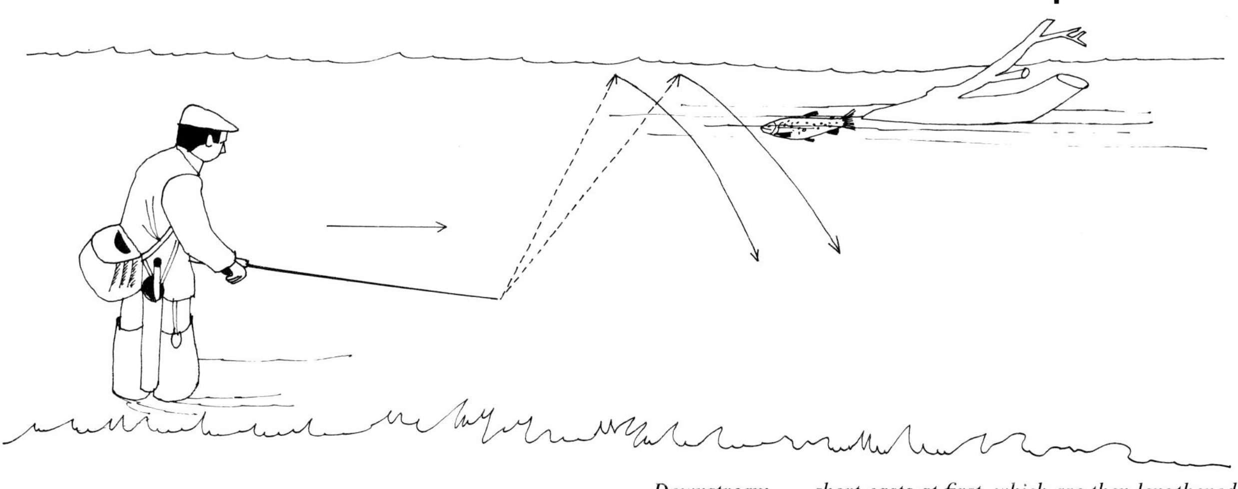

Downstream . . . short casts at first, which are then lengthened to the presumed hiding-place of the trout.

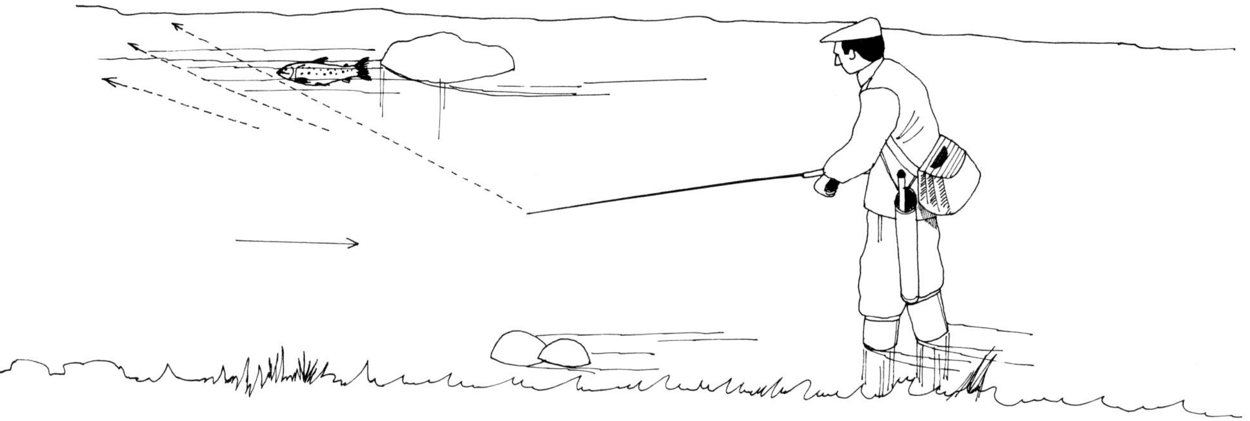

Upstream . . . long casts at first, which are then shortened to bring the lure near the trout's location.

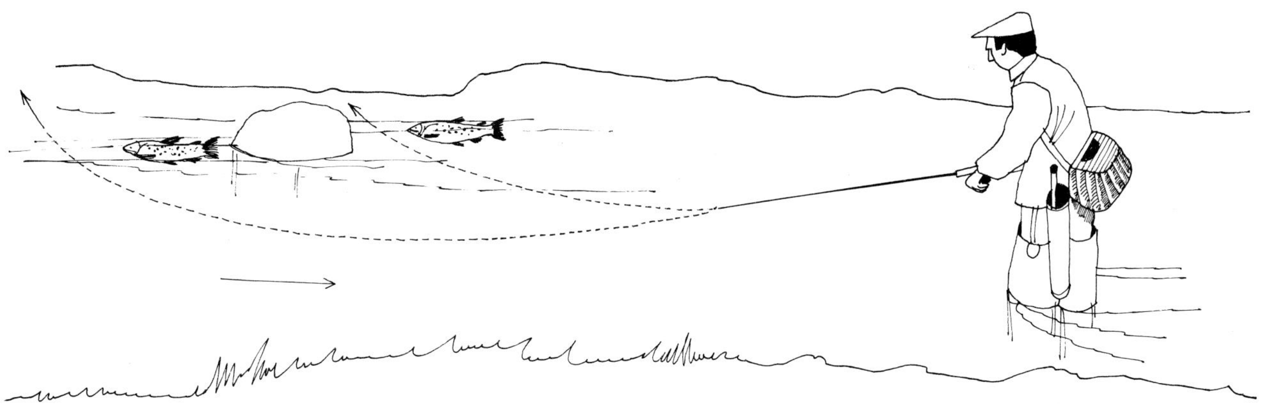

How a trout takes advantage of natural shelter.

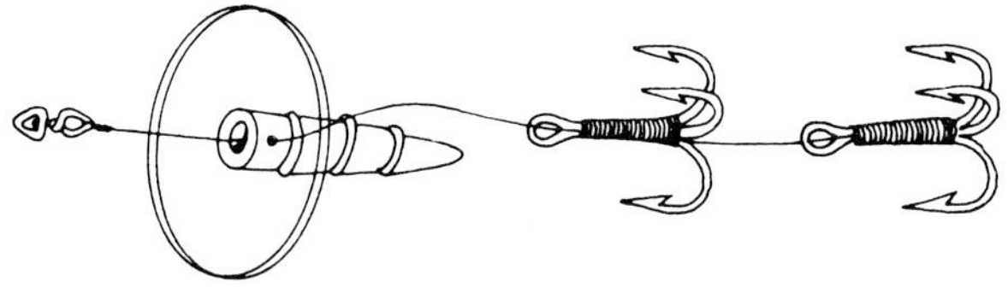

Tackle for mounting a dead fish for wobbling.

most cases. It should be of medium strength, allowing a weight of $\frac{1}{3}$–$\frac{3}{4}$ oz (10–20 g) to be cast, and equipped with a fixed-spool reel containing 80 yards (75 m) of 2–4 lb b.s. (900 g–2 kg) nylon. This combination is suitable for fishing with a spoon, a devon or a minnow.

There are two differing techniques: one for upstream, the other for downstream fishermen. Both should be learned, as each method can be successful in the right conditions.

If fishing upstream the fisherman cannot be seen by the trout, and the current drowns any noise made while wading; however, the fish may well catch sight of the line passing in front of it before the lure does so.

If fishing downstream, on the other hand, the fish will see the fisherman more easily and any noise will be directly transmitted through the water. Conversely, if a short cast is made and then gradually the length is increased the fish will see only the lure. This is the method generally used in salmon fishing, but there are good and bad points in both techniques.

While not wishing to cause even more arguments among fishing experts, it seems good advice to fish downstream in large rivers, taking care to be extremely quiet, to merge with the surroundings so as not to be seen, to walk as softly as possible and to search every lie, remembering to concentrate on the spots most likely to hold trout.

Alternatively, if fishing in small streams, rough water or very restricted spots where ultra-fine tackle with tiny lures must be used, fish upstream, taking care not to frighten the fish by casting too often in one place.

If it is a swim which is practically unfishable, pick the one spot where a trout may lie, and present the lure as well as you can without letting the fish see too much of the line.

With the minnow it is possible to fish either upstream or downstream, but remember that a minnow is always very easily taken across the current. So, fish down and across, allowing the bait to drift, but checking frequently to make it appear lifelike.

It should be mentioned at this stage that only freshly killed minnows should be used.

Take a pail of live minnows with you and transfer some of these to a plastic bottle half filled with water and tightly stoppered. This way there will always be a live minnow handy when one is required.

It has taken experts a long time to realise that the dead minnow preserved in formalin or glycerine, or even frozen, is nothing like as good a bait as the freshly killed one, which can yield surprising results.

Beside spinning, don't forget that trout can be fished for with a live bait, using float tackle, in the same way as fishing for perch. Try a minnow, a small gudgeon, a loach or a bull-head. The minnow is probably the best because, although not very durable, it has less tendency to hide, to swim under stones or get tangled up in weeds.

the artificial fly

Trout fishing with the artificial fly has inspired many writers on fishing and there are scores of books in the fly-fisherman's library. Halford, Skues, Louis de Boisset, Tony Burnand, Dr Barbellion, Raymond Rocher and many others are among the names of famous fishermen who are also authors.

Of course, in a general study, it is impossible to deal with all the subtleties of this magnificent branch of angling—fishing for trout with the artificial fly.

So, apologies are offered to the dry-fly expert no matter what exclusive club he may belong to, as we offer a few words of advice on general dry-fly and wet-fly fishing.

tackle and technique

For dry-fly fishing the type of tackle needed can be divided into five items:

1. A whippy 7–9 ft (2–2·50 m) two-piece rod (split-cane or hollow fibreglass).
2. A floating tapered line (silk or plastic), with sufficient backing.

Lures for all fish and all tastes.

1. *Alta-Minnow—S. T. P. Z. BB.*
2. *Plucky—P.* BB.
3. *Ondex—P. Z.* PE. *BB.*
4. *Flopy—*P.
5. *Voblex—S.* P. *Z. BB.*
6. *Luxor-Rafale—S. P. Z.*
7. *C.P. Swing—*T. C. *P.* PE.
8. *Plug—P.*
9. *Suissex—P. Z.*
10. *Bob—BB.*
11. *Mepps-Aglia—*T. C. PE.
12. *Plug—*BB.
13. *Vivif—P.* BB.
14. *Eira—*S.
15. *Trifacette—S. Z.* PE.
16. *Adys shrimp—S.*
17. *Flipper—P.*
18. *Dam-Turbler—P.*
19. *Spicky—P.*
20. *Stingsilda—*S.
21. *Articulated plug—P. Z. BB.*

These lures are recommended for the following fish; the best ones are in italics:
Salmon: S. *Trout: T.* *Charr: C.* *Pike: P.*
Zander: Z. *Perch: PE.* *Black Bass: BB.*

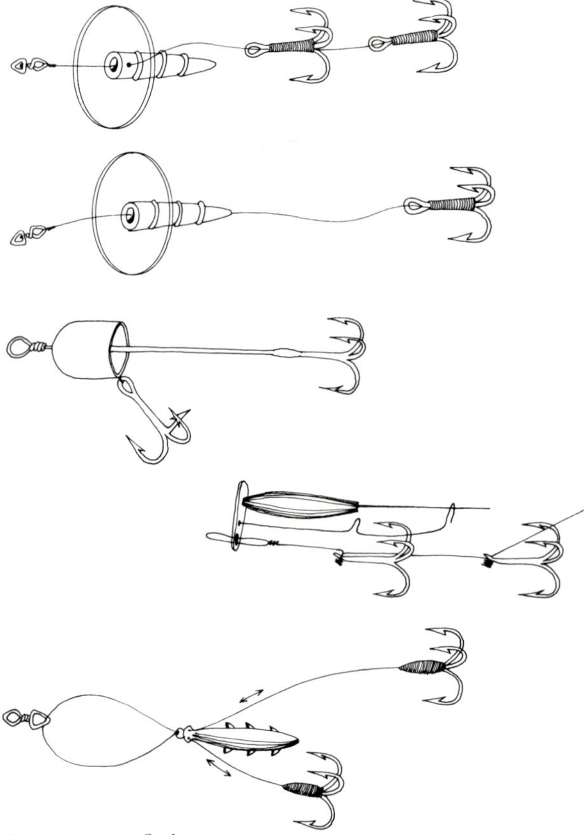

Some minnow flights:
1. *With swimming disc and two exterior hooks.*
2. *The same, but with a treble hook and line threaded through centre.*
3. *Hooded flight.*
4. *Weighted flight with swimming vane and needle (Donzette).*
5. *Drop minnow tackle.*

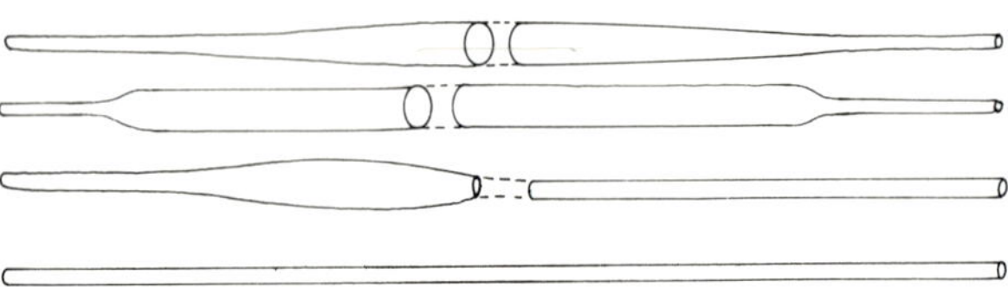

Three diagrams of fly lines. Above: a double taper line; centre: a weight-forward line showing the tapered tip and the belly (left); below: a level line.
The advantage of a double taper is that one is able to reverse it. The advantage of the weight-forward. which is non-reversible, is that it brings the rod into play with only a short length of line out, and at the same time can be recommended for long casts and fishing in high winds.

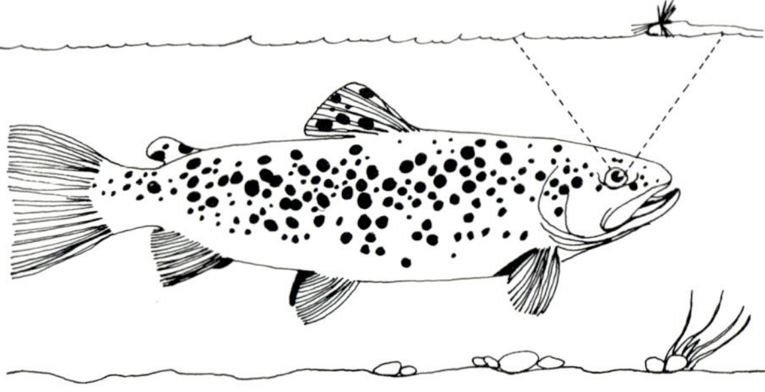

Specialists do not agree on the question of the trout's keenness of sight: when selecting a fly, does the trout go by its shape or its colour? The fisherman must take into account these two factors in order to select the right fly.

3. A tapered nylon leader to match.
4. A fly oiled to make it float.
5. A fly-reel.

Wet-fly tackle is identical, although sometimes stronger, and it is sometimes used with one fly but more generally with a team of three or four, which are not oiled and can thus sink. Sometimes wet flies are lightly weighted.

In a discussion on fly-fishing in general it is important to emphasise that rod and line should be correctly matched. In this type of fishing, involving continuous casting, rod and line are intimately linked, and the effectiveness of the technique depends not only on the fisherman but also on the balance of the tackle. In the chapter on salmon the standard AFTM line numbers are given. It is advisable to refer to them. Generally, in fly-fishing, the line serves as a weight (replacing the lead used in spinning) and the rod as a spring. It is the latter which shoots the line forward. However, this most satisfying of the angling arts does not easily give up its secrets either in wet-fly or dry-fly fishing.

A word about French-made equipment for fly-fishing.

Pezon and Michel of Amboise have maintained their high reputation for quality in split-cane rods for a long time. Of these, among the most beautiful and effective rods in the world are the "P.P.P." fly rods.

There are fine fly rods in the "parabolic" series, which are tempered split-cane rods of top quality, especially selected and finished. In a way these are the "Rolls-Royce" of fishing tackle.

In hollow fibreglass the new Mitchell series is excellent, and of course the famous Hardy rods, the finest in Britain, must not be forgotten.

As far as lines are concerned the natural silk lines have been overtaken by the synthetic lines made in different plastic materials, buoyant for floating lines, or denser for sinking wet-fly lines. It is difficult to recommend specific lines for fly-fishing and the fisherman should take the advice of the rod manufacturers, who determine both the strength of the rod and the correct line for it.

After the line comes the leader. Today gut and

other materials have been rendered obsolete by the use of nylon. Nowadays knotless tapered nylon leaders can be bought; for example a 9 ft (2·50 m) one may be 2 lb b.s. (900 g) at the point and 19 lb (8·50 kg) at the butt end.

Many fishermen prefer to make up their own leaders, as in this way they can manage to construct them with a better balance for specific conditions, such as for fishing in a high wind; Charles Ritz, for example, created his famous "rafale" for squalls.

A typical 9 or 10 ft (2·50–3 m) leader can be made by taking three or four lengths of nylon: one of 15 lb b.s. (6·80 kg), the next of 12 lb (5·50 kg), the third of 5 or 6 lb (2–2·70 kg), and ending with a point of variable length in 2 or 3 lb b.s. (900 g–1·30 kg). The blood-knot is recommended for joining the lengths of nylon.

the reel

The part played by the reel should not be neglected, although its importance is limited. It balances the rod in the hand, and during casting or false casting contributes to the rhythm—the timing—at which the British in particular are masters.

Some consideration must be paid to its qualities. It must be light and hold between 50 and 75 yards (46 and 70 m) of braided Dacron backing line, spliced to the fly line as a reserve on which to play big fish.

Nowadays the standard single-action reel in France has given way to the automatic-retrieve reel. Whether it is an Abeille (Bee), a Tru-art, a Flymatic, a Martin or a Mitchell, the principle of the automatic reel is the same. A spring is wound up which, when released, enables the spool to turn, and line to be retrieved.

Too many automatic reels have over-strong, ultra-sensitive springs which retrieve too quickly, and when dealing with a sudden slack appearing in the line during a fight with a fish may cause a break. The first requirement of an automatic reel must be the progressively increasing action of the spring. In this aspect the Abeille reel seems to have earned a deserved reputation.

the rod

Having dealt with the field of trout fly tackle in general, there are some other points worthy of further consideration.

For example the power and length of the rod is subject to conflicting opinions. Some prefer long powerful rods, others the shorter, more flexible ones. It is impossible to advise the tyro; it is a question first of the angler's physical strength and then of the conditions of the locality where he fishes most often.

However, for wading a short rod is preferable $7\frac{1}{2}$–$8\frac{1}{2}$ ft (2·30–2·50 m). For fishing in large rivers (say, wet-fly fishing with a team of several flies at the start of the season), use a 9 or $9\frac{1}{2}$ ft (2·50–3 m) rod, enabling longer casts to be made. The easier action and greater length will help to avoid getting the back cast caught up in vegetation when fishing from a river bank or in restricted areas.

There is no need to resurrect the old theories of fishing writers of the start of the century; nowadays the most popular length of rod is around $8\frac{1}{2}$ ft (2·50 m). With this it is possible to fish either a dry or wet fly in all rivers.

A word on the action of the fly rod. The tip action, or American fast action, is gradually taking over from the parabolic action created by Pezon and Michel.

The parabolic action, as its name suggests, came from the curve of the rod, which enabled the fisherman to cast a line smoothly with a minimum of effort, but this action is difficult to obtain with synthetics like hollow fibreglass.

As most fibreglass rods have a faster action, with less movement of the butt, the action depends on the top joint or the upper part of it. Casting is very different, but few fishermen brought up on the classic and supple butt action of split-cane are unable to get used to the more modern makes.

It should be mentioned, however, that Hardy manufacture the "Jet" series of fibreglass fly rods with a spigot joint in place of the usual ferrules. These are top-quality medium-action rods giving a smooth cast and yielding good results.

The French "Vario-Power" rod has succeeded in combining the synthetic fibreglass action with

A big male brown trout (11 lb (5 kg)) caught on rod and line on the Bresle (Somme). ▲ ▲

Rainbow trout in its characteristic livery, uniformly speckled with black spots. ▲

Paul Boyer wet-fly fishing in an Asturian stream in spring, during the mid-day rise. ▶

◀ *Picture of an evening catch on the fly on the Driva (Norway): six sea-trout and two brown trout.*

1. *A stonefly or perhaps a gnat has caused this trout to rise to the surface.*

2. *This Bavarian rainbow trout has taken the bait, and has been successfully played out.*

3. *Care should be taken of the fish's last struggles, even when it appears exhausted.*

◀ *The Lunain (Seine and Marne), a typical flat and open count trout river.*

Spinning in a northern river making its way towards the sea a difficult narrow channel.

Fly-fishing in July.

◀ *This brown trout has taken a fly that has fallen into the wate Unfortunately for him it is an artificial fly.*

that of split-cane. This $8\frac{1}{2}$ ft (2·50 m) rod is made with a hollow fibreglass butt and a high-quality split-cane tip, with the usual cork handle, reel fitting, a bronze-nickel ferrule and whippings of silk.

The action of this rod seems rather strange at first, but the user soon adjusts to it, so that today many anglers who have a somewhat sentimental attachment to the split-cane rod, even while recognising the qualities of modern materials, use it and are very pleased with it.

Fly-rod handles are usually constructed of cork, which is rounded or slightly oval to ensure a better grip, particularly for the thumb, which is essential for flexing the rod. The plastic imitation-leather handles (made by Mitchell to fit the hand) are also excellent as they ensure a natural hold, so that the fisherman can easily tighten his grip. They are constructed with a hollow for the thumb, which prevents the rod from turning in the hand during rapid casting. Finally, to close this chapter on fly rods, a word must be said about rings. This again is a controversial subject. Firstly, how many rings? Does the number of rings improve the rod action? Do fewer rings really lighten the rod? Should it have chrome bridge rings or simply light snake rings?

There is no doubt at all in the minds of most expert fly-fishers, and most of the best rod-makers, that hardened-chrome snake side-rings with loop type hardened chrome tip and either a wide-section hardened chrome or tungsten carbide butt ring are the best combination, the snake rings being half the weight of bridge rings. It is because so many anglers *demand* other types of ring that bridge rings, etc., are used at all. Agate-lined rings, once popular, are difficult to obtain today, and once the agate cracks the line is quickly damaged by abrasion.

In lake and reservoir fly fishing it is often necessary to cast 30 yards (27 m) of line, or more, to reach rising trout. This branch of angling has developed to a high art in Britain where many anglers use shooting heads (also called shooting tapers) backed with monofilament nylon of about 20 lb (10 kg) test to attain such distances regularly. Of course, more powerful rods are also often used, perhaps averaging 9 ft 3 in (2·80 m) in length and with AFTM 7–9 lines. The long-casting technique so developed was "borrowed" from the American west-coast steelhead fishermen.

artificial flies

In a general book such as this it is quite impossible to go into detail about trout flies; there just isn't the space. In brief, however, there are two main types of trout flies: those that float (dry flies) and those that sink (wet flies). Dry flies usually imitate winged flies of both water- and land-bred nature that the fish find floating on the surface, such as Mayflies, olives, gnats, daddy-longlegs, ants, among others. Wet flies usually imitate insects and other small animals trout feed on under the surface, such as nymphs and larvae and pupae of various water-bred flies, plus shrimps, snails, baby fish, sticklebacks and the like. Imitations of many of the water-bred fly nymphs etc. are known as nymphs in the angler's jargon.

There are other flies that are fished beneath the surface which are not called wet flies or nymphs. These are the lures, larger than the wet fly proper, and sometimes dressed on long-shank hooks: lures may be subdivided into bucktails and streamers, the bucktails with wings of hair, the streamers with wings of feather. Both can be just garish affairs that are drawn through the water and cause trout to strike at them by arousing the predatory instinct—the "if-it-moves-kill-it" reaction. Some lures, however, look sufficiently like small fish, tadpoles and other creatures to be useful in fooling fish feeding on such things.

Some anglers find entomology a very absorbing subject and combine a study of insects with fly dressing, to produce the closest imitations they can; others use flies that are a bit like many natural insects, or like none at all. Both types of anglers catch trout.

Such is the interest and following in fly-fishing today that beginners can usually rely on the flies and the advice offered by reputable dealers.

Let us take a brief look at some of the insects of great interest to the angler.

The **Ephemeroptera** are the upwinged flies, such as the Mayfly and the various olives, and are bred in the water, the life history or cycle being egg, nymph, dun, spinner. The nymph ascends to the surface, hatches into a winged fly (dun) but at that stage is still wholly covered by a gossamer skin, then sheds the skin to become a spinner, mates and then dies. The spinner stages last only a few hours. Besides upwings, the flies have long tails.

The **Trichoptera** are the sedge flies and the life cycle is egg, larva (this is the caddis which has already been mentioned as a trout bait), pupa and adult. Sedge flies, or sedges as anglers call them, are moth-like flies with long antennae, no tails and hair-covered wings which are carried in a roof shape over the the back at rest. Sedge flies are a feature of late evenings at the waterside when they appear in great numbers beside and over the water, causing trout to leap at them as

the casting of the fly

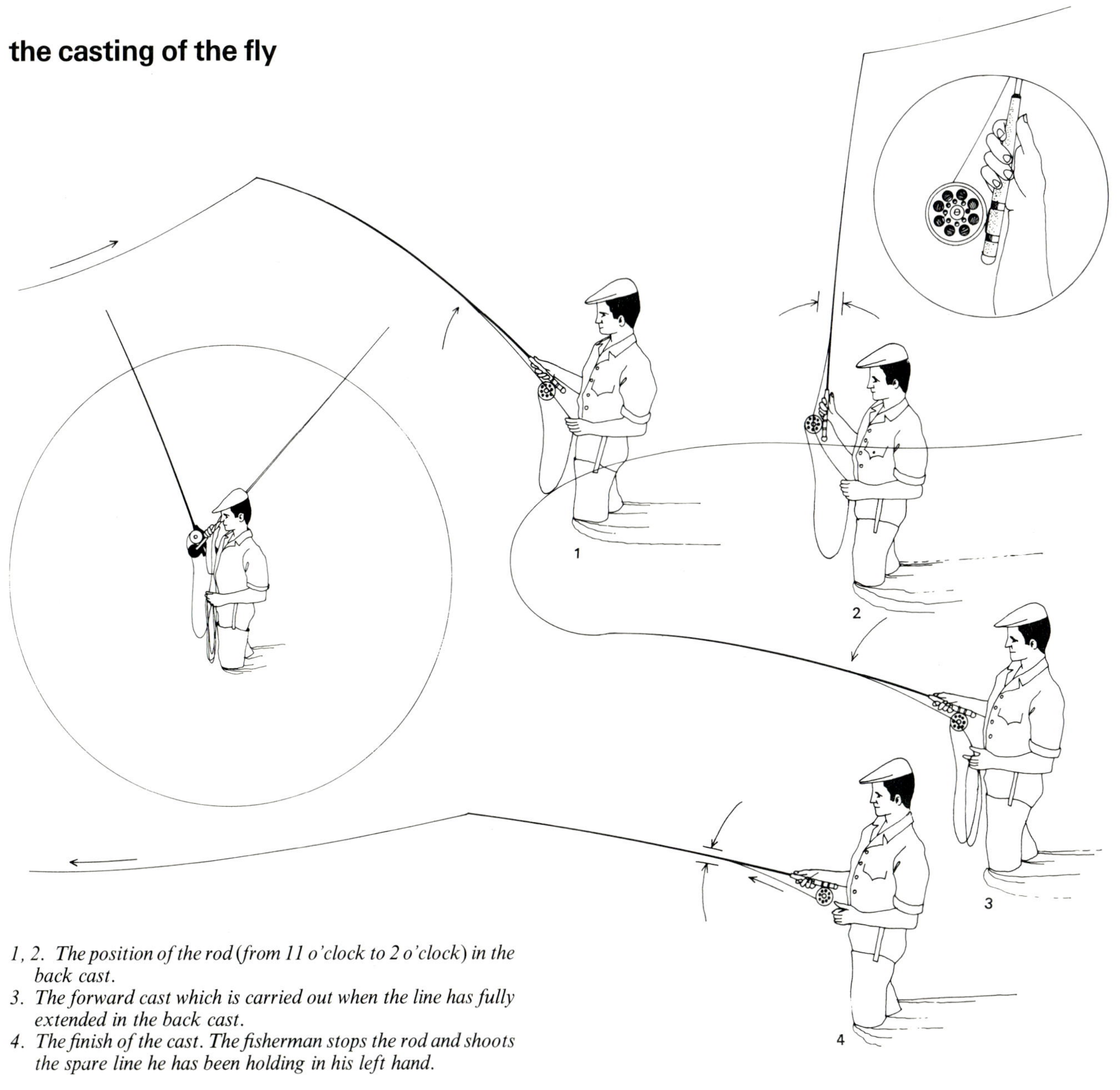

1, 2. The position of the rod (from 11 o'clock to 2 o'clock) in the back cast.
3. The forward cast which is carried out when the line has fully extended in the back cast.
4. The finish of the cast. The fisherman stops the rod and shoots the spare line he has been holding in his left hand.

1

3

2

1. *A French angler worm fishing for trout.*
2. *Spinning for perch in the Allier valley.*
3. *A French fly-fisher using dry fly upstream in spring.*

they skitter clumsily, half flying, along the surface.

The **Diptera** or flat-winged flies include the midges, crane flies (daddy-longlegs), mosquitoes and house-flies and is a very large order of insects. Most important to anglers, specially on still-water fisheries, are the water-bred midges whose life cycle is egg, larva (the bloodworm that wriggles in figure-of-eight movements in stagnant pools and rainwater butts), pupa (a hook-shaped stage during which it hangs in the surface film of the water at times when the surface tension prevents it breaking through to hatch) and adult. The crane fly, which hatches from a larva living in the soil on dry land, is also important in the summer months.

The **Plecoptera** are the so-called hard-winged flies, examples of interest to the trout fisher being the stonefly and the willow fly. They are found in numbers on rocky and stony rivers, but some also inhabit still water. The life cycle is egg, nymph, adult, and the stonefly nymph, which is large and ugly, being well over an inch long, is often used as natural bait, in much the same way as the caddis, specially in the north of England.

The **Coleoptera** are the bettles, the example illustrated being the Coch-y-bondhu (*Phylloperta horticola*), the angler's artificial bearing the same Welsh name.

The **Hymenoptera** include such insects as wasps and ants, and the Alder fly larva shown belongs to the sub-order of flies **Megaloptera**. The adult looks similar to a sedge fly, except that the wings are hard and veined, not hairy.

Finally, the other adult fly illustrated is the March Brown, a species of ecdyonurid, which favours stony rivers and hatches during the period late March to early May. It is a very important angler's fly on some rivers, and quite unused on others. The nymph is another ecdyonurid.

The grasshopper illustrated is copied by a few fly dressers, and is of some use on Irish lakes. Grasshoppers belong to the order Orthoptera.

The upwinged flies are of most importance to the angler who fishes in chalk and limestone streams, and who uses dry flies to simulate them, and nymphs cast upstream to trout previously seen. But upwinged flies are not confined to these alkaline waters and many hatch on rough stony waters.

The sedges are important to both chalk-stream, rocky-river and still-water fly-fishers and they are one of the few floating artificials which is actually moved across the surface to create a wake, specially at dusk, when the naturals are behaving thus.

The midges and crane flies are of most use to the still-water fly-fisher, and are, in fact, the staple diet of trout in most still waters (midges, that is). In summer, when hot, calm conditions make still-water trout fishing difficult, an artificial crane fly, cast out and allowed to sit on the water without moving, will often bring up a fine fish.

In fly-fishing, quite apart from the general intention to simulate the size, outline and colours of the natural insect, there is the matter of copying the movement of the naturals. In running water this may simply be attained by allowing the current to carry the floating fly or nymph back downstream towards the angler, or letting the current wash the wet fly down and across.

But in still-water fly-fishing, apart from a few instances of dry-fly technique, the angler needs to activate his artificial by drawing in line or lifting the rod.

Then there is the question of depth to consider. Trout often lie near the bed of the river or pool and will not rise to the surface to take the artificial. Then, the need is to use a fly that is heavy enough to sink quickly, and a long thin leader, wiped with detergent, to permit it to go down quickly through the surface film. But if the need to fish a nymph suspended 6 in. (15 cm) below the surface is the case, then the angler greases his leader to within about 7 in. (18 cm) of the fly, uses a floating line, and thus presents his offering suspended where the fish are eating the naturals.

There is much to fly-fishing, much more than a matter of casting and letting a trout take the fly. Fly-fishing with the artificial is a self-imposed problem, made to produce an art-form in catching what is, in effect, a greedy fish that scoffs a live worm or maggots or minnow without caution.

the flies and their imitations

Ephemeroptera

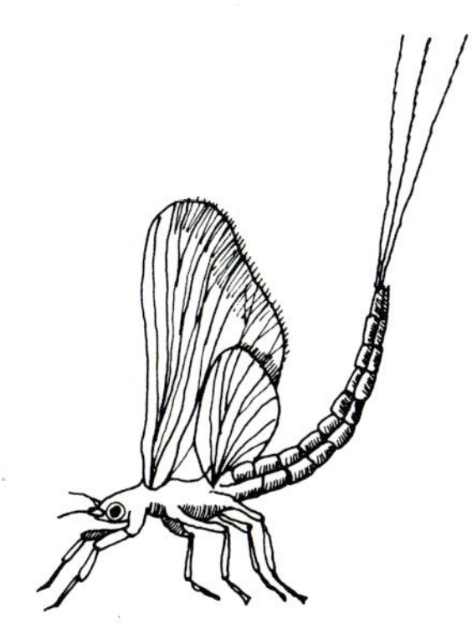

mayfly (Ephemeridae) at rest

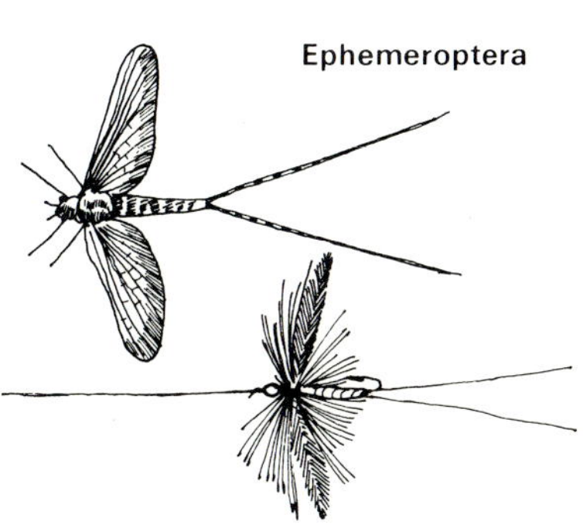

olive spinner and imitation (Baëtis)

sherry spinner (male) and imitation (Ephemerellida)

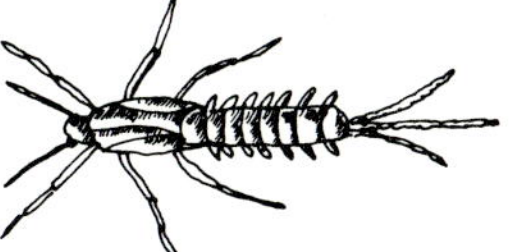

Ephemerid nymph

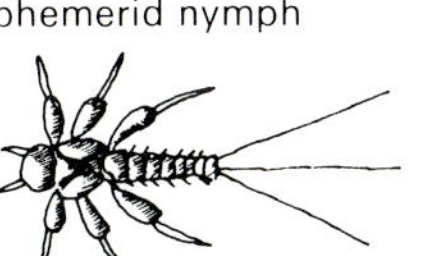

Ecdyonurid nymph

blue-winged olive male and artificial (Ephemeridae)

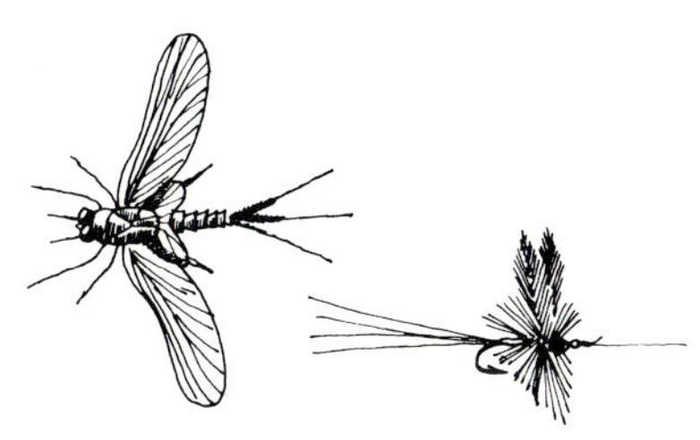

March Brown, imitation of Ecdyonurid

Megaloptera

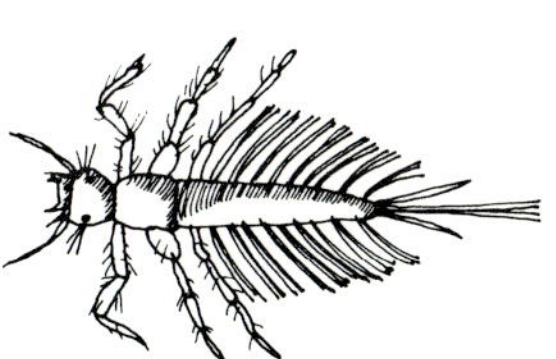

larva of alder fly (Megaloptera)

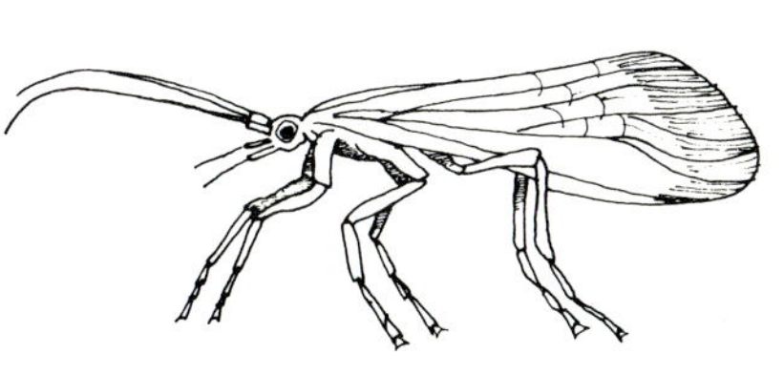

sedge-fly at rest

Trichoptera

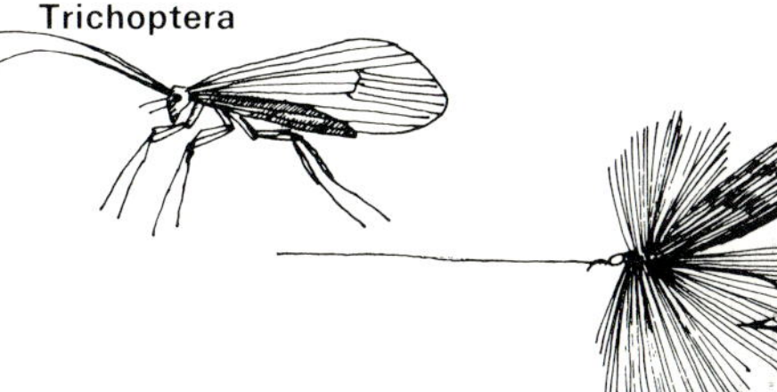

adult sedge-fly and artificial

Coleoptera

coch-y-bondhu: imitation of a Coleopteran

Plecoptera

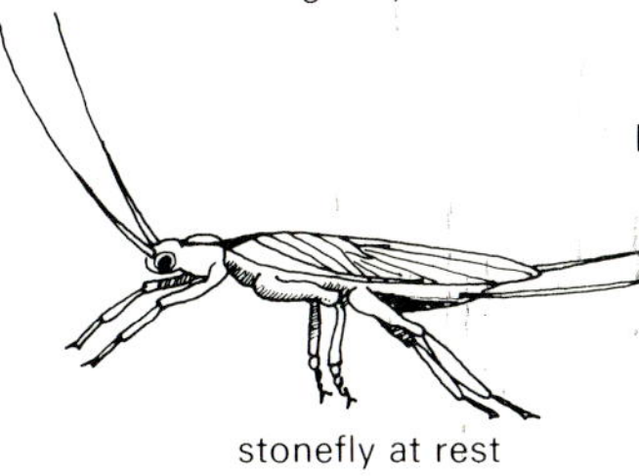

stonefly at rest

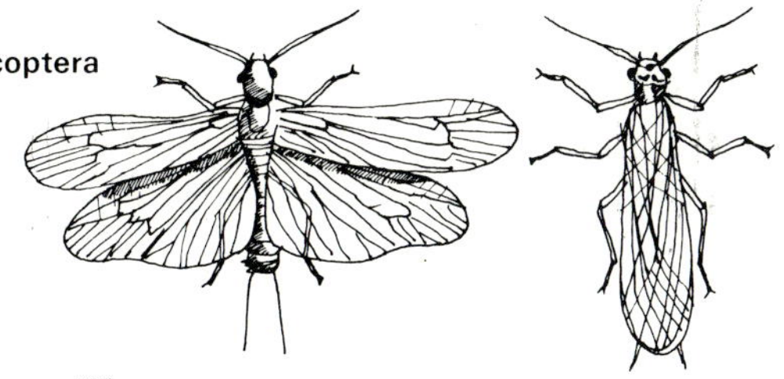

stonefly

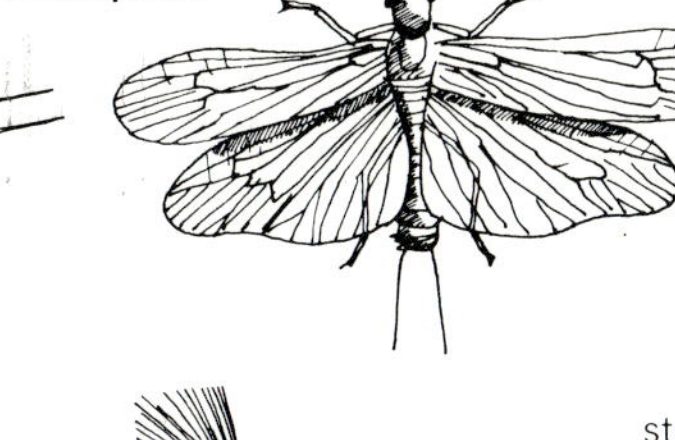

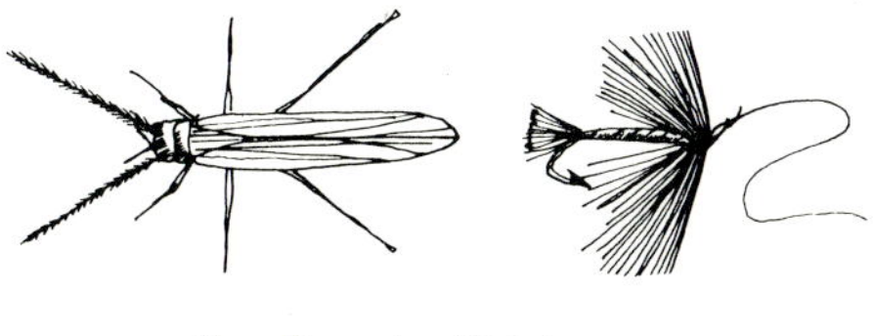

willow fly and artificial

Diptera

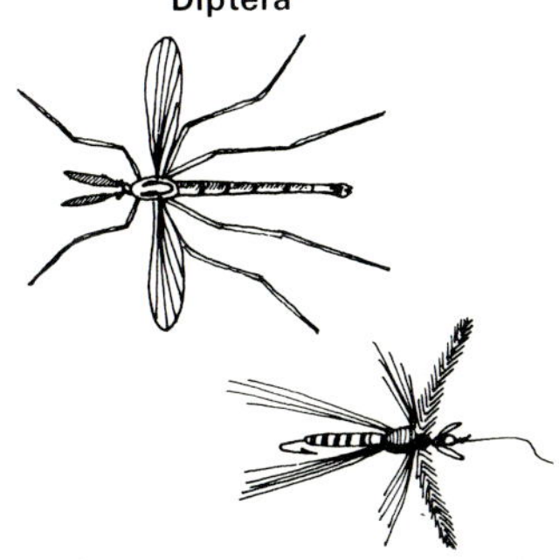

mosquito and artificial

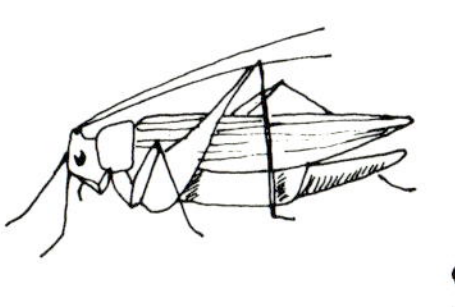

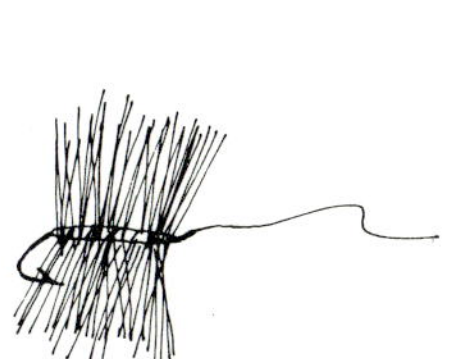

grasshopper

Hymenoptera

flying ant and artificial

Sea trout

1. *Gold Cock F.*
2. *Silver Blue*
3. *Teal and Red GB. Sc.*
4. *Ibis Cardinal*
5. *Silver Doctor GB. Sc.*
6. *Butcher F.*
7. *March Brown GB. Sc.*
8. *Yellow Fox E.*
9. *Black Boy E.*
10. *Special Doctor*
11. *Streamer (long shank)*
12. *Streamer (short shank)*

Salmon

13. *Shrimp Fantaisie FB.*
14. *Bonnenfant FB.*
15. *Kate E.*
16. *Corrib GB. Sc.*
17. *Lemon Grey FA. FG.*
18. *Black Doctor (blaireau) FA. FG.*
19. *Colonel Fuller*
20. *Jock Scott FG. GB. Sc.*
21. *Silver Grey GB. Sc.*
22. *Black Squirrel E.*
23. *Dusty Miller*
24. *Black Dose E.*
25. *Durham Ranger GB. Sc.*

The undermentioned flies are the author's favourites in the particular countries below:
Great Britain (GB.)
France (F.)
Scandinavia (Sc.)
Spain (E.)
France-Allier (FA.)
France-Gave (FG.)
France-Brittany (FB.)

N.B. For salmon in Brittany please refer to the Breton Ragot series which is not listed here. For Scandinavian salmon good results are had with ABU tube flies.

Trout

1. *Gallica No. 29 d.*
2. *Gallica No. 28 d.*
3. *Gallica No. 36 d.*
4. *Stonefly d.*
5. *Gallica No. 27 d.*
6. *Tup's Indispensable d.*
7. *Gallica No. 26 d.*
8. *Gallica No. 23 d.*
9. *May (Parabolic) d.*
10. *Governor d.*
11. *May d.*
12. *Halford Mayfly d.*
13. *Purple May d.*
14. *French Tricolor d.*
15. *Panama male d.*
16. *Red Spider w.*
17. *Levriere w.*
18. *Red Tag w. G.*
19. *Coch-y-bondhu w.*
20. *Hardy's Favourite w.*
21. *Grouse and mixed d.*
22. *Din-Din de Dubos w.*
23. *Virelles g.*
24. *Bourguignonne*
25. *Bretton de Chamberet w.*
26. *Pallareta w.*
27. *Sawyer P.T. nymph B. w. G.*
28. *May Special w.*
29. *Ritz w. G.*
30. *Sarranymphe w.*
31. *Olive d. G.*
32. *Red Quill d. G.*
33. *Blue Dun d. G.*
34. *Black Ant d. G.*
35. *Jacotte d. G.*

Dry fly: d.
Wet fly: w.
Flies marked G are recommended for the grayling.

1. *Good dry-fly boxes must have many compartments, each large enough to accommodate the flies without damaging their hackles.*

2. *Forceps are indispensable for unhooking the fly without damaging it.*

3. *Arthur Cove, one of Britain's most successful still-water trout fly-fishers.*

4. *This close-up of a trout's head shows the shape of the operculum, the comparatively small scales and one of the sensitive pores.*

5. *Dave Collyer, one of Britain's top fly dressers, with hatband of samples.*

1

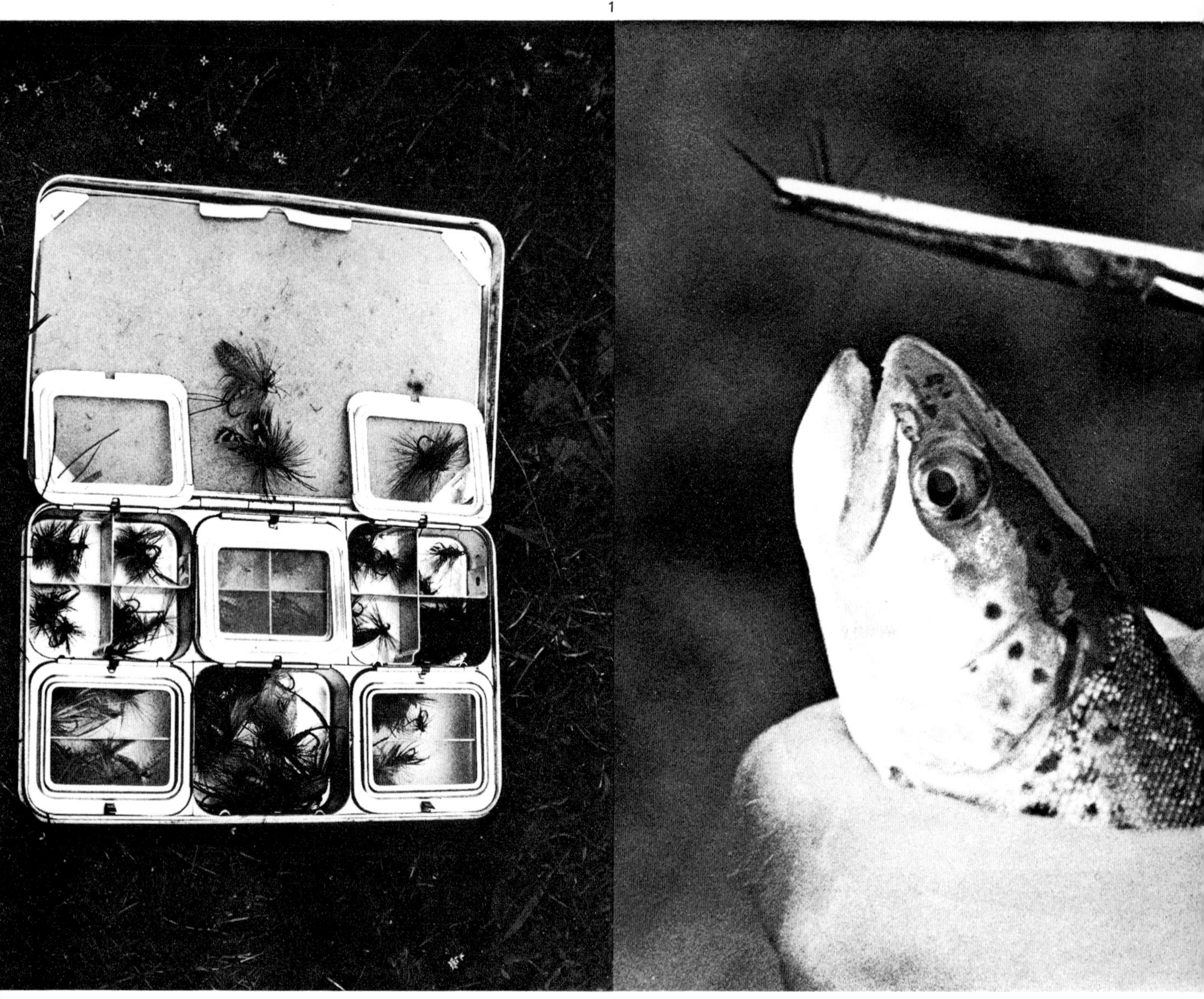

3

4

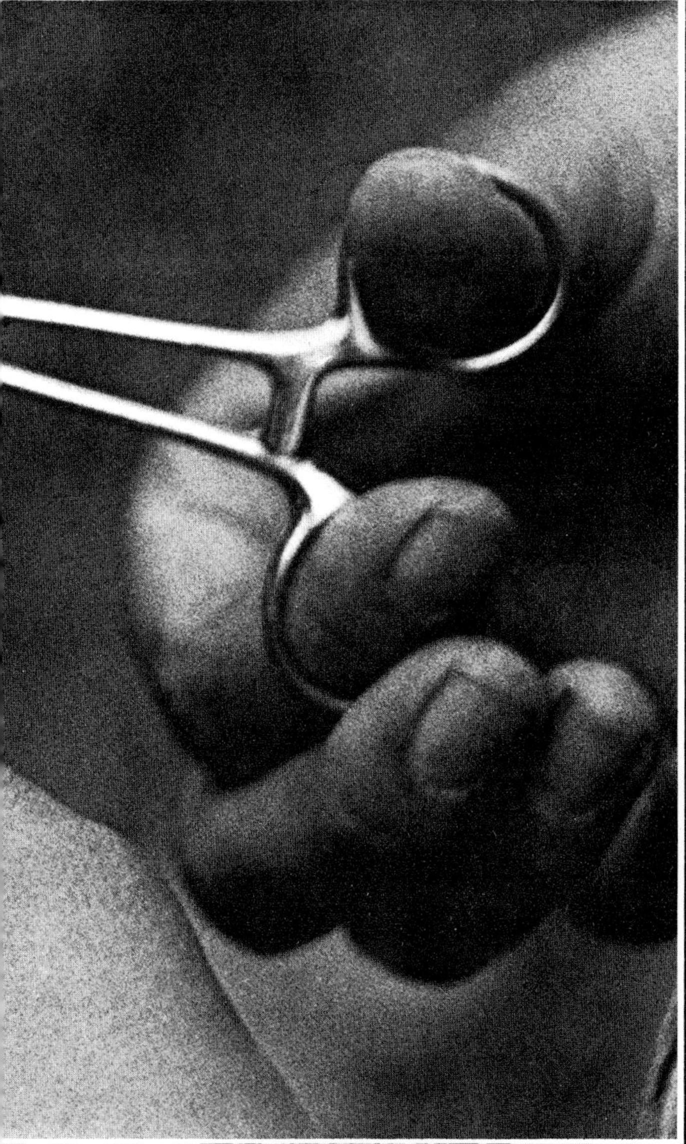

5

sea trout

Big sea trout are sometimes mistaken for small salmon, and vice versa, but there is no need for such confusion. There are a number of differences between them, the major visible ones being that (with mouth closed) the maxillary (jaw) bone of the salmon does not extend behind the rear of the eye, whereas that of the sea trout, and the brown trout of which it is a migratory form, does. Also, the sea trout has a thick wrist to its tail, which has easily crushed soft rays, while the salmon has a slim wrist and strong tail rays which permit the fish to be landed and carried easily by hand, the rays remaining a rigid wedge to grip. The spots on a sea trout are like asterisks and extend below the lateral line, while the salmon has fewer spots and very seldom any below the lateral line.

Sea trout do not migrate far from the shore as do salmon and return to breed like the salmon in the period March to October, the greatest runs taking place during July to September, spawning in late autumn and early winter.

The clear rocky mountain and highland rivers of northern Europe are home to the sea trout, but some clear lowland rivers also have them. They fight extremely hard and fly-fishing, mainly with wet fly (often best at night in high summer), spinning with small bar-spoons and devons, and worms, especially small redworms in bunches, are killing methods.

For fly-fishing a rod of between 9 and 10 ft (2·50–3 m) and line of AFTM 5–7 with leader point of 5–8 lb (2–3·50kg) test usually suffices. Flies are preferably bright and flashy, such as Butcher, Teal, Blue and Silver, Mallard and Claret, and streamers and bucktails also work well.

For spinning, line of less than 5 lb (2 kg) test is risky, as it is for worming, since sea trout of even 5 lb (2 kg) can test such gear to the limit, and beyond.

Norwegian sea trout have a special preference for certain flies such as the Teal and Red and the March Brown . . . but spoons, because of their shiny appearance and movement, attract them as well.

The Sheen, a sea-trout and salmon river in County Kerry, Ireland.

charr

fishing for charr

arctic charr

This salmonid, *Salvelinus alpinus*, exists in a number of clear, deep mountain lakes in the Alps, Scandinavia, Scotland, the English Lake District, Wales and Ireland. Seldom reaching 1 lb (450 g) in weight, the charr is fished with teams of flies, metal lures, worms and maggots, at depths in the region of 200 ft (60 m), and it is mainly fished for as a table delicacy. However, during late summer, these small lake charr sometimes migrate to the shallow shores and the surface and may be taken on tiny dry and wet flies.

The migratory form grows into the teens of pounds and is a far different prospect for the angler. Norway, Finland, Russia, Iceland and Greenland are the places to visit in September and October when these fine fish are moving up the rivers and inlets to spawn.

With spinning tackle and small bar-spoons, or with a fly outfit (as suitable for sea trout) the big migratory charr is a terrific fighter and is a superb fish, more so when in their spawning dress, with the belly and belly fins blood-red, especially in the cock fish.

Flies need to be flashy and highly coloured, and streamers and bucktails are most effective when fished on a slowly sinking line. The charr will often be found in very shallow, clear water in estuaries, inlets and rivers, and it is in such locations that the fly does best. The fish is best sought with spinner when the water is not very clear.

brook trout

Salvelinus fontinalis is not a member of the trout family at all but is more closely related to the charr. It is beautifully marked with a marbled effect on the back and at spawning time becomes brilliantly red, like the arctic charr.

The brook trout was introduced to Continental European waters in the late nineteenth century and in some areas, where the water is pure and cool, it has acclimatised well. It likes fast mountain streams and has not done well in British waters.

Although it fights in a lively fashion the brook trout is not highly regarded in its native land by the real *afición* trout fly men: the brook trout is too much of a simpleton to please men who deliberately try to make their sport more difficult by choosing to fish artificial fly in the

first place. A "brookie" will take pretty well any fly, particularly gaudy non-imitative patterns, and if it misses it, or gets pricked the first time, it will come again and again, until it ends up stuck through the jaw.

However, as a fish for the fly-fishing beginner to tackle, the brook trout is tailor-made. It can naturally be taken by spinning and bait, too.

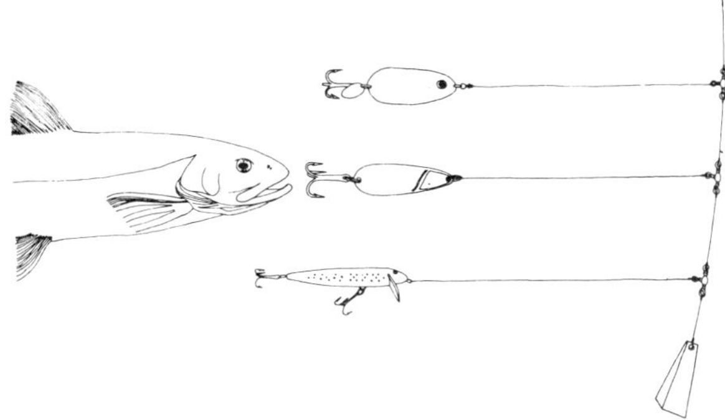

The lake charr is usually fished for by boat, trolling a series of lures.

A wading fly-fisher nets a fish. ▲

*A fine colour shot of an American brook trout (*Salmo fontinalis*) showing the marbling on the back and the stark white leading edges of pectoral, ventral and anal fins.* ▶▶

◀ *Deep mountain lakes have been the home of the smaller type of arctic charr for millions of years. This one is in the Alps.*

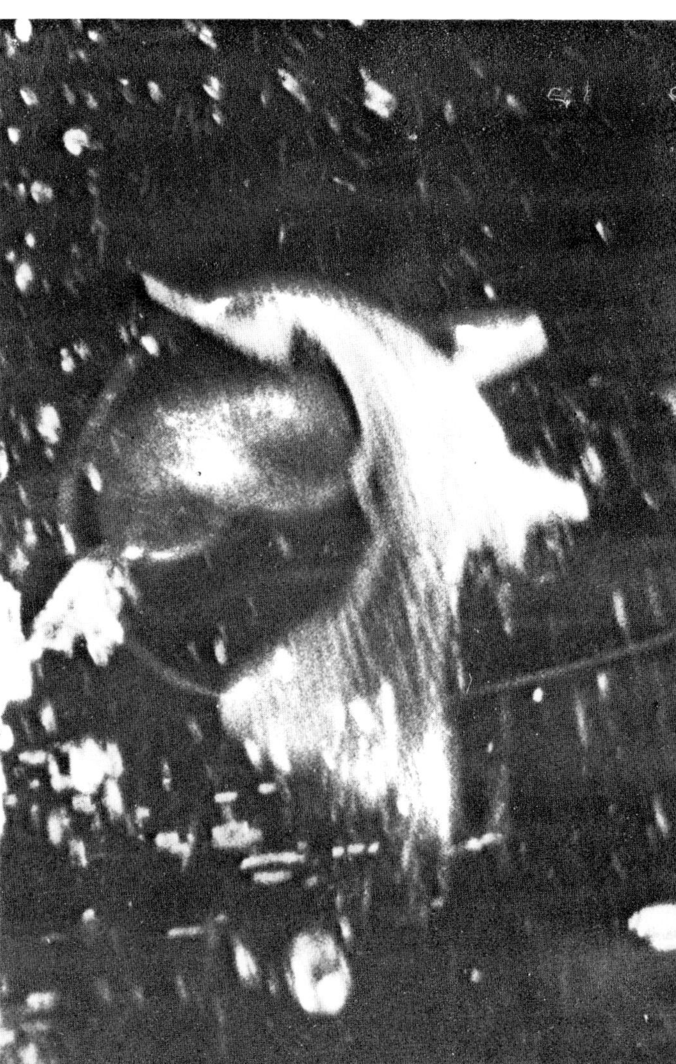

grayling

fly-fishing

When fishing for grayling you need patience, a well-fitted fly-box of small flies (there is an excellent series for grayling in the Chamberet and Deveaux collections), and very fine points of 1–2 lb b.s. (450–900 g). This, of course, refers to dry-fly fishing. The grayling is fond of gnats and little flying ants which have some fine imitations in the series already mentioned. With the wet fly, grayling fishing becomes much less sporting and when the fish are on the feed catching them becomes far too easy. The same happens when fishing with the nymph: the fish either refuses or takes too well. The grayling is a temperamental fish, but far from discouraging the angler, its behaviour tends to attract him. The grayling is not found in every river, so the first thing is to find out where it is present and to check on its nearest haunts from local fishermen or the local tackle shop. There is no point in indiscriminate fishing; search for the parts of the river which the fish loves. Generally speaking the grayling likes fairly deep water with a moderate current, and it prefers very clean gravel beds or sandy glides. This fish is so well camouflaged that it is always difficult to spot in the water. Like a flickering shadow its body passes over a clear patch then gently fades into a darker area and disappears, and the shimmering water adds to the impression that a vanishing trick has been performed. Apart from the spawning season when shoals of grayling congregate in shallow water it is a difficult fish to study. All discerning fly-fishermen can tell this fish from its take—a take which the expert can easily distinguish from that of a trout as it is slower and usually more delicate.

In some cases, the only possible way of taking grayling is on dry fly, using an 8 or 8½ ft (2–2·60 m) fly rod. The line should match the rod, and a 1 lb b.s. (450 g) matt nylon point is not too fine. Fish upstream and across, commencing almost upstream if need be. Ten, twenty, thirty times the carefully dressed fly may pass unheeded through

The grayling lies deep, but it often rises to the surface to take ants and gnats.

the fish's field of vision. Occasionally the grayling will rise to take some invisible morsel, but not the fly. If this happens the fly should be immediately replaced with a smaller one of a different colour, perhaps a small ant or sedge. In this way the right fly may be found. Downstream dry-fly sometimes works.

For wet-fly grayling fishing use a leader with either one fly, two flies, one on the point, the other mounted half way up the leader on a dropper, or, as is most common, with a team of three flies. The technique is totally different from that recommended for the dry fly. In order to keep the nylon leader out of sight of the fish it is advisable to cast downstream; or to make alternate casts, e.g. one directly across, then across and down in order to cover the whole swim. This method is not as selective as the dry-fly technique and as has already been said, on some days the grayling take too eagerly and on the wet fly these fish can be slaughtered.

bait fishing

The grayling takes natural bait very easily, and this is the most profitable way of fishing for it. Using freshwater shrimps it is possible to fill the creel more easily than with the dry fly but with less enjoyment. For fishing with natural bait a rod of 10–13 ft (3–4 m) should be used. (In France rods up to 18 ft (5·50 m) are used.) A centrepin or a small fixed-spool reel loaded with 2–4 lb b.s. (1–2 kg) line, a No. 14 hook, a 1½ or 2 lb (680 g–1 kg) hook link leaded according to the current, and a small float are the best equipment. *N.B.* A fairly small hook should be used because the grayling has a very small mouth, and the fineness of the line is important. The technique consists of carefully covering all pools with medium currents and slow glides. The bait (shrimps, small worms, maggots) may be lightly trotted along the bottom.

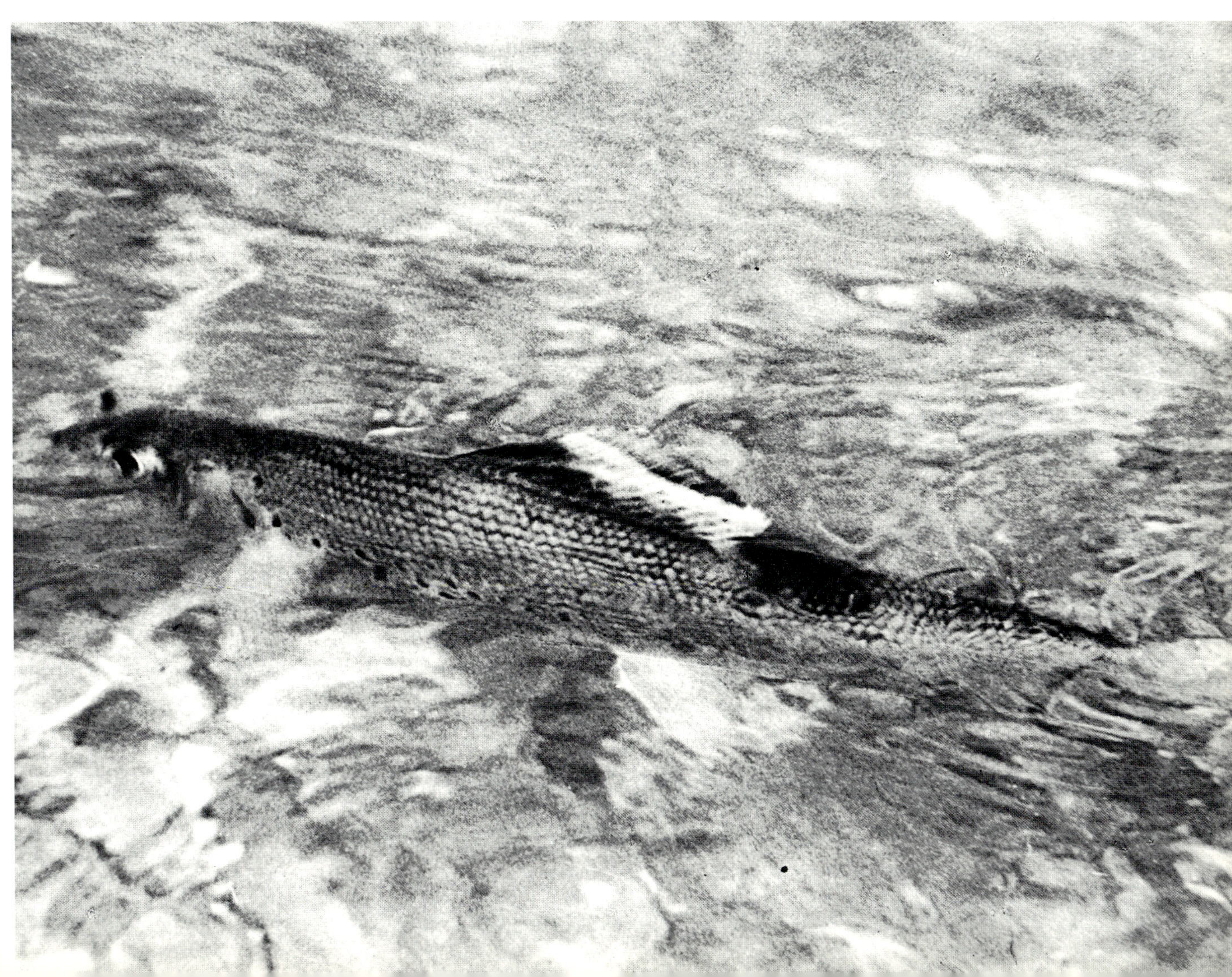

1 and 5. These fine illustrations depict a grayling in its environment. In addition to the general morphology, note the characteristics of this fish, especially its large dorsal fin and its small mouth.

2. A grayling takes . . . its prey is a tiny artificial fly and immediately the fight begins.

3. Fly fishing in the Allagnon at the end of September. Certain sections of this river of Massif Central are rich in grayling.

4. Perhaps there is no elegance in the action of this fly-fisherman —but there is certainly efficiency.

There is also a much less delicate method practised in the summer. When the water warms up, the grayling gather in the depths of the oxygenated currents. The previous hook link should then be replaced with a stronger one of 2 or 3 lb b.s. (1–1·30 kg) and a No. 14 or 16 hook; only the lead will change (a larger bullet mounted on a dropper). With this method let the lead sink to the bottom and wait a few moments before moving it; when a fish bites the strike must be immediate, as in a current the take is always fast.

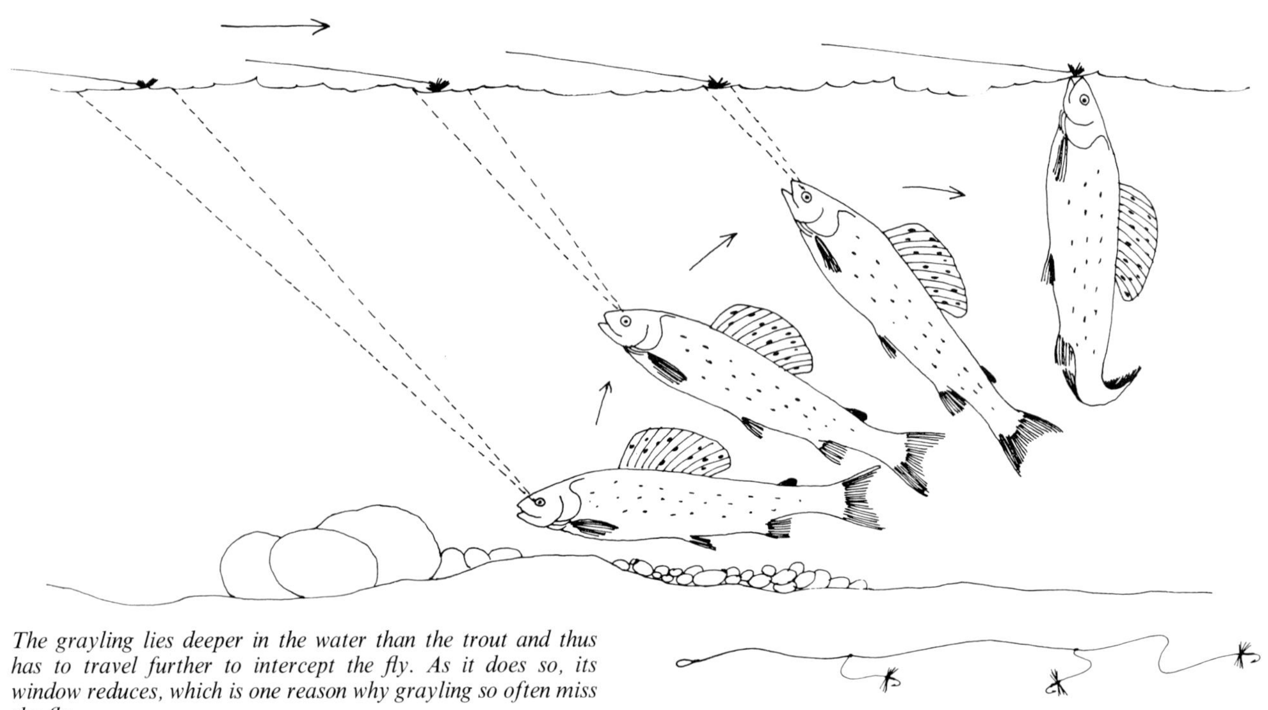

The grayling lies deeper in the water than the trout and thus has to travel further to intercept the fly. As it does so, its window reduces, which is one reason why grayling so often miss the fly.

A leader with three flies, two of them on droppers, often used when wet-fly fishing downstream and across for grayling.

the shoot

SHOOTING LINE WHEN FLY FISHING
Loops of fly line are held in the free hand and are let go at the moment the rod projects the line, the heavy head of the line pulling the loops up through the rings. Shooting line like this not only produces long casts but also helps to make the fly or flies alight gently on the water.

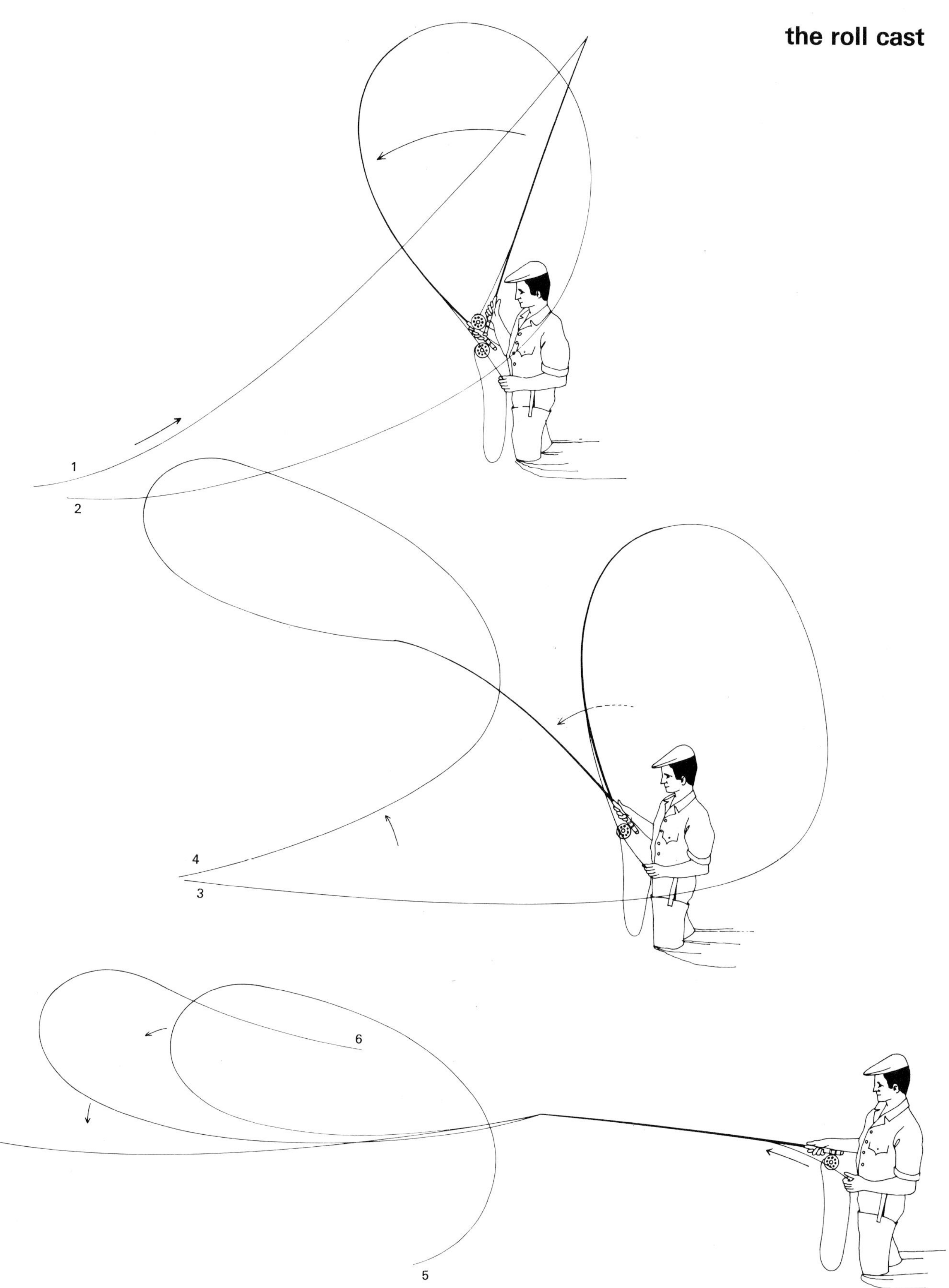

This cast is essential when fishing with a high bank or trees behind, so that a back-cast is not possible. In this cast the line hardly travels a yard or so behind but is made to perform a continuous circle which unrolls in front. The line is lifted from the surface (1) and when the loop is just behind the shoulder of the rod arm the rod is pushed rapidly forward and down (2, 3 and 4). The line comes off the water towards the caster and continues to follow the circular motion made by the rod (5, 6 and 7) and finally turns over at the tip to put the fly down on the water again. The left hand keeps the line between butt ring and the hand taut and then lets go as the line pulls the loop out, so gaining an extra yard or so of distance.

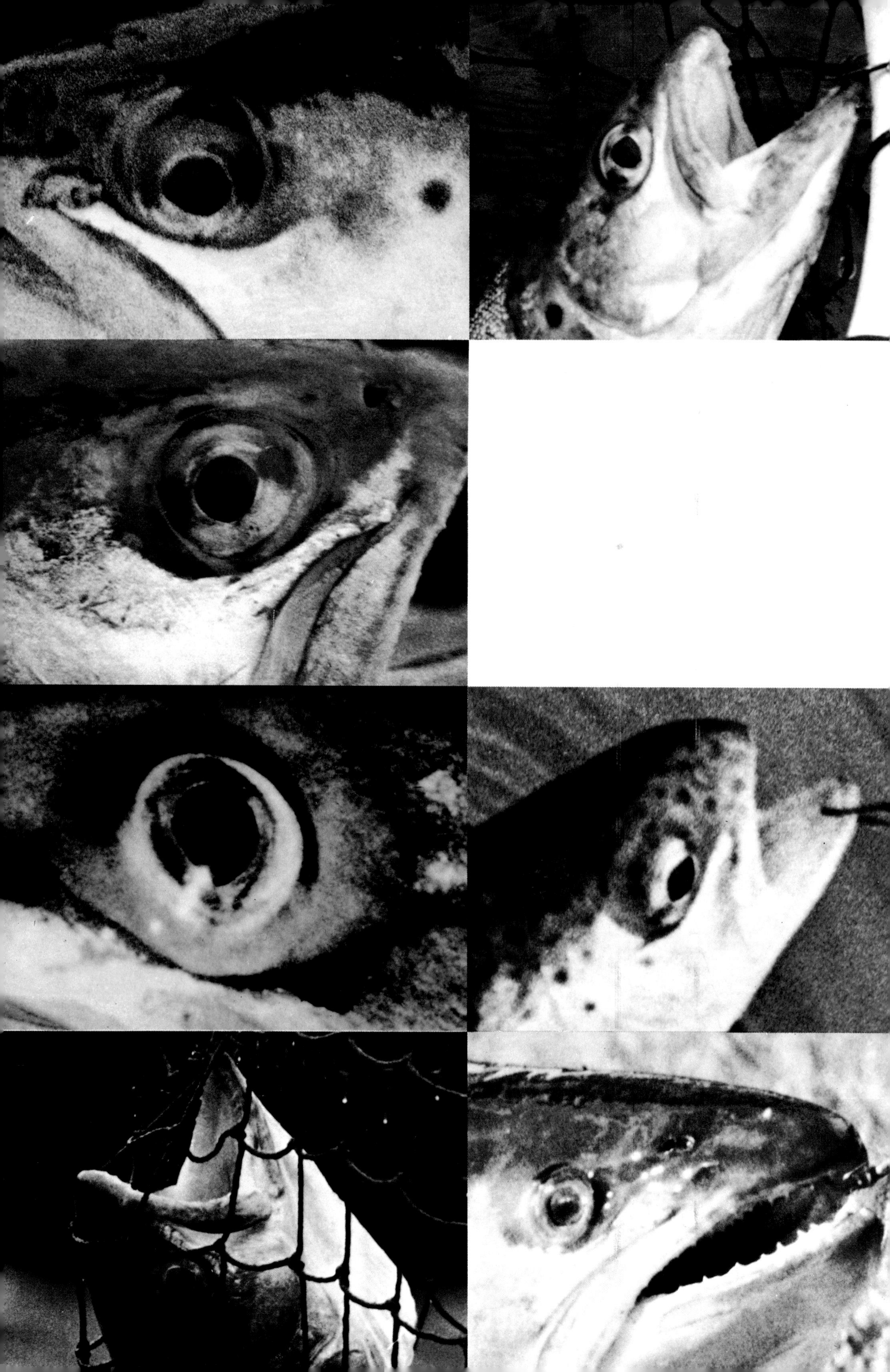

the salmon family

salmon

Salmo salar

The Atlantic salmon feeds in the rich, cold northern seas and spawns in the clean, rapid rivers. Big fish which run in February to April are called springers or spring salmon; summer-run salmon tend to be smaller, perhaps 8–12 lb (3·50–5·50 kg) as against the 15–25 lb (6·80–11 kg) or more of the springers. Smaller salmon returning after only one winter at sea (usually they return in summer) are known as grilse. Usually salmon return to the rivers of their birth.

Before spawning: red fish, ripe fish.

After spawning: kelt, spent fish.

The Atlantic salmon is a superb fighting fish and a superb table fish, but because of its fine pink flesh, which fetches high prices, and the disease UDN, pollution of rivers, and barriers in the form of dams and hydro-electric systems, it is tending to die out from the majority of rivers in which it thrived less than 100 years ago.

Atlantic salmon grow very quickly and sometimes attain the age of seven years. The world record is a fish of 83¾ lb (37·90 kg).

Fly-fishing for salmon is perhaps the most satisfying way of taking this noble fish, especially since the leverage the fish is able to put against the long rod makes it tough for the angler. There is a growing feeling that the Atlantic salmon is too valuable a world resource to permit commercial fishing to wipe it out. It is therefore suggested that more protection and conservation be organised to try to revive declining stocks and re-open many rivers now not holding them because of various examples of man's interference, that salmon be used only as a sporting proposition. However, anglers would have to sell some of their fish to permit the valuable food to reach the open market.

In Canada and parts of North America, where the Atlantic salmon was dying out owing to commercial depredations and unsatisfactory river conditions, the commercial fishermen have been "bought off" and angling restricted to fly-fishing only. This has had a remarkable effect and runs on many of the rivers have much improved.

brown trout

Salmo trutta

It was not long ago that it was thought there were well over a dozen different sub-species of brown trout, but now it is scientifically accepted that these slight variations of size, form and colour are due only to environmental conditions.

The brown trout is native to the rivers and to the big lakes of Continental Europe and the British Isles. A mature trout in a moorland stream with its acid water and poor supply of small fauna may measure only 6 in (15 cm) in length, but in a rich river or Irish lough, for example, and more especially when the water is alkaline, a mature fish may weigh 10 lb (4·50 kg) or much more.

Some trout have a yellowish brown background, with black and red spotting on their back and flanks, fading to a whitish belly; others, such as the native fish of Scotland's Loch Leven, are silvery with mainly black spots; still more may stray from pure fresh water into the lower parts of rivers where there is some salinity, even into the estuary itself. These fish, sometimes known as slob trout, grow to a good size and are highly prized.

In some lakes, in Ireland, Scotland, Scandinavia, Bavaria, for example, brown trout do attain great weights, 20 lb (9 kg) being not unknown and fish of 50 lb (22·50 kg) plus have been recorded. These great fish have become fish-eaters early in their lives and have grown rapidly as a result.

Brown trout demand clean, well-oxygenated water and since this can be provided as a by-product of water-supply reservoirs, some very good brown-trout fisheries have been provided on such waters. And the fish can grow to a much larger size than they usually do in the wild environment of rivers.

One of the reasons for the recently increased participation in trout fly-fishing in Britain has been the provision of trout fishing in the many water-supply reservoirs that have been and are still being built. The angling-water shortage, for fishing the fly to wild brown trout, meant that costs of fishing went too high, except for the minority of privileged or wealthy people. Now day permits are within the purse of many ordinary working people.

In reservoirs or lakes without gravel-bedded feeder streams, brown trout cannot spawn successfully, which is a problem. However, some seem to manage to live to a ripe old age and fish of 6 and 7 lb (2·7 and 3 kg) are caught most years on some of the best English reservoirs, such as Grafham Water, Chew Valley Lake, Hanningfield Water and Draycote.

Trout fishing seasons vary a little, but in general open either in early March or April and close at the end of September.

rainbow trout

Salmo gairdneri

The rainbow trout, native of the Pacific coast of North America, was introduced to Europe around 1880 and, like the brown trout, there are two types, migratory (sea run) and non-migratory.

Both types now exist in Europe: the sea-running type, *S. gairdneri irideus*, which is the steelhead made famous by Zane Grey in his stories of one of the fish's rivers, the Rogue, in Oregon, and the inland type, *S. gairdneri shasta*, native to the streams of the Sierra Nevada.

Rainbows grow much more quickly than do browns and rarely exceed four years of age. But in that short time, even in European rivers and reservoirs, weights of 7–8 lb (3–3·50 kg) have been attained, some even heavier. The rainbow is less selective than the voracious native brown, even, and this makes some anglers look askance at him. However, the rainbow is a magnificent fighter, making sizzling wild runs for maybe 50 or more yards (50 m), then leaping and cartwheeling across the water; often he throws the hook in these antics.

Rainbows are also very good to eat.

They are very easy to rear in fish-farms and are cheaper to raise than browns; they do not often acclimatise sufficiently in European rivers to reproduce themselves, although in one or two British rivers and in Austria and some other parts of the European continent they do breed naturally. Where they do, they are so successful that they tend to oust the native browns.

Rainbows, which spawn in the period November to May, the *shasta* strain earlier, the *irideus* later, are unmistakable when compared to browns: they are silvery, with black spots, including spots on the fins and tail, and generally have a rainbow-coloured band along their flanks, though in some the band is hardly noticeable.

It is worth noting that in certain large lakes, notably Pend Oreille in Washington, North America, the rainbow has reached 40 lb (18 kg) in four years; huge fish are caught in New Zealand (Lake Taupo for example) and in South America.

sea trout

Salmo trutta

The sea trout bears the same scientific name as the brown trout because morphologically it is the same, except that it and, as far as is known, its progeny migrate to sea to do their feeding, thus growing more rapidly than nonmigratory brown trout. In good sea-trout rivers specimens of 10 lb (4·50 kg) are not uncommon and fish of more than 20 lb (9 kg) are taken. The most famous of the European rivers for very big sea trout is Sweden's Em, where 15 pounders (7 kg) have been almost "two a penny".

Wales, Ireland, Scotland, Norway produce some fine sea trout. It may be caught both in salt and fresh water, and unlike the Atlantic salmon, when in the rivers some sea trout at least do feed, both on flies, fish and worms.

The differences between big sea trout and modest salmon have already been dealt with. As a table fish, the sea trout is held by many gourmets to be better than salmon.

Common names include many more variables than most other fish, and to include all, especially those to describe the small fish, would produce a vast list. The adults are variously salmon-trout, white trout (Ireland), peal (Devon, Cornwall), sewin (Wales).

American brook trout

Salvelinus fontinalis

This fish, the American brook trout, has nothing in common with the salmon (*Salmo salar*). It is a charr, a close relative of *Salvelinus alpinus*.

The American brook trout originated in North America, and was brought to Europe around 1880, becoming naturalised in different regions. In principle, as its name (*fontinalis*) suggests, this fish prefers the very cold, clear, oxygenated water of mountain streams. However, in reality it seems to be more tolerant of polluted water than the brown trout. Like all salmonids it possesses a small adipose fin between the dorsal and the caudal fins, but if its general morphology differs little from that of the trout, there are some variations of note: the brook trout has 109 to 130 scales along the lateral line, its dorsal fin is distinguished by 3–5 straight rays and by 8–10 flexible ones. In addition, its mouth is much larger than the trout's and its pectoral, pelvic and anal fins are fringed with white.

The colour of its livery is remarkable. The dark back carries lighter marbling which pales to a bright yellow near the belly, and its whole body is covered with small orange and red spots. These colours change during spawning, becoming more striking, with the belly of the male turning coral-red and the flanks reflecting a beautiful iridescent hue.

Trout-fishing methods are quite suitable for the brook trout, which is much less wary. The author has noticed on many occasions that if a brook trout is missed it will, unlike the trout, make several attempts to swallow the fly until it is finally caught. However, if it is easier to catch, it is certainly more difficult to land, because its fight is more powerful than the trout's.

Arctic charr

Salvelinus alpinus

(Non-migratory)

This fish is closely related to *Salvelinus fontinalis* but is more localised and non-migratory. It is found exclusively in lakes and is content with a diet which is poorer both in quality and quantity. Experts believe that this fish was originally a migrator but became landlocked during the glacial period and has since lived in mountain lakes.

It is found in Lakes Geneva, Du Bourget, Annecy, and in certain lakes of the Massif Central (Lake Pavin) and the Pyrenees, as well as the English Lake District, Scotland, Wales and Ireland.

Due to poverty of its environment this fish grows rather slowly and is never very large, the average weight being between 1 and 2 lb (450–900 g).

The Alpine charr has a greyish back with paler flanks, and a pink belly with light spots on the sides, which in the male change to a bright coral-red during spawning. The scales are very small, numbering about 200 on the lateral line.

It is a disappointing fish for the angler because it lives at a great depth, anywhere between 150 and 350 ft (45 and 100 m) down. Therefore, although a few bank fishermen spin and fly-fish for it, the main method is trolling from a boat towing a heavily weighted train of lures, usually spoons.

Arctic charr

(Migratory)

The migratory version of *Salvelinus alpinus* is an excellent sporting fish. It is found in rivers of the far North, in Greenland, Iceland, the north of Canada, the extreme north of Russia and Scandinavia. In autumn it spawns in rivers and descends to the sea where it completes its growth. In Greenland it is caught in three coastal rivers in the south near Narssarssuaq, where it reaches weights of between 5 and 7 lb (2 and 3 kg). Specimens weighing more than 20 lb (9 kg) have been caught in Canada.

The livery of this fish is similar to that of the freshwater charr but its head is totally different. The male has a hook on the lower mandible, like the salmon, the mouth is armed with a large number of teeth, and the gill-covers are much longer than the freshwater charr's.

When it runs up the coastal rivers of the North to spawn, fishermen use artificial lures, especially the wet fly. It prefers very brightly coloured flies such as the Royal Coachman or the Trout Fin.

grayling

Thymallus thymallus

The scientific name arises from the fact that a faint scent of thyme may be detected from a freshly caught grayling. It is a true salmonid, but a maverick, in that it spawns not with the majority of its kind, in late autumn and winter, but in spring, with the coarse fish.

Nevertheless, the grayling is a fine fighting fish for both fly and bait fishers, and is also a fine table fish.

Common names: umber (from the French *ombre*), lady of the stream.

Grayling must have clean, clear water and are the first fish to migrate from polluted water. They are less tolerant than trout of impure water or oxygen deficiency. Gravel-bedded rivers, chalk-streams, in fact places where trout thrive in general, are also favourable for grayling. In fact, the fish often live side by side, but the grayling is frequently more successful than the trout, which it often ousts from favourable water.

The fishing season for grayling usually begins in earnest about September, when trout fishing is closing, and they can be caught in winter on fly, even dry fly.

A pound (450 g) grayling is quite a nice fish, but two pounders (900 g) are not uncommon. In Finland grayling of 4 lb (2 kg) or so are regularly caught.

The grayling is easily recognisable by its silvery colouring, which is slate-grey and green on the back. The silvery flanks have scattered black spots and the regular positioning of the hexagon-shaped scales gives the impression of a striped livery. The huge dorsal fin, shot with purple, is covered in dark chequered spots.

This fish is also characterised by a forked caudal fin, a tiny adipose fin, a small mouth and a prominent upper lip.

Its eyes have been described by Professor Dottrens as "the most beautiful eyes of all river fish", and consist of gold-ringed pupils with purple and green irises.

The grayling swims of many rivers are being reduced by the building of numerous hydro-electric dams which, together with pollution, are changing the character of the water. The Loue, the Doubs, the Dessoubre, the Ain, the Upper Allier, the Allagnon and the upper reaches of the Loire and the Rhône are the best known French rivers which contain grayling. Many north-country rivers, Scottish streams and southern chalk streams in Britain hold grayling. The most usual fishing technique is with the dry fly, though trotting worm or maggot is also popular.

salmonids and predators

grayling
black bass
pike
perch
zander

predators

pike

The pike is always a fascinating fish, particularly to young fishermen and beginners. The tyrant of the fresh water, it is also a fish of legend. Since the Middle Ages numerous fables and misconceptions have built up around the pike. It is supposed to eat one and a half times its weight of fish a day, and, according to Isaak Walton, one monster is supposed to have bitten a washerwoman's hands and another to have attacked a horse while it was drinking.

Esox lucius owes its almost primeval name to the family Esocidae, of which it is the sole representative in European waters. Every autumn and winter fishermen set about catching the pike, and they stalk the fish, searching tirelessly along canal banks, in river back-waters, or by edges of weed beds in ponds and lakes. They dream of the enormous head and powerful well-armed jaws that one day might decorate their walls . . . if only the pike could be persuaded to take the bait and lures it is presented with.

Apart from the salmonids, the pike is the sporting fish *par excellence*, the truly voracious predator that can be taken through sheer perseverance, no matter how old and cunning it is. Fishermen have been known to search the same piece of water for years knowing that the fish is there because they have hooked it before, only to lose it at the last moment. They have found the pike again, probably chasing roach at the edge of a weed bed, and have hooked it once more, only for a broken line to end their hopes. They search for it and they wait patiently, while the pike lurks under the lilies or waits, motionless, on the bottom, merging with vegetation, for the occasional fish to come by within reach. The fishermen catch jack pike but what happens to the big one, the enormous pike which puts on at least a couple of pounds more every year? At last in the early morning mists of a November dawn they see the float run slowly but surely; they wait for a minute, then two, then three; at last they strike and . . . they cannot believe it. Here it is at last, the big one and the fight is on. The pike will sell its life dearly, but they have taken every precaution this time: steel trace, reinforced hook, strong line and a heavy-duty reel. This time all the odds are in favour of the fishermen, and after a Homeric battle it comes to the net. There he lies, on the grass, the big pike, caught at last.

trolling

Only the most commonly practised methods of pike fishing will be discussed here. Perhaps the most boring is trolling, a technique used on very big lakes, such as the Irish and Scottish waters, or in Bavaria.

Briefly, trolling (or trailing, as some anglers insist) involves pulling an artificial lure or a dead fish on a spinning or wobbling flight, behind a boat, usually by rowing slowly, although it is possible to use an outboard motor, throttled back until it is only just turning over.

The angler or anglers simply wait for the pike to take, signalled by the reel (put on check) letting out a scream, or, if the angler holds the rod, a terrific yank, then play the fish. An advantage on vast lakes is that trolling does cover a lot of water whereas stationary fishing, or working from the bank, could not. Either long wobbling spoons, up to 8 in. (20 cm) in length, plugs, or a herring, sprat, roach or whatever is available will do the trick at times.

A typical pike swim on the Loing. ▶

Lip-hooked on a revolving lure, balanced forward by a weighted anti-kink head. ▼

Though the pike is a voracious fish, it is not the "shark" that Izaak Walton called it. ▶

A 13 lb (5·8 kg) pike caught in the lake, by trolling with a wobbling spoon.

A refinement of recent years involves the use of echo-sounding devices rigged to the boat so that the anglers may know exactly the depth of water and the configuration of the bottom. Then, by adjusting boat speed and/or weight of lure or bait, the contours can be fished selectively; and approached in this way trolling can be a less boring pursuit.

Since casting is not necessary, the reel may be a centrepin, or a multiplier, loaded with about 150 yards (140 m) of 10–15 lb (4·50–7 kg) test monofilament line, used with a medium salmon spinning rod of 8–9 ft (2·50–2·70 m). Leads may be necessary on many occasions to get the bait or lure to the correct depth, a foot (30 cm) or so above the bottom. Usually depths up to 25 ft (7·50 m) will prove most rewarding, the greater depths seldom producing pike in numbers.

The edges of drop-offs and around extensive weedbeds are the places to search carefully; the boat should, of course, be stopped as soon as a pike strikes.

It is a mistake to think that letting out more line will get the lure down deeper; it may have the opposite effect. Depth must be gained by the lure itself or the lead a few feet ahead of it. It is seldom good practice to have more than 40 yards (36 m) of line out, since line-stretching at long range can result in the failure of the hooks to take hold in the pike's jaws.

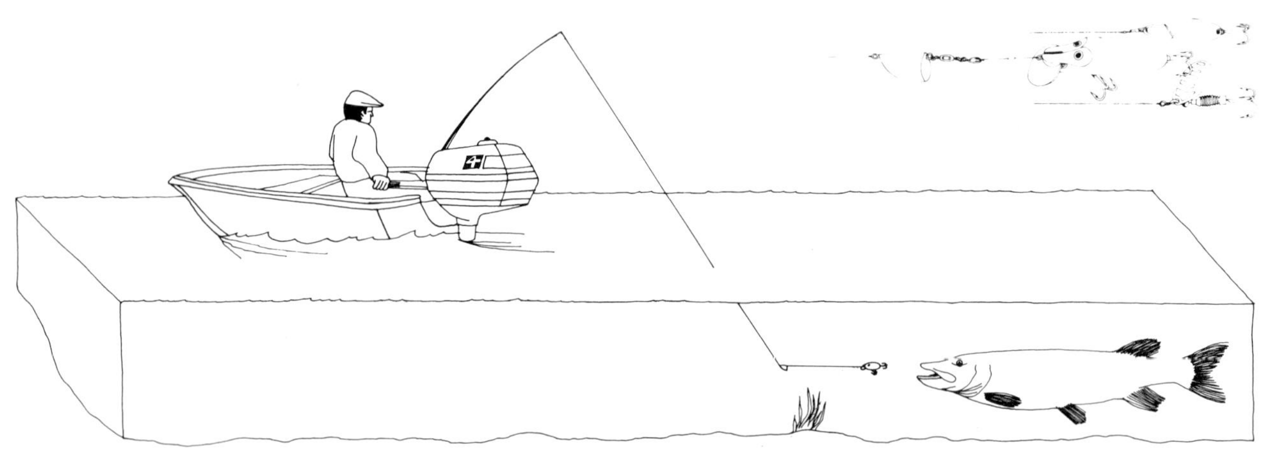

For pike trolling plugs can be used or all types of spoons. ▲

Michel Duborgel and Roger Danten fish for pike early in the morning on an Irish lake in Roscommon. ▼

live-baiting

Live-bait fishing for pike demands both patience and perseverance, for the pike is often dozing in its lair, and so it is necessary to tempt it when it goes in search of food, by placing the live-bait in its path. In the main, the difficulty has been to find places likely to hold pike. An eddy, a little backwater, weedbeds, reedbeds, water lilies, stumps, dead trees and holes in the bank, these are all pike haunts. The pike has to be persuaded to come out of these places for the fisherman to have the best chance of catching it.

Although the pike will find a bigger-than-average bait attractive, the author prefers to use smaller ones, for if they are not taken by the pike they may well be snapped up by a perch, a zander or another predator.

To catch a large pike, a 6 or 7 in. (15 or 18 cm) roach is probably best, but this size is not binding. Pike have been known to attack fish as large as themselves, so quite small pike can be caught with a 1 lb (450 g) roach. The roach should be baited if possible through the back with two double hooks, fixed to a wire trace, a fairly heavy lead and a float whose sensitivity will not be its main function. In order to pinpoint the position of the line after the take some fishermen still use pilot floats, which are simply oval floats placed at intervals above the main float. The standard French pike rod is 13 to 16 ft (4–5 m) long, made of cane with a fibreglass tip, or hollow fibreglass (9–11 ft (2·50–3 m) in UK). A multiplier, centrepin, or fixed-spool reel with at least 80 yards (75 m) of 10–15 lb b.s. (4·50–6·80 kg) is needed. This method can also be used with an ordinary spinning rod but if fishing in depths greater than the length of the rod there will be difficulties in casting. In summer when the water is very warm

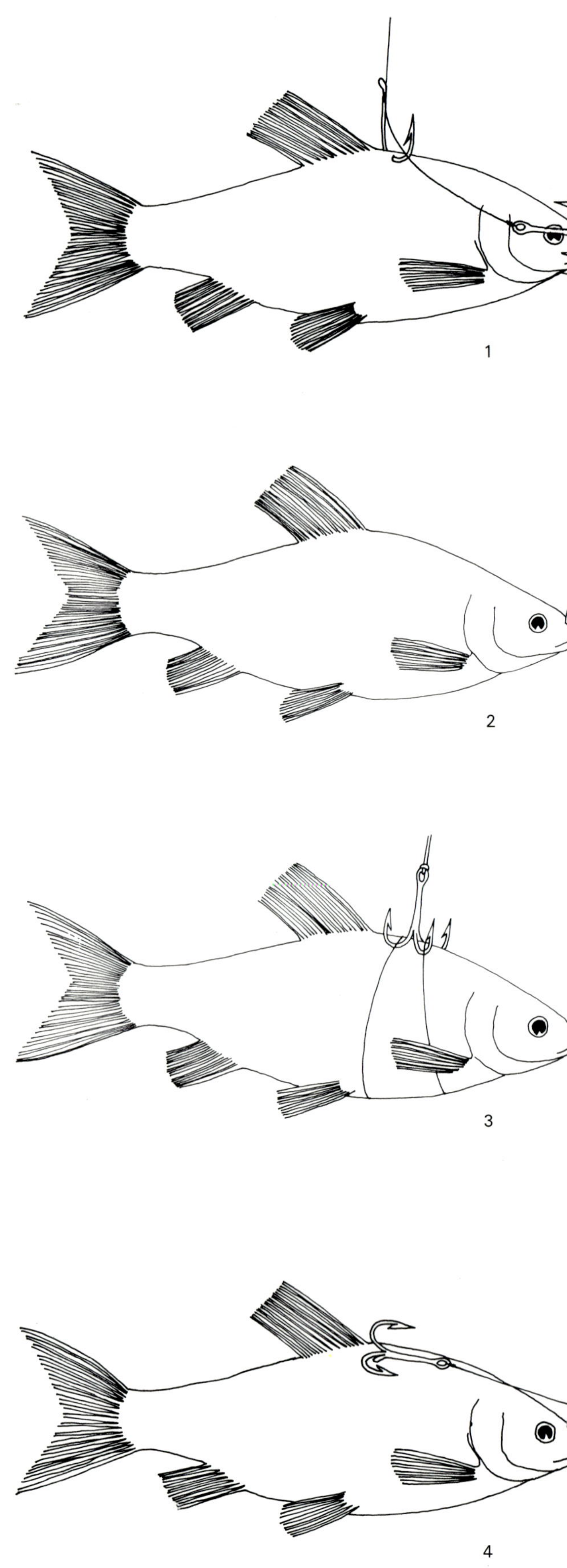

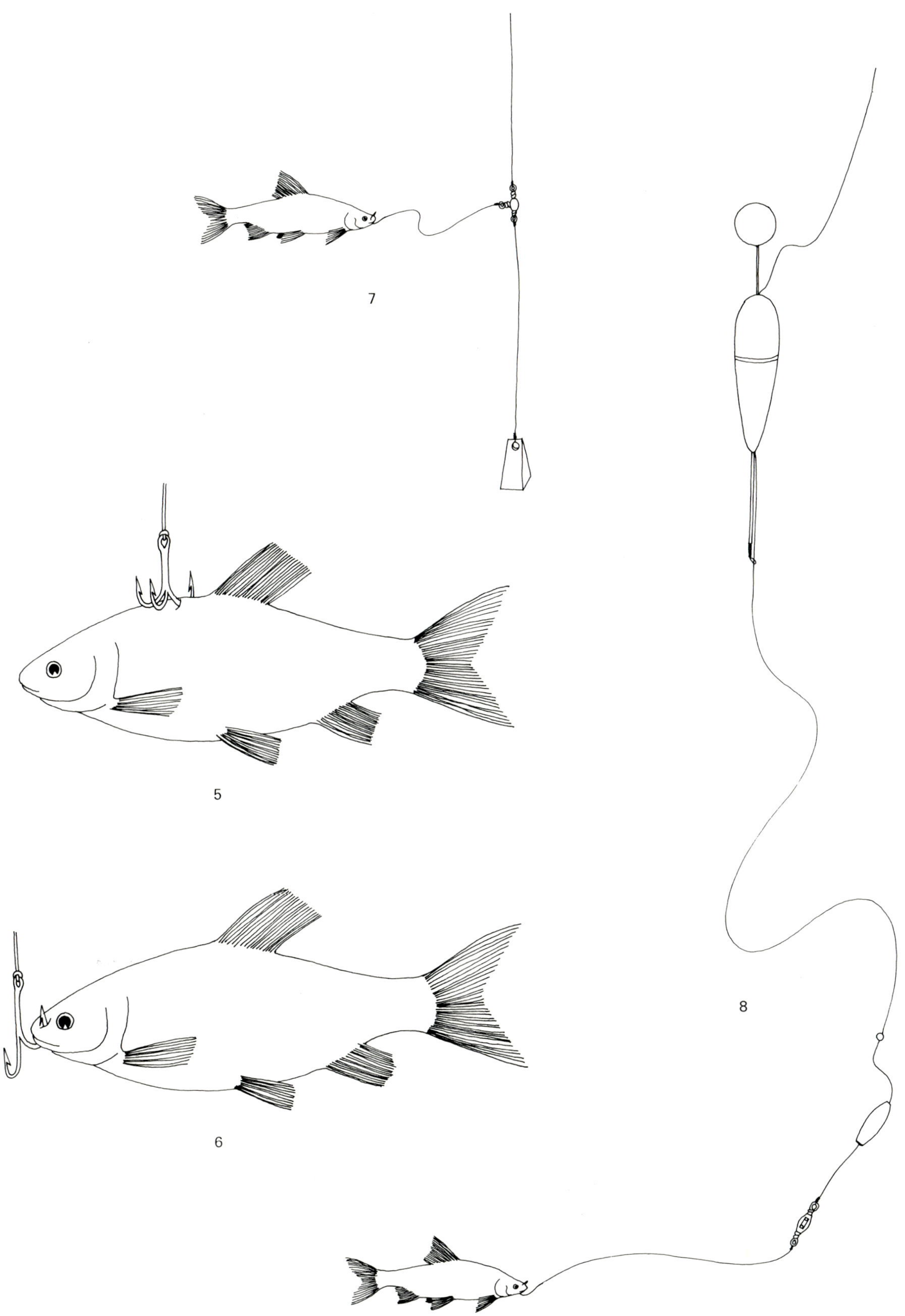

1. *Live-bait with single hook through fin root, one hook of treble in top lip.*
2. *A treble hooked through both lips of a live-bait.*
3. *A less cruel mounting: the fish is fixed to the hook with an elastic band.*
4. *Rig for live-bait in fast water.*
5. *A simpler kind of baiting with a treble hook whereby the bait is hooked through the skin in the front dorsal fin.*
6. *Baiting a live-bait through both lips.*
7. *Mounting for fishing with weighted or free-swimming live-bait. The dropper is fixed to a three-way swivel.*
8. *A more classical mounting with a sliding lead, stopped above and below by a split shot and the swivel to which is attached the trace.*

it is advisable to fish at mid-water; if the live-bait is swimming fairly strongly the pike will often come from a distance to take it. In autumn or winter when the temperature drops considerably, fish deeper, even quite near the bottom, thus allowing the bait to be worked near the pike, which is usually skulking on the bottom in the weedbeds.

Another method of live-baiting, using a long rod, is legering, especially for fishing a long way out, with a wire trace and a fairly heavy lead, and, of course, no float. A bite is signalled by the rod tip, or by the scream of the reel as the pike runs with the bait, or with a bite indicator or alarm.

Returning to the subject of live-bait: the pike feeds on all species of fish: minnows, roach, bleak, small chub and carp, small bream and tench. He likes everything; in rivers which hold gudgeon this small fish is a choice bait which even a large pike finds hard to refuse. For effective ways to mount a live-bait see the diagrams.

The technique of live-bait fishing is very simple because the live-bait does the work; it is a fish, a living bait, it swims and attracts the pike by behaving naturally. However, as when fishing with dead bait, this presentation can be improved, at the risk of snagging, by working the bait into very restricted corners and giving little twitches on the line to give the bait more mobility. This is often the time when the attack occurs; the pike emerges from the shadows, seizes the fish in its powerful jaws, sometimes pauses for a moment and then moves off with its prey; it is at this moment that most misses occur. The inexperienced fisherman often tends to strike too soon. When live-baiting for pike it is better to wait. The old fishermen at the turn of the century used to say, "There should be time to roll a cigarette between the take and the strike." This picturesque appreciation of the necessary time lapse still retains an element of truth. The delay is necessary because the pike first seizes the bait crosswise in its jaws and then turns it head first preparatory to swallowing it. But using multi-hook rigs the strike may be made as soon as the pike stops running.

From the moment of striking, a terrific struggle, albeit a short one, begins. The pike is a fish which makes short but violent efforts to escape, and it tires quickly. It leaps out of the water, tries to reach its lie among the weedbeds and then turns in circles which decrease as it loses its strength and finally it is possible to bring it near the net or the gaff. The pike is not caught yet, for it always summons a reserve of energy for the final phase of the battle. However, the strength of the modern nylon line means that the odds are against even the largest specimens escaping.

An English angler fishes an active deadbait technique.

dead-bait fishing

Dead-bait fishing—sink-and-draw or wobbling—for pike is more sporting than live-baiting. The fisherman needs to be continually on the move, continually casting and retrieving and perpetually on the look-out for likely lies. It is of little importance what bait is used provided it is fresh. It must look alive, and so it has to be moved all the time, sinking and drawing to make the dead fish seem to be swimming slowly, wounded or in difficulty. This method calls for more skill on the part of the fisherman than does live-baiting as his know-how is tested at every moment, his knowledge of the water, his knowledge of the pike and its haunts. Dead-bait fishing is practised with a light or medium-heavy spinning rod of 8–10 ft (2·50–3 m) in length but powerful enough to cast a 6 in. (15 cm) bait weighted according to the mounting (*see diagram*) and well armed. The trace has to resist the pike's sharp teeth so steel must be used. A swivel to prevent kinking is also recommended.

In Britain, many anglers simply leger a dead-bait for pike, often without any lead at all—just a herring, dead roach, or a sprat (with a running lead).

1. *Mounting with a treble hook through the tail and a single hook through the lips.*
2. *Mounting with fluted lead and with a plastic swimming disc. This mounting necessitates a baiting needle to attach the bait to the hook. The line is passed through the fish before the hook is attached to the line. This method is recommended by the author.*
3. *Mounting with a weight and two single hooks.*

▲ *Beautiful 6 lb (2·70 kg) pike taken on live-bait.*

Though its jaws were clamped together by the two hooks of the spoon, the gaff—which should have been gently inserted in the front of the fish's lower jaw—was still needed to lift this pike from the water. ▶

Who said the pike is not a sporting fish! (previous pages).

Two pike taken on live-bait at the beginning of autumn at Gewässer (Germany) (previous pages).

Snow, frost, falling temperature are conditions for fishing with live-bait (previous pages).

fishing with lures

Plastic minnow, minnow spoon and Mepps tandem spoon.

The various positions of a pike.
1. Intense activity. *3. Rest.*
2. Medium activity. *4. Complete rest.*

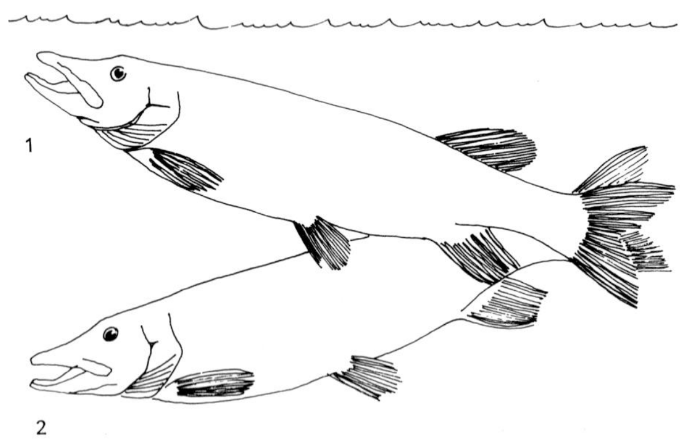

It is very difficult to choose from the large number of pike lures on the market: revolving spoons, tandem spoons, wobbling spoons, minnow spoons and plugs.

Pike spinning has its own fashions, and it is difficult to say, for example, whether the revolving spoons with their red woollen tags or the tandem and minnow spoons are more attractive to the pike than the simpler lures.

The Mepps tandem spoon is very popular; it has revolving oval vanes which lengthen the outline of the lure and give out vibrations. The minnow spoon, originally armed with a natural fish, now uses a plastic one (Alta-Minno, Mepps-Minno).

Fishing with such lures poses no great problem. There is no point in trying to improve on the action of the lure by moving the rod top because this may affect the rotation of the lure's vanes which are turning anyway. Just cast in the right spot and retrieve slowly, accelerating from time to time to break the rhythm or to lift over obstacles, and getting as near to pike lies as possible.

The attraction of the wobbling spoon may be greatly increased by action of the rod to give it a semblance of life as in dead-bait fishing; the same applies to plugs, which, because of their shape and their realistic action, are at present the most deadly bait for large pike. Light, well-balanced lures seem to be the best; the ones which suddenly disappear under the surface and pop up again gently after a short tug are the most efficient, as they are extraordinarily life-like and deceive the wiliest pike.

Light spoons, specially the bar-spoons like the Mepps, Ondex, etc., are best fished with a rod of about 7 ft (2 m) with a fixed-spool reel loaded with 7–10 lb (3–4·50 kg) line. Good distances are achieved with this outfit, but in playing big pike the fixed-spool reel tends to kink the line, since it is being pulled off one way and wound on in another.

1. *Blue Creek Chub.*
2. *Mepps No. 4.*
3. *Sosy perch 2 oz. (60 g).*
4. *Plug with diving vane.*
5. *Jointed plug.*
6. *Rapala CD 13.*
7. *Creek Chub Tiny Tim.*

A last zooming leap before the exhausted fish is brought to the gaff . . . then finally to the fisherman's hand.

Following page: a pike demonstrating its sporting qualities.

Usually, especially in Scandinavia and Britain where there are plenty of big pike, anglers who fish in summer, or at any time where the water is weedy or snaggy in other ways—and holds big pike—choose to use the multiplier reel and the short baitcasting rod with offset handle. Such a combination, specially with plugs, is extremely accurate casting among heavy growth, yet with its direct drive (through gears it is true, but not "round the corner", as in the fixed-spool) the multiplier can handle big fish in tight corners; and the line will not be kinked.

perch

The most striking aspect of the perch is its amazing instinctive intelligence. This makes it extremely wary at all times except when it is hungry. It usually fasts for several hours and then joins a shoal to hunt for food. Its need for food overcomes its wariness and at these times it can be caught with anything, live-bait, all natural baits, sink and draw and even with certain insects which are surface-dwellers. The perch present a splendid sight, swimming on their way nonchalantly and majestically with jaws closed and dorsal fins half deployed. Often they stop and remain motionless for a while, suddenly darting instinctively forward with their mouths open as a shoal of minnows passes by. The violent onslaught panics the small fish and the perch snap up as many as possible before descending once more to the bottom to wait, motionless, for new prey.

The perch prefers very small fish, all sorts of fry, including its own, minnows, small gudgeon and tiny chub. The largest perch usually hunt alone but the smaller ones are more gregarious and hunt in shoals, predatory hordes, chasing the small fry in back waters, or little bays in very shallow water. These hunting expeditions take fishermen by surprise although the most experienced can recognise them by the panic the perch cause when slashing at a shoal of fry. The author has often seen small fish jump on to the bank to escape from the perch. Yet apart from these aggressive periods this redoubtable striped fighter lives among his future victims without frightening them.

live-baiting

This chapter on perch fishing will begin by refuting the great Plato, who maintained that fishing was an occupation unworthy of a well-born gentleman because it demanded more skill and cunning than strength and, unlike hunting, it did not provide young people with healthy exercise. Skill and cunning are certainly needed to catch the perch, but in certain methods exercise is also obtained by searching for, and presenting a lure or bait to, individual specimens.

How are the favourite perch lies recognised? When it is not actually feeding, the perch, for all its strength, is lazy. It lives in calm, often very difficult stretches, in the holes under tree roots, around submerged stumps, rocks and among weeds and water lilies, reed beds and all such places. Faced with such variety the difficulties of perch fishing are obvious. Except when it leaves its favourite haunts to feed, its whereabouts are very difficult to find, causing the angler many problems, and the numerous hazards and loss of tackle sorely testing his patience.

Times of high water in autumn and summer are favourites for perch fishing. During these periods fish, including the small fry, move to the eddies which are more or less sheltered from the current. With their food there the perch soon follow. This is the time to use live-bait, traditionally the minnow. For live-baiting for perch the tackle is very simple: an Avon-type rod of about 11 ft (3 m) with 3–4 lb (1·30–1·80 kg) line on a centrepin or fixed-spool reel. A buoyant float to

Mitchell

This fisherman is casting for perch in the Allier at Azerat under the pale October sun.
◀
A splendid 1½ lb (680 g) perch.
▶

A certain ferocity is characteristic of the perch.

support the bait and a swan-shot or equivalent, hooks Nos. 4–8, and a live minnow mounted through the lip. It is not necessary for the live-bait to be fished on the bottom as the perch will detect it from a distance and take it in mid-water. If the perch is present and hungry, the live-bait is pursued the moment it disappears beneath the surface, the float bobs, moves sideways and then bobs two or three times before disappearing completely. The fisherman must not be in a hurry and must strike gently. Few perch are missed on the strike, but its mouth is soft and quite large specimens have been known to escape when almost netted. However, if the perch is absent or perhaps sulking motionlessly a few yards from the live-bait there may be a very long wait. In this case it is a good idea to lay down the rod with which you are fishing for perch, and throw in morsels of bread, etc. to get a shoal of fry active. The perch may well begin to feed.

Among the lures for the perch are: the revolving spoon, Celta, Voblex, Suissex, and the small wobbling Orkla (from top to bottom).

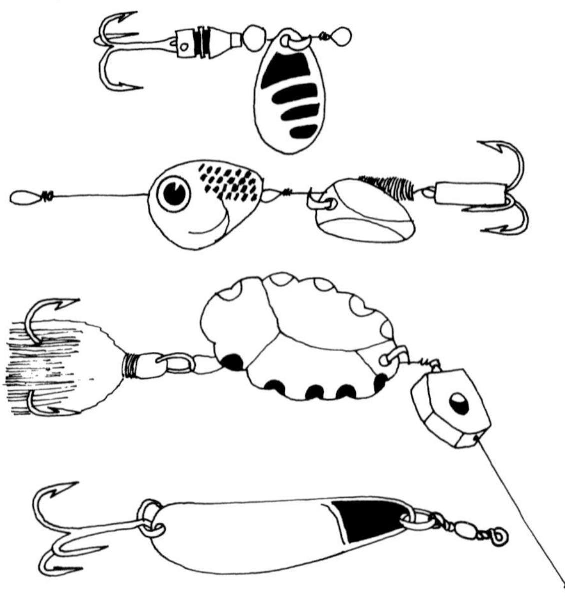

The perch takes the live-bait head-first, so the hook point faces forward.

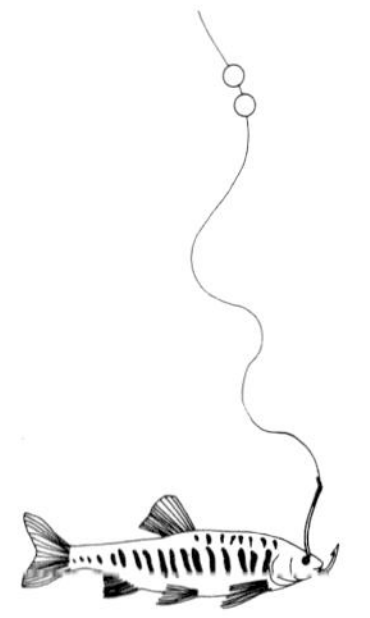

Diagram of sink and draw technique. Note the direction of movement—down and up—given to the drop minnow. ▼

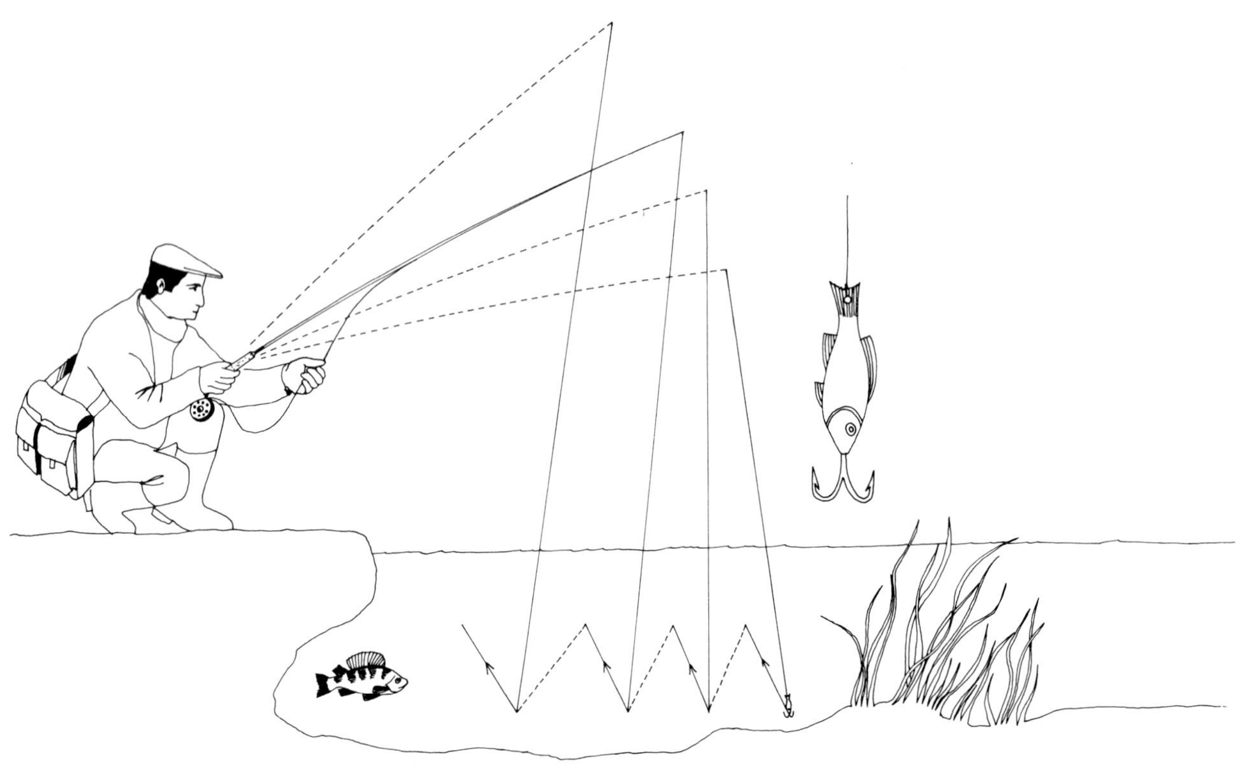

worms, maggots, shrimps and caddis grubs

Worms, maggots, shrimps and caddis are good for light float fishing. Use an Avon-type rod of 10–13 ft (3–4 m) and, depending on conditions and your technique, a centrepin or fixed-spool reel loaded with 3–4 lb (1·30–1·80 kg) test line.

Hooks sizes Nos. 12 to 8 are suitable. If using worm as bait it is best to use the small red worms as they are more attractive and lively than the sluggish black-headed ones. The best method of mounting shrimps is to use two on the same hook, one threaded from the back of the head to the tail so that the shank is hidden, and the other simply threaded at one end. If this method is used the perch has difficulty in seeing the hook and so takes the bait without hesitation. Another excellent method is to thread a large shrimp completely on the hook and attach a smaller one by its tail close to the barb of the hook. The main attraction of this method is that the shrimp stays alive and thus is a very natural looking bait. Fernand Biquet, the author of a very complete study of the perch and how to catch it, is a great advocate of the leather jacket. This is the larva of the daddy-longlegs and, although difficult to procure, is a particularly deadly bait in summer. The eggs are usually laid underground in the roots of grass, or vegetables, and these are the most likely places to find the grub. The adult insect is also valuable for fishing for trout and chub.

sink and draw

As its name suggests sink and draw is a method involving movement of the artificial bait. It is possible to sink and draw with small dead fish or a natural bait, but the best known is the drop minnow (a small metal fish the size of a minnow or fry), which is armed with a single, double or treble hook, attached to the line by the tail, and made to wriggle from the bottom of the water to the top, at the edge of perch lies. This method is generally used when the water temperature is low and the fish have taken refuge for the winter in the shelter of rocks and weed beds. It is a difficult time for perch, a time of permanent hunger, and its aggression and inquisitiveness tend to unsettle everything in its neighbourhood. This metal lure, which is roughly comparable to the devon, gives good results if well fished, but it needs to be given constant movement, because it is useless when still (*see diagram*). A dead minnow with the line threaded from mouth to tail and the hook, with a small barrel lead on its shank, pulled back into the mouth is deadly. This is the English technique and it catches trout, chub and pike, too.

spinning

If fishing for perch with lures use trout spinning tackle, an average-size reel loaded with 80 yards (75 m) of 3–6 lb b.s. (1·30–2·70 kg) nylon and a 6–7 ft (1·80–2 m) rod. Identical lures to those used for trout fishing are effective, such as Mepps or Rublex spoons (Celta, small Voblex, the red Virex), and large perch will go for a Colorado—the author has caught several in this way while fishing for pike or salmon. Little needs to be said about the technique of casting. If possible, fish upstream to avoid being seen, casting up and across and retrieving quite quickly to arouse the perch's curiosity and aggressive nature. With a plug it is advisable to cast directly downstream, retrieving in a hesitant or jerking fashion to give some life to the lure. Perch fishing with a dead minnow is carried out in the same way, retrieving it with a jerky zigzag action. Just one hint in spinning for perch: do not be afraid of losing the lure or bait, for the more the difficult lies are searched the more chance there is of finding the fish.

zander

Living in deep or turbulent waters the zander has to be sought by different methods from the perch and pike even though the baits are roughly the same. Since it feeds at deep levels it is pointless fishing for zander either on the surface or even at mid-water. As voracious as the other predators, the zander behaves very differently when taking its prey. It is a fish which the angler will often hook and then lose because of its habit of biting, then chewing the bait, spitting it out, taking it again, sometimes swallowing it and sometimes leaving it. As the zander plays its cat and mouse game with the bait it is important not to hurry the strike. The same advice that was given for pike fishing is equally applicable here—it is better to strike too late rather than too soon.

live-baiting

Although the zander will take a minnow, a slightly larger live-bait such as a gudgeon, bleak or small roach, mounted not through the lip but the middle of the back is advised.

dead-baiting

This is a very deadly method provided that the fish are feeding, and there are frequent instances of fishermen taking huge quantities of zander by it. Unlike some other carnivores the zander has no objection to a dead fish on the bottom, so the best recipe for success is to search the river bed moving the bait in fits and starts, sometimes leaving it motionless for a fraction of a second, and not striking too quickly if a zander bites. There are two methods of mounting the dead fish: one consists of threading the fish between the eyes on a large single No. 2, 3 or 4 hook; the second of attaching the dead fish on a mounting with two double hooks.

The zander is not a great fighter but it can put a fair bend in the rod when it reaches weights of 8 lb (3–4 kg) or so.

live- and dead-baiting

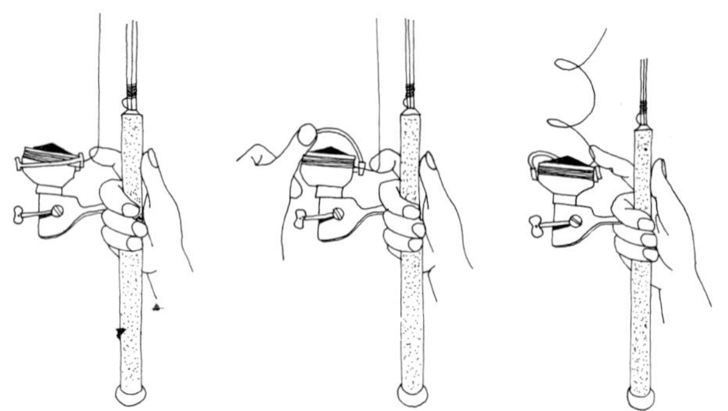

Picking up the line, opening the bale-arm, and line release when casting with a fixed-spool reel.

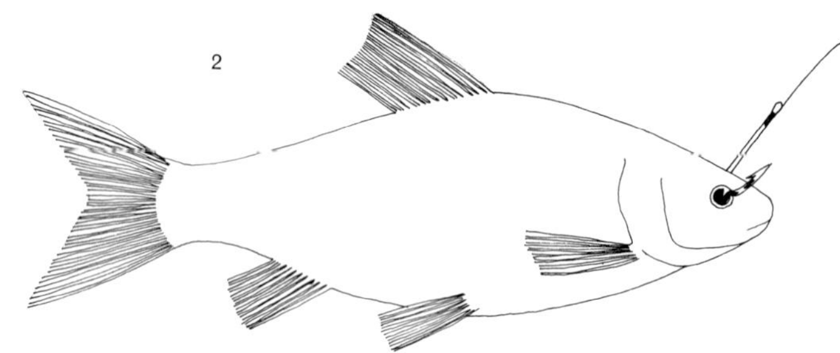

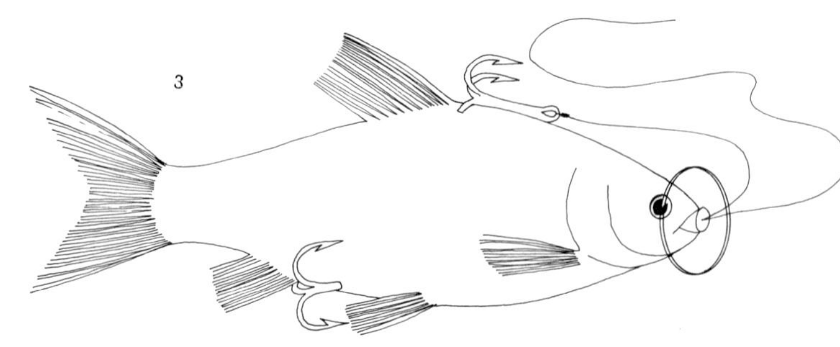

1. *Live gudgeon hooked by the back on a treble hook.*
2. *Dead young roach fixed between the eyes on a large single hook.*
3. *A dead fish mounted on two treble hooks with wobble vane.*

lures

The zander can be caught on lures, but they are not the ideal bait. This fish is far less likely to take a lure than a live or dead bait, although the author once caught a 2·2 lb (1 kg) zander on a Voblex while fishing for salmon in the Sélune, but this was a pure accident. However, if pike or perch fishing with a spoon in a river or lake which also contains zander, the lure should be weighted more or retrieved more slowly so that the lure hugs the bottom where the zander is. To fish with the best possible chance of success with zander a small live roach, bream, or gudgeon, or dead-baits of similar species should be fished on the bottom, either on straight running-leger rig or with a float-leger or paternoster. Although the zander is a very fine fish to eat, unfortunately it does not fight at all well, and line of 5–7 lb (2–3 kg) test is quite strong enough. It does have a mouthful of sharp teeth, however, and in England a thin wire trace is used; one top English zander angler has said in print, "I fail to see how the Continentals fish successfully without them, for good sized zander (say 5 lb plus (2 kg) fish) are quite capable of biting through nylon monofilament." Fishing in winter for zander is popular, and they seem to feed well in very muddy water conditions when other fish are not on the feed, especially pike.

The zander's dorsal fin has 14 spiny rays.

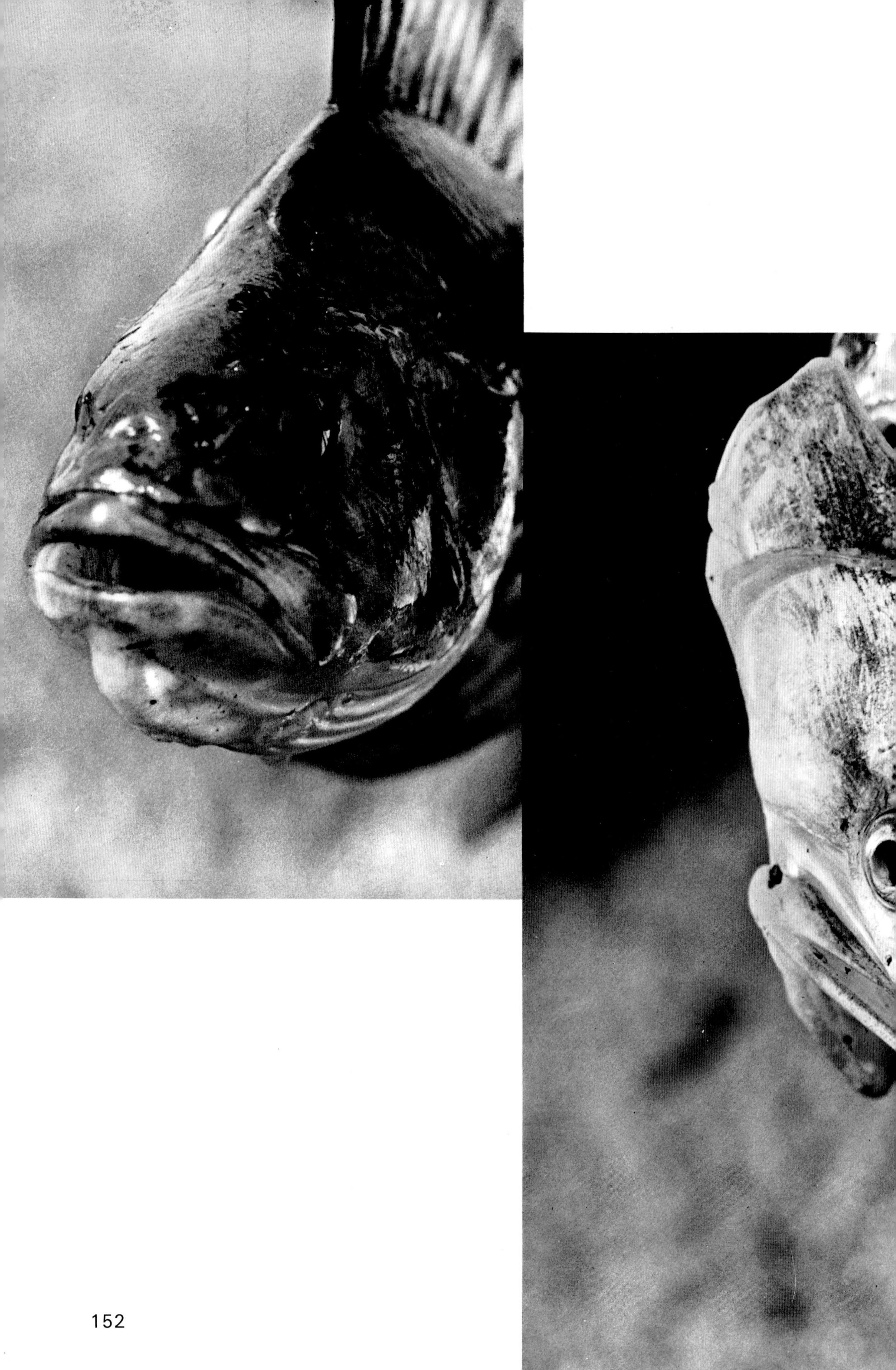

Three heads of carnivorous fish: the perch, the zander and the pike.

black bass

The large-mouth black bass (*Micropterus salmoides*) is a marvellous sporting fish, not only because it is a predator, but also because of its fighting qualities and the fact that it is almost omnivorous. It will take almost anything—live-bait, lures, frogs, insects and artificial flies.

There is no comparison between the take and the fight of a black bass and that of a pike or a zander. It is a violent fish and its effort is sustained: it fights fiercely and long. If a plug passes within its reach the fish slashes at it, relentlessly pursuing it. Like the sea trout it puts up a terrific struggle, leaping again and again from the water in the effort to get rid of the hooks in its jaws. To see a carnivore taken on a natural fly is strange for a European angler, but the black bass also takes insects. If a black bass is seen apparently asleep at the surface of a pond, drop an appetising grasshopper somewhere near and it will soon be seen that the sleep was a pretence. Nor does it hesitate to snap up a little green frog (not quite so cruel if a rubber one is used); frogs are perhaps its favourite food.

In general, methods recommended for the perch are also suitable for the black bass; but there are two or three special ones.

frogs

A medium-strength spinning rod, 6 lb b.s. (2·70 kg) line, no lead but a simple No. 6 treble, with an appetising little green frog attached by the nose or tail. After the black bass has been located cast the frog near its lie, retrieving slowly so that the bait does not sink deeply and avoids snags. As the frog moves, keep it on the move, then make it run away, and this usually triggers off an attack by the bass.

earth worms

This is the multi-purpose bait and most fish can be taken with it. The author has never caught one by this method, nor seen one caught, but his colleague Michel Duborgel has had many fine bags of black bass in Béarnais ponds with his own method, which is as follows: a fine hook link, a reel with a well-stocked spool of $2\frac{1}{2}$ lb b.s. (1·13 kg) nylon, a No. 5 single hook and a big black-headed worm which needs no shot. With this tackle cast near the weedbeds or water lilies and retrieve slowly and jerkily. This method is much more deadly if one casts to visible fish. A few snags or breaks may occur in the weeds, but it is very exciting, and one may land fish which would otherwise be uncatchable.

Lure box divided into different compartments.

Coarse fishing, from a boat, in a Central European lake.

When legering it is important to check the bait frequently.

insects

If the swims are fairly clear fly-fish with a fly line, a tapered leader and a No. 8 or No. 9 hook baited with a natural insect, such as a grasshopper, a cricket, a cockroach, a cockchafer or other fly. If the area is too restricted it will be necessary to change to spinning tackle using a bubble float. If the bass are taking on the surface mount a bubble float on the point, and 3 or 5 ft (1 or 1·50 m) higher, a dropper with a hook to fine nylon and an insect mounted on it. The drawback of this method is that some fish may be scared off by the bubble float trailing during the retrieve or by the sight of the nylon a few inches above the surface.

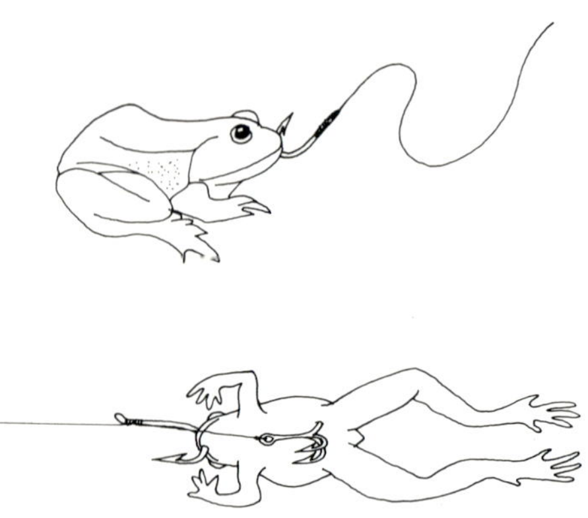

The two best methods for baiting with a frog (top for live frog, bottom for dead one).

Crayfish hooked in the end of the tail.

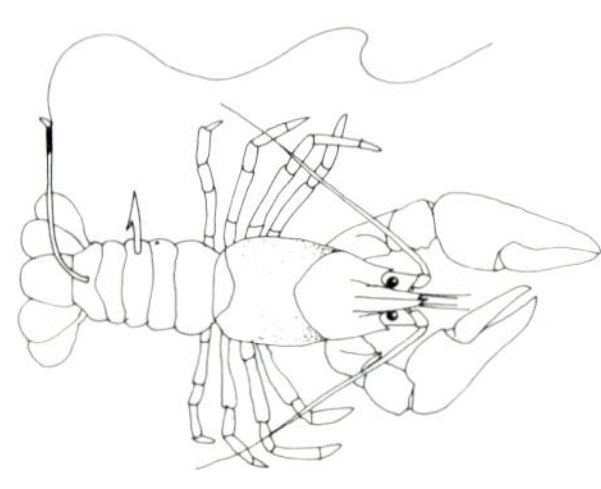

The black bass may also be taken on all the large wet flies of the streamer type (minnow-fly), and the whole range of plugs, including the eccentric American ones. One last piece of advice: fill all available ponds and stretches of water with black bass now, and there will be many happy hours of fishing to come.

Unfortunately for British anglers, there are only about two pools in the kingdom holding bass and these are not open to the public, being on club membership access only. Also, Britain's Ministry of Agriculture, Fisheries and Food is not in favour (it constantly says) of importing any foreign species—quoting the grey squirrel in England and the rabbit in Australia. Yet it has no hesitation in bringing in fish like Chinese grass carp, which are intended not for additional anglers' sport but to clear water weeds, they hope, more cheaply!

Fishing for the predators.

The fight a black bass gives before it is netted. ▶

predators

pike

With a scientific name of *Esox lucius* it comes as no surprise to find the wolf-like teeth of the pike bearing a similarity to that savage animal's. Inhabiting most European fresh waters, and some others that are brackish, the voracious "freshwater shark" is built to pounce like lightning from ambush among weeds, tree-roots or holes in the banks. A lean, slender body terminating in a duck-billed jaw, with dorsal and anal fins, both large, just ahead of the round-lobed forked tail to provide maximum and instantaneous acceleration, plus baleful forward-looking eyes and a dappled green and yellowish coloration make the pike the perfect assassin.

Although it bears a certain similarity of head to the zander, the pike cannot be confused with any other European freshwater fish, although it has relatives on the North American continent, including the mighty muskellunge. Pike grow to vast sizes, and fish of 50 lb (22 kg) certainly exist, although the British rod-caught record is open at the time of writing for entries over 41 lb (18·50 kg). Many 30 lb (13·60 kg) fish are being taken today with so many refined techniques being used.

Pike spawn in weedy shallows in lakes and up backwaters and feeders on rivers during the period February to April. The females are far larger than males, male pike seldom attaining weights over 12 lb (5·40 kg).

Although fish form the basic diet of mature pike (fish of 4 lb (1·80 kg) upwards), they will also grab at voles, frogs, newts and waterfowl, and will even try to attack fish in an angler's keepnet.

On the continent of Europe pike are eaten with relish, but in Britain few are killed and most of those caught by dedicated pike anglers are put back alive, although some anglers more interested in catching lots of small fish kill pike in the belief that they are saving their infant fish from a killer. In fact, in large waters pike help to preserve the balance of the fish population by thinning out cyprinid species which often tend to overpopulate a water and become stunted.

perch

The perch (*Perca fluviatilis*) belongs to the Percidae family in the Percomorphi order. This predator, an excellent sporting fish, has many regional names. It can be found in most slower-flowing rivers and also in rougher water if sufficient food is available.

The main characteristics of this fish are that the dorsal fin is armed with 13–15 spiny rays, that a second dorsal fin is situated further back with 14–16 soft non-pointed rays, and that there are 8 or 9 soft rays and 2 spiny ones on the anal fin, while the number of scales on the lateral line varies from 65 to 70. The greeny-grey, sometimes dark-brown back has 5–7 vertical bars, which are almost black in the upper part and extend three-quarters of the way down the flanks. The perch's livery changes according to the water and the region, but its tail and fins are almost always red. The perch has a relatively small mouth for a carnivore of this type. Its top lip is especially soft and many anglers have lost fish because of this. With all its fins displayed in its own element, the perch looks a redoubtable and even ferocious fish. Right up to the last moment the angler must take care, particularly if he has no net, for apart from the dorsal fin with its particularly sharp spines the gill-cover also ends in points which often leave painful souvenirs on the hand of the imprudent fisherman. Finally, the quality of its flesh is incomparable. The river perch living in clear, running water has equally as good flesh as, and sometimes better than, that of the brown trout. The average length of the perch is between 8 and 12 in. (20 and 30·50 cm) although there are exceptional specimens more than 18 in. (46 cm) long, weighing 4 lb (1·80 kg). Conversely, young perch which have excessively overstocked some still waters multiply without getting any larger. This is called dwarfing. Thus in some waters an 8 in. (20 cm) perch is a good fish.

zander

The zander, which bears the scientific name *Stizostedion lucioperca*, is often called pikeperch because its head bears a resemblance to that of the pike while it has the humped back and spiny dorsal fin of the perch.

Introduced into western European rivers, and into a few enclosed waters in England, it was later deliberately introduced into the Great Ouse, from which it has spread quickly. It likes warmish water with plenty of oxygen and it is an extremely voracious predator, rapidly cleaning up stocks of smaller native fish; it is for this reason that many anglers do not like the zander.

The zander is native to eastern and central Europe, but it is claimed, though not yet proved, that the American pikeperch, known in its native land as a walleye (*Stizostedion vitreum*), is also present in smaller numbers. The walleye, which owes its name to its large opaque eyes, is distinguished from the zander by its brassy oblique lines on head and body, by the distinct black spot on the membrane at the tail-end of the first dorsal fin, and by the dark flecks on the pectoral and pelvic fins, which on the zander are unmarked.

Among the individual characteristics of the zander are its teeth, which include a pair of canines in each row. Its first dorsal fin has 13 to 15 straight rays, the second has 2 spiny rays and about 20 soft ones and between 130 and 150 scales have been counted on its lateral line. The colouring, which varies according to its environment, is usually grey-green on the back with a yellowish belly, black stripes on the sides and dark spots on the dorsal and caudal fin. This carnivore, which was recorded at between 10 and 15 lb (5 and 7 kg) in western Europe only a few years after its introduction, may measure more than 3 ft (1 m) and weigh 33 lb (15 kg) in some central European lakes.

The zander spawns in spring, and the female lays on average 50,000 eggs per pound of its weight. The young hatch out shortly after the eggs are laid and less than two months after its birth the little fish has reached 2 in. (5 cm) in length.

black bass

The prototype sporting predator, the black bass has not acclimatised in Europe as well as its qualities deserve. Belonging to the Percomorphous order like the perch and the zander, the black bass is a member of the Centrarchidae family from North America. It is the only representative in European fresh waters. The main characteristic of the Centrarchidae is that they are nidifactors: unlike most freshwater species this fish builds a nest on the river-bed and defends it jealously, until the eggs are hatched. There are two sorts of black bass: the better known large-mouth (*Micropterus salmoides*), and the small-mouth (*M. dolomieu*). Ichthyologists are not agreed on the spawning period of the black bass, some maintaining that it occurs in April and May, others that it begins in May and lasts throughout the summer months. The shape and colouring of the black bass have given it the nickname perch-trout in some regions, but if it can claim some resemblance to the perch, particularly in its spiny dorsal fin, it has none with the trout. Its dorsal fin is in two parts; the first is spiny and has 10 rays and is smaller than the second, which is not spiny and has 12 or 13 rays; there are three spiny rays on the front of the anal fin, and the pelvics are set slightly behind the pectorals. Its lower jaw gives it a malevolent look. There are 65 to 70 scales on the lateral line. The large-mouth has 10 rows of scales on the flanks. Its colouring camouflages it well in its environment as it has a dark-green back, occasionally mottled with brown, black or dark green patches, and flanks and a whitish belly. As has been said, the black bass has had difficulty in acclimatising in European waters, although it is sometimes found in private ponds, canals or dykes, which it seems to find to its liking. The black bass average between 1 and 3 lb (450g–1·30 kg); however, exceptional specimens have been caught over 2 ft (70 cm) long and weighing up to 11 lb (5 kg).

cyprinids

carp

the queen of the cyprinids

The carp is considered to be the queen of the cyprinids for a variety of reasons. The first is because of its weight, which often reaches impressive proportions, 66 lb (30 kg) carp having been caught in some waters of south-west France. Apart from its weight, this fish is very shy and extremely powerful. It is a veritable locomotive which, although lacking the spasmodic rushes and the leaps of the salmonids, pulls powerfully and long when it is hooked.

Its instinctive wariness enables it to detect the most ingenious traps. It might be thought that a large fish would be less suspicious than a small one and that because of its size it would eat thinly disguised bait, or come and eat out of the hand of the fisherman like the domestic carp in ponds, public parks or castle moats. However, this is not the case; the carp is a very clever and cunning fish, and carp fishermen, the true ones, who devote all their time to this fish, are well aware of this.

When the author was a young fisherman, he was fortunate enough to read a series of articles which appeared in *Au Bord de l'Eau*, edited by Dr. Sexe, the great expert on carp. He had been struck by the fact that a member of the medical profession (who usually tend to prefer game fishing) could be so passionately interested in carp. The author owes his first successes as a carp fisherman to these articles which, though sometimes boring because of their technical nature, were essential for success in attracting the grandfather carp and persuading them to take. Thus he caught a few quite respectable carp in the deep pools of the Allier around Vieille-Brioude. He was using parboiled potato as bait, and in those days a 0·01 in. (0·50 mm) diameter line had a breaking strain of only 17 lb (7·50 kg). The writer confesses to fishing for carp with this line and sometimes even with a 0·02 in. (0·60 mm) one, used also for early salmon fishing. Later a fisherman from Clermont, frequenting the same swims taught him the subtleties of fishing for carp with a 6 lb b.s. (2·70 kg) line and with small bait such as maize, corn or beans.

The bigger they were, the more difficult they were to deceive. They could be seen every day when the sun was high, swimming nonchalantly in single file, out of reach of the rods. During the day there was nothing doing. Often one killed time fishing for roach while waiting for the fateful hour of 5 p.m., for these carp fed only between then and nightfall. As soon as the shadows covered the water, and the sun went down behind the mountain they became active and went cruising in search of food on the bottom. The author regularly brought them food every day; a bucket of 10–20 lb (5–10 kg) of crushed, boiled potatoes serving as ground-bait. A week before, it had been necessary to bait up daily even more massively to alert all the carp in the area and bring them to the swim. Once they got into the habit, they came every morning and evening, but, if they took the ground-bait they were less attracted by the hook-bait. With his battery of three rods the author waited on his folding stool for the sound of the reel ratchet that would signal a bite. Then the line tore off the reel and a carp streaked away towards the other bank, about 50 yards (50 m) off. It was necessary to get up promptly and adjust the brake before making any attempt to take command, for during the first few minutes nothing stops a 15 lb (6·80 kg) carp, not even a 15–25 lb b.s. (6·8–11·40 kg) line, which it can rapidly wear through with its sharp dorsal fin and which often becomes snagged in roots or chafed through on sharp rocks. With

Mirror carp at the moment of exhaustion. ►

the rod upright it is important to keep firm contact and not to panic. Simply wait for the fish to tire itself out while attempting to prevent it from going towards the obstacles near the bank or on the bottom. If the battle develops at mid-water, there is every chance that the fish will gradually weaken, turning in small circles which decrease as the fish loses strength. That is the moment to pump, just as when playing a salmon, by lowering the rod point and retrieving a few yards of line, then lifting the point and repeating the operation. The effect of this is to bring the fish closer until it appears at the surface, on its side, absolutely worn out. However, the battle is not over, as the final phase is very hazardous, particularly with a big carp for which the net never seems large or strong enough. If fishing for very large carp it is better to avoid telescopic nets, which might give way under the strain. A large reinforced net with a big cane handle is ideal even though it may look clumsy and difficult to carry. Most large carp (leather carp in particular), summon up reserves of energy when they see the net, and make a last dash for freedom. They can cover short distances at great speed and several attempts may be necessary before the fish is safely landed.

fishing for carp

It would take an entire book to explain all the techniques and skills used in carp fishing. However, there are a few very important tricks to persuade the fish to bite. The author does not entirely agree with those fishermen who say that the carp can be caught on thick nylon as readily as fine. Many a time roach fishermen, using the finest of lines, have felt a tug as a carp has taken off for the wide-open spaces like an express train, with a tiny No. 18 or 20 hook buried in its leathery lip. Then inevitably the carp has won, despite the modern rod or the fixed-spool reel and its slipping clutch. There is no doubt that it can be caught more easily on a fine line, so to be fair, if thinking of fishing for carp weighing no more than 5 or 6 lb (2·20–2·70 kg), do so with a 6 lb b.s. (2·70 kg) line; for fish weighing more than 10 lb (4·50 kg), and in relatively weedy swims, a 12 lb b.s. (5·40 kg) line is useful. Nowadays the lines called "Nylorfi", "Platyl-strong" or "Super-Mimicry", with a diameter of 0·01 in. (0·35 mm), are strong enough to play a 15 lb (6·80 kg) fish quite comfortably without risking a break each time it runs. In view of the carp's wariness, the colour of the nylon should be matched as nearly as possible to that of the water.

Unless they are living in close proximity to people—such as those often fed bread by children in public park lakes—carp are notoriously shy fish. Although when fed bread like this they can be quite easily lured by an angler fishing with bread, on the bottom or floating on the surface, while he is sitting in full view, carp in the wild, as it were, are quite different. A heavy footfall, a shadow on the water, a flash of rod varnish, a splash from tackle . . . all these will frighten the fish, which will be unlikely to take the offered bait.

Many carp anglers fish at night, when the fish tend to roam more round the margins and when they are more approachable. They fish with electric buzzer bite alarms on their lines, or with glowing leger bobbins clipped to their lines just ahead of the reels.

Carp fishing can be divided into two parts: fishing a bait on the bottom and fishing a bait floating on the surface. Although sometimes a carp will pick up a No. 6 hook baited with maggots, even with the hook showing, it pays to conceal the hook—except for the point—when after carp. Among the successful baits for bottom fishing are bread paste, flake, crust, boiled potatoes, cooked beans and peas, luncheon meat and sausage meat, bunches of maggots, worms, cheese mixed with bread, and many smelly concoctions involving either high-protein content or high-smell content—such as cat food mixed with bread paste.

A useful French tip when using potato is to ream a cylinder from the potato with a tube of metal, pass the nylon line through it with a baiting or plain needle, then tie on a treble hook. The hook is pulled gently back into the potato

The fleshy lips in which the hook is embedded, to remain there ◀ *until the fish is subdued and comes to the net.*

and nicks made ahead of each point to permit easy penetration on the strike. In Britain, though, treble hooks for carp are frowned upon.

Much carp fishing on the bottom is done with just the hook on the line, the bait giving the weight for casting. The rod is placed in V-rests and the line arranged so that when a fish takes the bait and swims off line is drawn easily from the fixed-spool reel. A running-leger lead, stopped by a split-shot between 2 and 24 in. (5–70 cm) in general, from the hook, is used when weight is a necessity to attain long casting range, or when anchoring a buoyant bait (such as bread crust) above a muddy or weedy bottom! If carp are biting very shyly, a slim float with the tackle lightly lying on the bottom, may be used.

Most surface carp fishing is done with bread crust, often at night and suspended just under the rod tip in the shallow margins. Sometimes the angler goes in search of feeding carp and drops the crust ahead of the fish, or even casts a bait of maggots or worms in its path to sink to the bottom.

Ground-baiting is very important in carp fishing. Carp, more than most fish, seem to go off certain baits on which they have been caught before, and anglers often have to experiment with strange baits, and samples must be put into the water beforehand to get the fish used to feeding on the new bait.

Such is that attraction of carp fishing for many anglers that whole week-end trips are made, fishing continuing throughout day and night, the anglers cooking their food by their rods, well concealed of course, and cat-napping in bed-chairs.

Carp are very powerful fish, almost as strong as a fresh-run salmon, and it is this great fighting quality, plus the vast size of the fish's potential, that makes the carp such a popular angler's fish. Many carp sessions can be disappointing, and it is fairly common for some keen anglers fishing difficult waters for very big fish, to go a whole season without catching a fish! And these men will not be daunted, and will be trying again next season. In every carp angler's breast lies the hope that a 50 pounder (20 kg) will one day take his bait. . . .

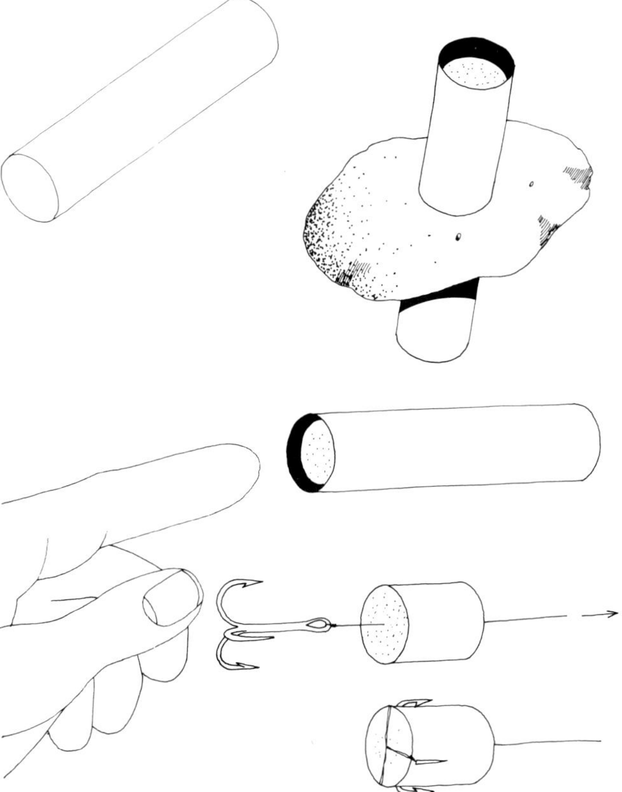

This is the way to bait up with a cylindrical piece of potato: take a tube the width of a treble hook, push it into a cooked potato, extract the cylinder, through which you thread the nylon, then tie on a hook and pull the hook back into the potato, leaving the points free.

How to put an earthworm or a bunch of maggots on a hook.

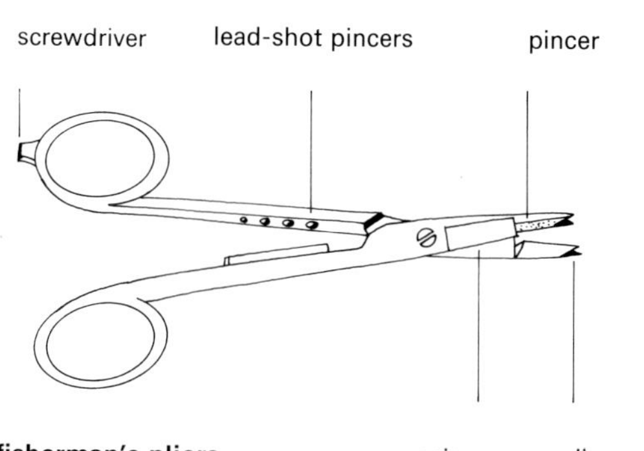

A catapult would have saved this fisherman a lot of effort when ground-baiting at a distance. ►

A 5 lb (2·20 kg) sparsely scaled mirror carp. ▼

Mind the branches! ►

Plenty of room, a quiet retreat—these are the usual refuges that the really large fish seek (bottom right).

Two rods mirrored in a calm pond. ▼

A river of the Tarn and Garonne.

The Loing at Montigny.

Winter carp fishing in Kent: an angler braves the cold to net a 10$\frac{1}{2}$ lb. (4·80 kg) mirror carp as dusk falls.

The beautiful $10\frac{1}{2}$ lb. (4·80 kg) mirror carp, seen being landed on previous page, is held up for the camera by its captor.

The Essone in winter. ▶

▼*A 6 lb (2·70 kg) carp.*

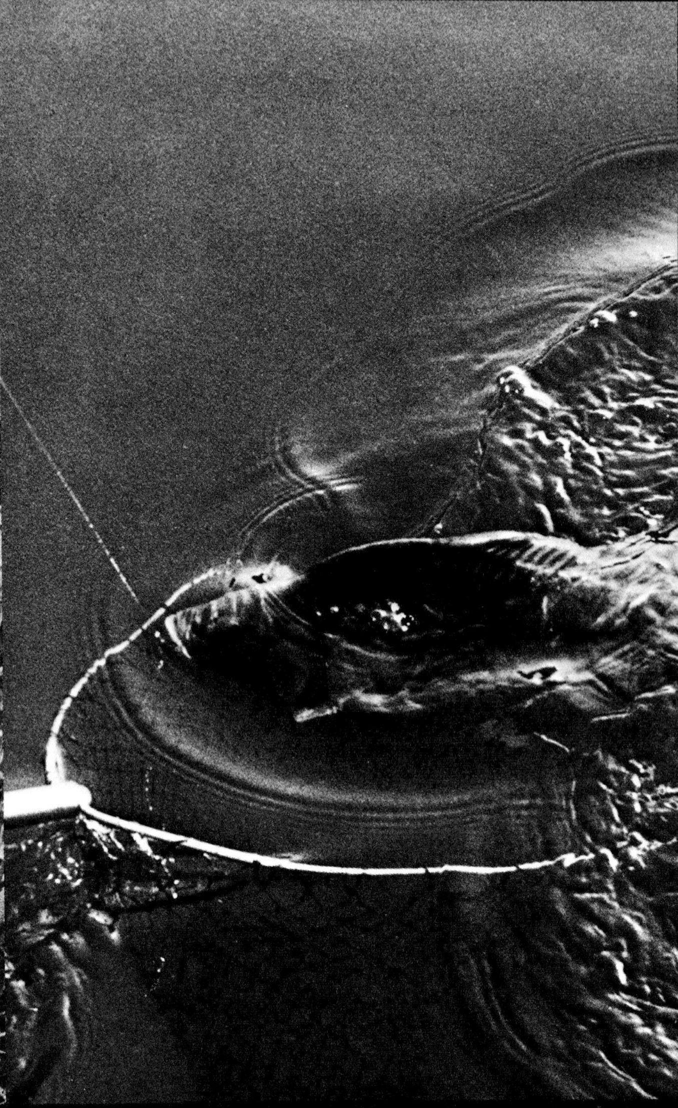

Bottom-fishing or surface fishing—both produce carp.

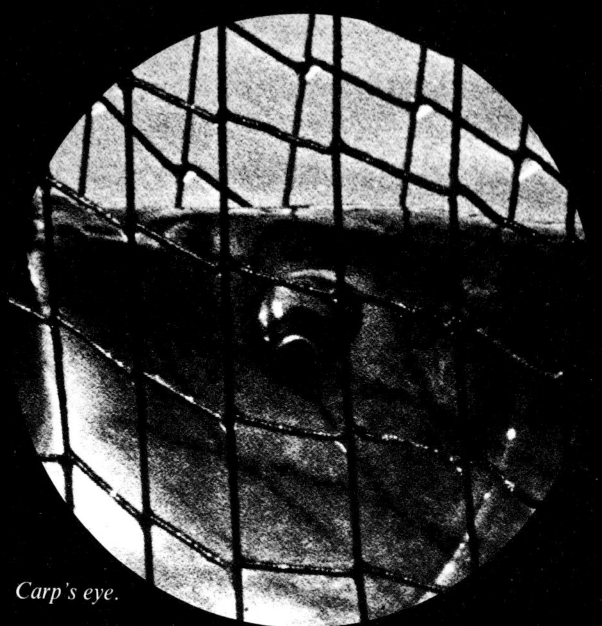

Carp's eye.

chub

Chub fishing poses an obvious problem, for the chub is truly catholic in its tastes. It can be caught in summer on the natural fly, artificial fly, insects, ripe fruit, aquatic larvae and worms, and in winter on dried blood, bits of bacon, pellets of bread, etc. This omnivorous fish is a kind of bonus to the fisherman, because it is often caught without the fisherman really trying and it causes many a surprise. The different coarse-fishing activities for chub will not be discussed, as the more sporting methods such as the fly, stalking, and in winter blood fishing, are more worthy of consideration.

fly-fishing

The chub should be fished by this method in swims where it is most vulnerable, that is to say in currents, fairly broken water or along river banks. For all surface fishing, it is vital to be absolutely quiet and to remain invisible, both when fishing from a distance or round a bend. Fly-fishing for chub is very like fly-fishing for trout. A supple rod, a braided line in silk or synthetic fibre, a nylon leader, a hook of appropriate size and a fly or natural insect, such as a stonefly, winged ant, house-fly, oak-fly, bluebottle, grasshopper, or cricket, are required. Chub can be caught either by casting to individual fish or by covering the water. The first method is more satisfying, because it allows the fisherman to observe the reaction of the fish to the bait, to see if it is refused or if it alarms the fish. This type of fishing needs a delicate touch and a certain dexterity like fishing for trout with natural fly. If the fisherman

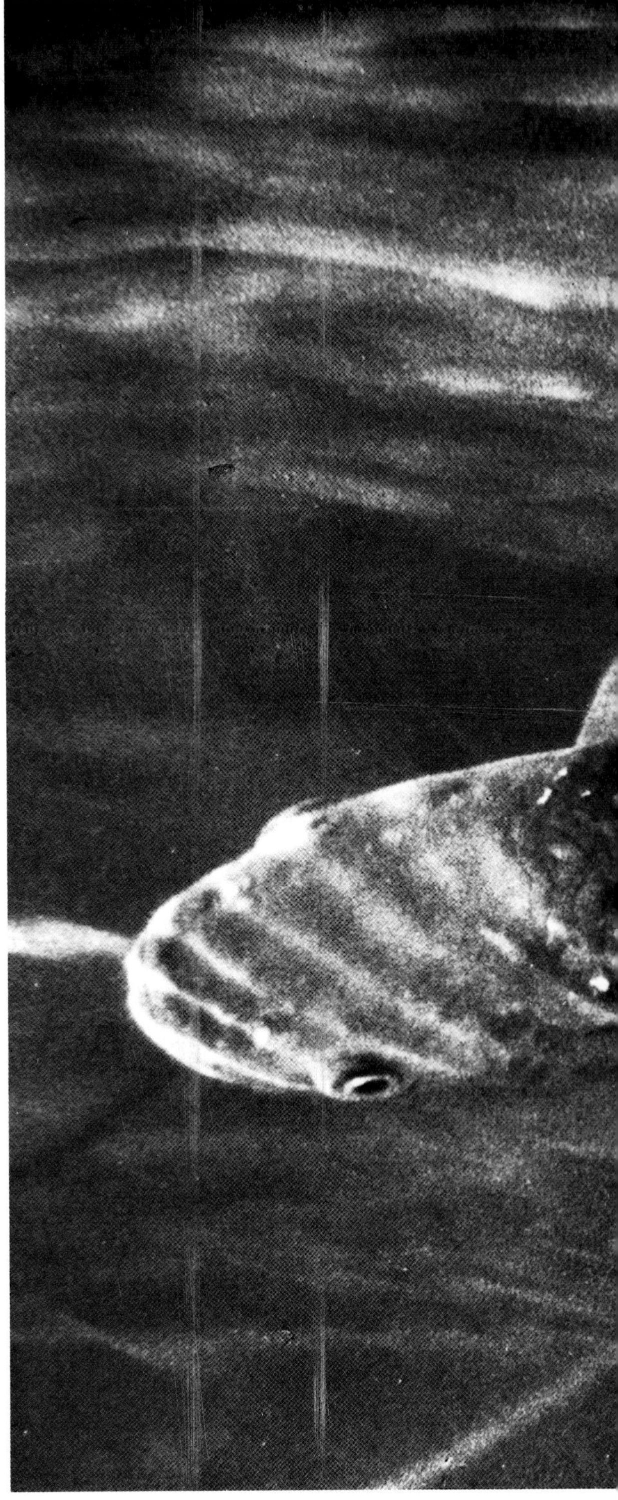

A chub on the surface . . . taken by surprise.

A play of light on the silvery scales of a chub under the rippling water. ▶

▲
With his Roubaix rod D. Maury prepares to teach the roach a lesson.

The lower the sun sinks, the more the magic of fishing during the evening reveals itself. ▶

Trotting on the Hampshire Avon with a centrepin reel—this is excellent water for big chub. ▶▶

casts too strongly, the fly or insect will be flung off at the first cast. It often happens that the bait, submerged by a wave or ripple, sinks. If this happens it is advisable to let it remain, while keeping control of the leader which is still on the surface. In this way a bite will be seen, as the leader and line will sink; this is the moment to strike. On the other hand, when the chub takes on the surface, it sometimes makes no noise but is clearly visible and the bite is slow enough for an effective strike to be made.

stalking

Numerous precautions must be taken when stalking chub, but the tackle itself may be very simple as it has little influence on the effectiveness of the method. As its name indicates, stalking is a method designed to surprise the chub. The fisherman fishes at close range, about 10–13 ft (3–4 m) away, by silently working up a bank between trees, in the tall grass, in France with a powerful split-cane or fibreglass rod about 14 ft (4·50 m) long and without a reel. Directly attached to the tip is a short length of braided line 12–16 in. (30–40 cm) long, then a length of 5 or 6 lb b.s. (2·20–2·70 kg) nylon, about 5 or 6 ft (1·50–1·80 m) long on which a No. 8 or 9 hook is tied. For bait a grasshopper is used (*see diagram*). In Britain, the rod would be between 10 and 12 ft (3 and 3·60 m) in length and used with a centrepin or fixed-spool reel. With a minimum of noise, taking each pace very quietly along the bank, with no unnecessary movement, hiding behind tree trunks, sometimes crawling, move the rod gently forward to the edge of the water and wait for a chub to go by. It rises nonchalantly to the surface with its dorsal fin just breaking the water, swallowing an ant here, a fly there. Let it pass the rod-top, then raise the rod, and let down the grasshopper, which falls gently behind the fish; at this moment the chub, detecting the fall of the insect, turns round and without examining it, swallows it immediately. The fisherman must strike quickly and immediately, before the fish has time to dive, applying maximum pressure,

Fishing the lake over a rim of ice; anglers have to be hardy. ▶

risking a break. This method gives excellent results in very warm weather, under shaded banks and in overcast conditions, although it is useless in rain or high winds. Never stay long in one place; move along a few yards, for the chub in the immediate vicinity, alarmed by the capture of one of their relations, are unlikely to bite.

blood-fishing

French anglers use blood from the abattoir for winter chub fishing: the liquid blood mixed with bread and sand as ground-bait, clots of blood on the hook. Sometimes chicken entrails or cubes of bacon fat are the hookbait.

In Britain, trotting for chub down the smooth-flowing rivers is very popular, the centrepin reel being free-running to pay-off line as the float is pulled downstream by the current—some anglers use fixed-spool reels. Also successful is legering with lumps of cheese, cheese mixed with bread paste, bread flake and crust, worms, slugs and maggots.

Often British anglers free-line, simply letting the bait—flake or a bunch of worms or a slug—sink slowly and drift downstream, without anything on the line but a hook. This can be very effective, too, as can the same technique with a crust of bread on the surface.

SCABEP

Tackle must be prepared with meticulous care before each fishing session.

For successful coarse fishing it is important not to neglect the bait.

The eternal problem: choice of the line or terminal tackle.

Previous page (inset): A young but already dedicated fisherman, intent on the art of expertly baiting up a hook.

Previous page: Feet in the water, sun in the sky, rod in the hand . . . and hopefully soon a fish on the hook.

roach

The roach is certainly the traditional coarse-fisherman's quarry. It abounds in quieter waters, in rivers and ponds. Therefore, it is generally caught on float tackle.

The impression of roach fishing given by game fishermen who laugh at the patient coarse fisherman waiting for the roach to work up an appetite, must be recognised as false. Do not think that roach fishing is easy; on the contrary, patience and a perfect knowledge of the habits of the fish are required to allay its suspicions. The roach is wary of everything from the thickness of a nylon line to the colour of the hook, the disposition of the lead, and of course, the bait. It sees everything, and even in muddy water it is never easy to deceive. However, good fishermen do catch them, and some catch a lot, but as has been said, roach fishing is a fairly specialist technique.

baiting-up

The roach is not truly omnivorous, but prefers vegetable matter and grubs. In very hot weather it is fond of rising to the surface to suck down gnats. So it can be fished for in several ways, according to the season and the environment.

Ground-baiting is not absolutely necessary, but it does help to get fish to feed in the chosen swim. There is plenty of choice where ground-baiting for roach is concerned: earth or dung mixed with gentles, bloodworms and all types of meal and bran, sold in the trade, which are soaked in water and mixed with the appropriate material, soaked bread, hempseed, etc. It is advisable to ground-bait lightly in order not to overfeed the fish, if possible using the same material as the hook-bait. For instance, if fishing with wheat, as soon as the frequency of bites begins to diminish, throw a handful of wheat slightly upstream of the float. Beforehand ground-bait more heavily in order to keep the fish in the swim.

The baits which roach prefer during the summer season are hempseed, wheat, the crumb of the loaf, pieces of potato or bean, and most animal baits: worms, maggots, freshwater shrimp and caddis.

In winter or in colder water vegetable baits give way to animal baits such as the bloodworm or the small red worm. Roach can also be fished for either with the natural flour-based pastes or egg yolk mixed with hempseed oil, or with different-coloured synthetic pastes like Mystic. This method is recommended for beginners. It is important to remember that all vegetable baits such as wheat, potato, hempseed, etc. must be cooked.

tackle

The specialised technique of most French match fishermen has brought about considerable advances in roach tackle and more particularly in the design of lines for roach fishing. However, before talking about lines, let us begin with the rod, the basic instrument for roach fishing. Firstly the conventional rod. The Fréjus cane rod has definitely been abandoned in favour of hollow fibreglass. Nowadays there are a great variety of rods available between 11 and 26 ft

A selection of floats used by French anglers.

1. *Poulet*
2. *Lora*
3. *Ideal*
4. *Jupiter*
5. *Méduse concours type*
6. *Boréal type*
7. *Cluny*
8. *Versailles*
9. *Droger*
10. *Micro*
11. *Porcupine*
12. *Régence*
13. *Conducteur*
14. *Bouchon poire*
15. *Cigare à boule type*
16. *Glisseur "Steph"*
17. *Plastic Plume*
18. *Piston type*
19. *Colibri type*

(3·50 and 8 m) or more. There are rods with the traditional cork handle, there are telescopic rods; in fact there is a rod for every taste. Secondly, there are the Roubaix rods, which have a piece of elastic fitted between the rod-tip and the line. These Roubaix rods are extremely stiff, which permits a rapid strike, and their effectiveness is increased by the action of the elastic buffer which prevents breaks when heavier fish are struck or being played.

The length of the rod is left to the choice of each individual French fisherman who will make up his mind according to local conditions. The same applies to the action of the rod. Some prefer long, whippy rods, others the short Roubaix ones. It is pointless to have a rod with any kind of rings, since a reel is quite unnecessary for roach fishing.

(British anglers occasionally fish the ringless and reel-less rod, but normally use 12–13 ft (3·60–4 m) quick-action rods with rings and fixed-spool or centrepin reels, especially on fast-flowing rivers.)

There are many tight-line rigs but the author prefers one that combines many attributes and is easily modified.

The author uses a straight bronze No. 16 hook and a hook-link of 1 lb b.s. (450 g) nylon. A tiny shot is placed about 8 in. (20 cm) from the hook. Above the blood-knot, which connects hook-link and the 1½ lb b.s. (680 g) main line is a sliding weight, stopped by the knot, or a fixed shot with the weight giving perfect balance to the line. Finally, a quill or a balsa float with long antenna, or a small Versailles float is attached. The main thing is to ensure the balance of the combination so that at the slightest bite the float is seen to move.

The size of the hook will vary according to the bait chosen. Thus, to fish with a bloodworm, you will choose a smaller hook (No. 20). To fish with a maggot, a slightly larger hook (No. 14) is needed. With regard to the colour of the hook, the experts recommend that it is as near to the colour of the bait as possible. Thus, when fishing with corn or bread or light pastes, you would use a gilt hook, whereas when fishing with animal bait in dark hues, you would use a bronzed hook.

techniques

Roach-fishing technique is very important, even more so than the choice of tackle, although both are complementary, as always, to successful sport. First, the shoal of roach must be located, although there are well-known swims that nearly always hold them, differing in summer and winter. In summer faster water, up to 5 ft (1·50 m) deep, in rivers will tend to hold roach; in the winter they often move into deeper (up to 15 ft (4·60 m) or so) and slower water or pools, and like submerged lily beds and gravel bottoms.

Float tackle is most useful for roach, and one should adjust the float on the line to fish from about half the depth of the water at first, gradually increasing depth until bites are seen and fish caught. In summer mid depth will be the norm, whereas in winter the bait is most likely to find fish on or just above the bottom.

Although trotting the float down the current in rivers is usually most effective, in lakes, and in rivers in winter, a legered bait will often prove to be most killing.

The fisherman must keep a permanent hold of the rod, keeping the line taut, checking at the end of each swim and several times while retrieving the line. The wary roach is most often taken by a moving bait, so when the line and the bait sink bites are difficult to detect. On the way up they are felt more easily. A roach is sometimes caught without striking, but if it is necessary the strike must be fast. It is more rapid with a Roubaix rod where the movement is not slowed down by the suppleness of the cane. That is why there must be no slack in the body of the line between the float and the rod-tip. In a word, the success of tight-line roach fishing depends on the sustained concentration of the fisherman, so that he is always ready to strike on the slightest shiver of the antenna. Whether it rises slightly or sinks just as slightly, or moves sideways . . . strike immediately.

After striking, if the fish is hooked, it is still necessary to act with care in order to bring it to the bank. On a 1 lb b.s. (450 g) line a small roach can be lifted straight out, but if it weighs around 10 oz (300 g) it is better to use a small net to land it.

Winter fishing in Central Germany. ▶

other cyprinids
angling methods in brief

tench

The tench lives mainly in still, weedy waters, near reed beds or among the water lilies, in fact anywhere where the vegetation provides abundant food and a chance for it to hide from men or predators.

This very wary fish is difficult to catch. Its unpredictable behaviour is well known and it is possible to fish for days without a bite, in spite of plentiful and carefully laid ground-bait. Then suddenly one fine morning, it comes on the feed, and good bags are easily taken.

Tench mainly feed over the bottom of the pond, lake or slow-flowing river, and most fishing is done on the bottom or just above it using lobworms, red worms, maggots, bunches of bloodworms, bread baits of all types, potato and swan mussels. However, tench sometimes feed higher in the water and then a slow-sinking bait on light tackle, or a bait suspended just under lily leaves, etc. will catch them.

The months June to October provide the best of the fishing, with June and July the cream. Early mornings and the evenings usually produce most activity, but on some deep waters tench feed all through the daylight hours.

Float fishing with the last shot just touching bottom or with a running lead stopped inches or feet away from the hook works best as a rule. As for tackle, a flexible rod that will curve into a quarter circle yet not break 5 lb (2·20 kg) line is a reliable weapon: 10–14 ft (3–4 m) may be necessary and lines of 3–7 lb (1·30–3·10 kg) test to suit open or snaggy/weedy waters.

Ground-baiting over a period of days before fishing is widely practised, but is not essential. Throwing in a garden rake-head on a line and dragging the bottom and weeds is a recognised practice, and tench will often be caught within 15 minutes of the disturbance!

Tench are very strong fighters, boring strongly into weedbeds, which they like to inhabit. Fish of 4 lb (1·80 kg) are good and a 6 lb (2·70 kg) fish a real specimen. Whatever size hook is needed—say No. 14 for small red worms or maggots or No. 8 for bread or lobworm—it should be strong with a flat forged bend.

bream

The common or bronze bream is a sluggish bottom feeder living in slow rivers and in still waters, though occasionally in faster rivers. It mainly fights very feebly when hooked—though there are exceptions—and is generally regarded highly only by competition anglers, because they are normally easy to get feeding and weigh heavily at the end of the day.

Bream of 12 lb (5 kg) or more have been caught but the average weight is about 2 lb (1 kg). Roach tackle and laying-on tactics, rather as for tench, will usually work well enough: the float not quite cocked and a shot or a running lead lying on the bottom. In rivers a float trotted down with the bait dragging bottom will also work.

Heavy ground-baiting will attract and hold a big greedy shoal of bream, and baits of lobworm, red worms, maggot, bread in various forms, and stewed wheat are normally accepted.

Ordinary legering is the tactic chosen when bream swims are a long way out—in big lakes for

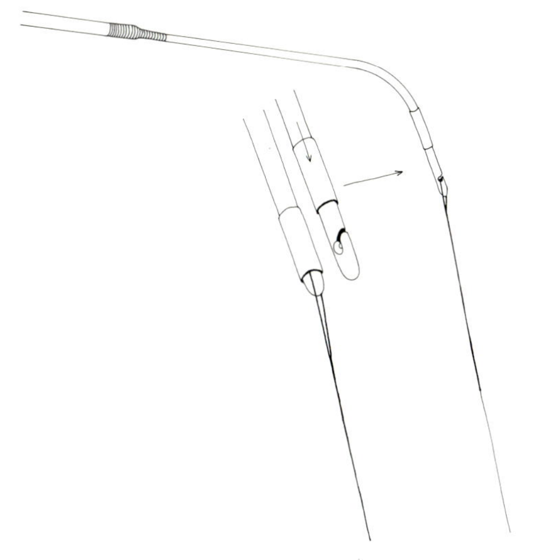

How the elastic shock absorber at the curved extremity of a Roubaix rod is fitted.

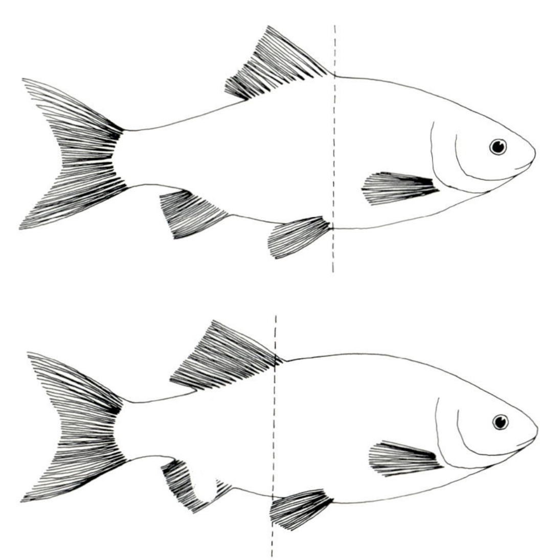

This shows the difference between a roach (above), and a rudd (below), with the dorsal fin of the rudd clearly placed further back.

float tackle rigs for small fish

French-style float tackles.

1. *Roach line (long cylindrical leads).*
2. *Bleak line with two hooks.*
3. *Line with the float on a separate length of nylon.*
4. *Jigging a line to give a bait movement.*
5. *The position of the shots on the bottom for tench.*
6. *Toulouse tackle for gudgeon.*

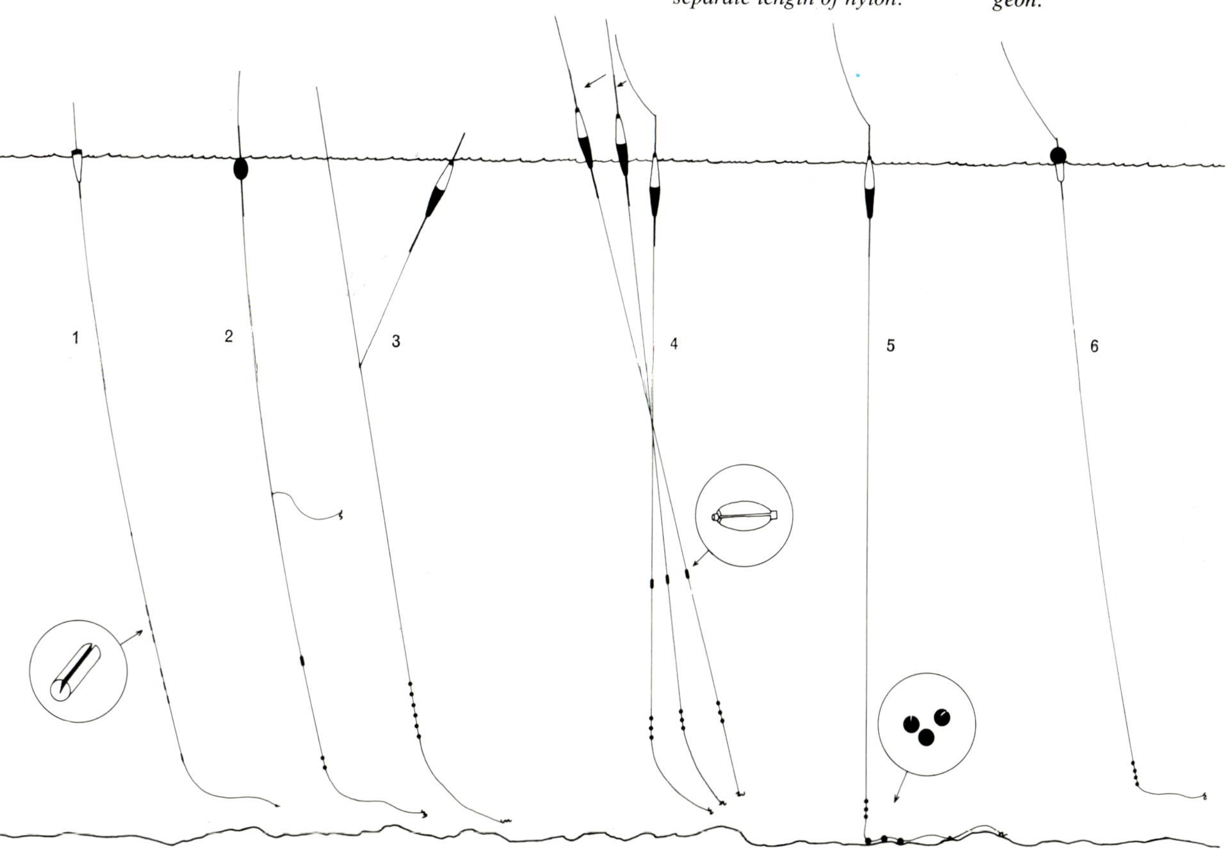

example. In addition, to get the bait and the ground-bait together, a swimfeeder is used: this is a tube of plastic film, with lead on one side threaded on the line like a leger lead. The tube is filled with maggots, mashed bread, etc., and the hook baited. The ground-bait comes out of the swimfeeder and is deposited near the baited hook.

A feature of float fishing on the bottom for bream is that, when the fish tilts head-down to pick up the bait, then straightens up again, it lifts the lead or shot and the float often comes up to lie flat on the water. It is possible to strike then, or one may wait until the float is drawn along and under.

rudd

Rudd are often confused with roach, but rudd have longer lower lips than upper lips while in roach the reverse is true. Also, rudd have fins more orange coloured than roach. Rudd prefer to live in still water and roach tackle is suitable, except that rudd in summer tend to feed right on the surface, and floating bread or a dry fly will provide good sport. Rudd are good fighters and their average size is better than that of roach. This being so, it is strange that rudd are of lesser interest to most anglers; perhaps it is due to the fact that there are fewer good rudd waters than there are roach waters. Rudd, small ones in particular, are a pest to anglers fishing in still waters for big carp, tench, etc., since they often nibble at the bait and cause constant false bites and bait replacements.

dace

Dace do not grow to much heavier than 1½ lb (680 g), and a half-pounder is a good one. But what the dace lacks in size it makes up for in numbers and fight, and an enjoyable day can be spent in filling a keepnet. With maggots or bread constantly going in, a shoal can be kept feeding for hours.

At the bottom or at mid-water the dace takes maggot, red worm, the water shrimp and other larvae. On the surface it has catholic tastes, particularly for tiny flies and relatively small insects no larger than a little grasshopper. In currents it can be taken on both dry and wet flies, particularly "spiders", lightly dressed on a No. 12 or 14 hook. It is also caught with baits that are not meant for it. It is worth mentioning that although this fish bears a certain resemblance to the chub, its bite is quicker, its speed is much greater and misses are much more frequent. So, no matter what tackle is being used, be very careful to strike immediately at the slightest bite or nibble.

barbel

In France some anglers do not fish for barbel because the fish is not very good to eat, there being so many bones—which is where the French and British attitudes to fish differ so much. The barbel is rated among the top three coarse fish in the United Kingdom—it is not found in Scotland or Ireland—simply because it is such a strong fighter.

With its steeply sloping forehead and flattened belly the streamlined barbel is built to withstand strong river currents, and this is where it is to be found. Barbel like clean, clear rivers with gravel beds and boulders and preferably an abundance of weed. They lie in deep or shallow fast runs, almost invisible—until one rolls to dig in the gravel for food, when a flash of golden flank may be spotted to locate the fish.

Most barbel fishing is done between mid June and early November, although in mild winter spells a few fish may be caught. Legering is one successful method, sometimes with a swimfeeder, but in good swims with more open water trotting, with a fairly heavily shotted float to keep the bait trundling the bottom and the float upright in the turbulent surface, is a very killing method.

Baits for barbel are legion: early season sport can be good using live or dead minnows, legered or trotted, and maggots, worms, bread, cheese, luncheon meat, sausage and hempseed have all done very well.

The tackle for barbel needs considerable attention since the fight of even a six pounder (3 kg) in strong water can last a long time on 4 or 5 lb (2 or 3 kg) line. The line can be between 4 and 10 lb (2 and 4·50 kg) test, depending on the size of the fish expected and the nature of the water—snags, current, etc. Barbel attain weights of nearly 20 lb (9 kg) and a fish of that size could fight almost on a par with a spring salmon.

The rod must be flexible down to the handle. As for tench, which in some respects the barbel's fighting tactics resemble, the hooks—be they a No. 14 with two maggots or a No. 8 with cheese on—must be strong, with forged bends. One good thing about the fighting barbel is that its underslung mouth is very tough and makes an excellent hold once the barb is home.

The traditional French method is called *à la pelote*, and is in fact the one-time old English method of clay-balling. The bait is hidden inside a hollow ball of soft clay the size of an egg, along with ground-bait such as maggots, worms, hempseed, etc. The barbel dig out the food and then take the baited hook.

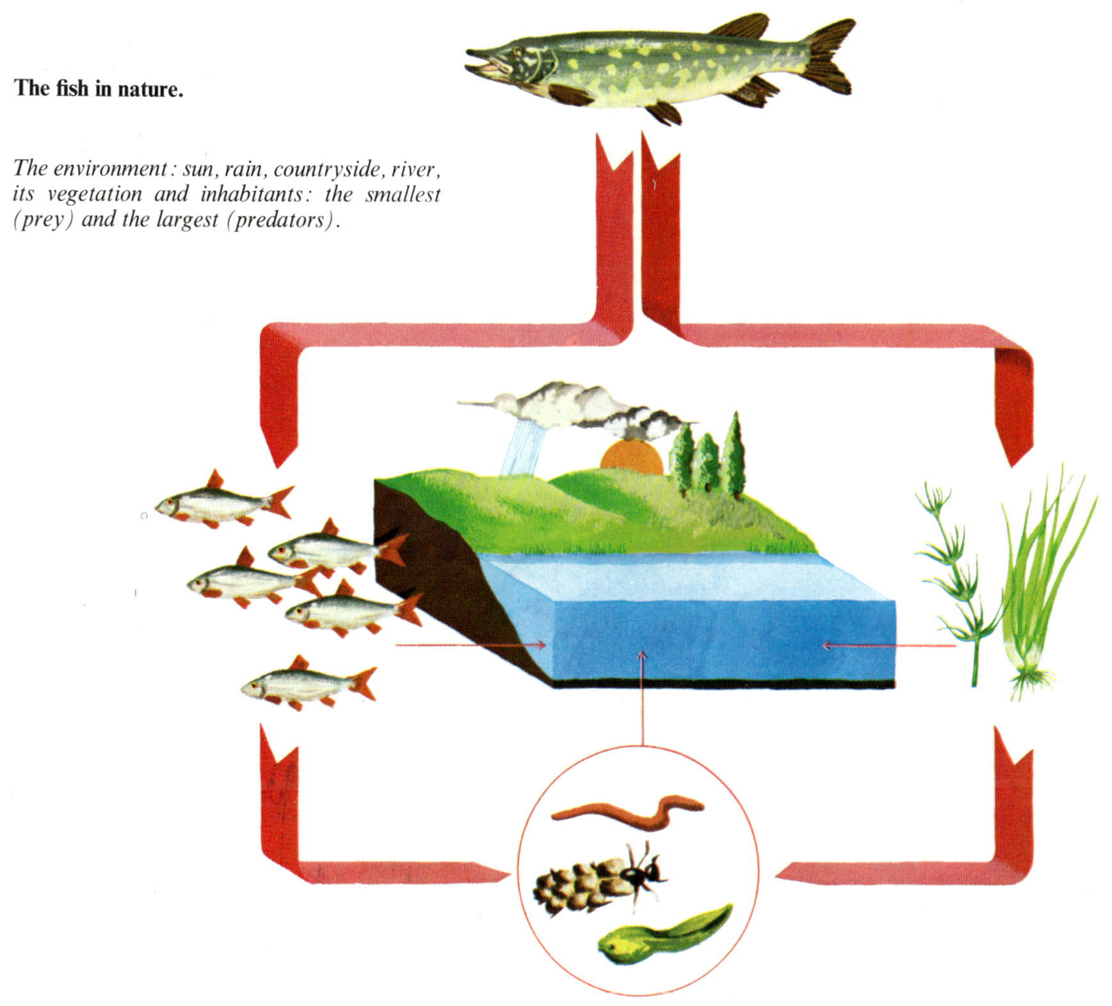

The fish in nature.

The environment: sun, rain, countryside, river, its vegetation and inhabitants: the smallest (prey) and the largest (predators).

nase

The undesirable hotu or nase (*Chondrostoma nasus*) is a migratory fish originating from the Rhine basin. It invaded many beautiful rivers in Western Europe to the chagrin of fishermen who quickly realised the damage it does. A gregarious fish which moves in large compact shoals, it likes streamy, oxygenated water and penetrates as far as the grayling zone, where it destroys everything in its path. However, it is not a predator. It is a deep-water fish with a very underslung mouth and an extremely hard, sharp, bony lower lip. It scours the stones and the rocks and when there are two or three of them together in a swim, it is a catastrophe, because the other fish disappear through lack of food.

However, this fish is elegant in appearance and movement. It has an ash-grey, sometimes greenish back, silvery flanks, white belly and 55 to 63 scales on the lateral line. Usually it is between 12 and 14 in. (30–35 cm) long but it can measure up to 20 in. (50 cm) and weigh nearly 4 lb (2 kg).

It is found in medium-strength currents in between 3 and 10 ft (1–3 m) of water. The presence of a shoal of nase can be detected by the numerous silvery flecks on the flanks and belly which are very noticeable when they are searching the riverbed for food. It is caught by the usual long-trotting method, a 1½ or 2 lb b.s. (680 or 900 g) line, No. 14–16 hook with baits such as maggots, bread pellets, silk weed or small red worms.

small fry

All small fish such as the bleak, gudgeon, minnows can be caught in the same swim. Therefore, if fishing for gudgeon it is possible to catch minnows or bleak and vice versa, though the gudgeon does lie deeper than the other fish.

Elementary methods of catching small fish may be used, with very simple, inexpensive tackle. Yet however small these fish are, they are no less wary and some consideration should be given to the choice and quality of the tackle. First, the rod: this should be very light and consist of several joints for easy carrying. At present there is a very wide range of tackle available, including telescopic hollow fibreglass rods and rods of more traditional type. The length of the rod must not exceed 12 ft (3·60 m) and it should have a flexible tip to improve the strike. Lightness and suppleness are the main qualities to look for in a rod used for catching small fish.

lines

If fishing in less than a foot (30 cm) of water the float can be dispensed with, although the author would recommend that it be used. The thickness of the line is important; the main line may be of relatively strong nylon of ¾–1 lb b.s. (340–450 g), but the leader must be much finer: about ½ lb b.s. (220 g). The main problem is the choice of the hook, particularly the size. For the minnow use a No. 20 or 22 hook, for the bleak and gudgeon use a No. 18, but if the water is very clear and the fish unusually wary choose a slightly smaller hook and make sure it is very sharp. In many cases the float will be superfluous, but its use does ensure that the bait is presented at the right depth. It is not necessary to be specific about the choice of float because there is an impressive range of floats on the market these days. The float simply needs to support the bait and stay invisible to the fish but easily seen by the fisherman, and its resistance to the fish when it bites must be negligible (e.g. Micro model). For small fish the number of shot and their positioning on the link or line are of little importance. The set-up which the author has used since his early days as a fisherman, and which has been very successful in catching bleak and gudgeon, is a traditional one like that previously described. Two hooks are used, one mounted on a dropper. With frequent checks, a gudgeon may be tempted on the lower hook, which is baited with a little piece of red worm, and a bleak can be taken on the upper one, which is baited with a small maggot or water shrimp. As this method is usually employed in fairly strong currents and therefore with fish which are more active and less wary than in still water, nylon of $\frac{3}{4}$ lb b.s. (340 g) mounted with No. 20 hooks can be used.

baits

The question of whether or not ground-baiting should be employed is difficult. The answer seems to be that if there are enough fish in the swim ground-baiting is unnecessary, but if the bait is untouched after a few casts and there appears to be no fish about then ground-baiting can be tried to tempt fish into the swim. For bleak use a small cloud of traditional flour-based ground-bait (all competition baits are suitable), but for the gudgeon heavier ground-bait is necessary. Many fishermen have had great success with ground-bait composed of balls of clay mixed with hempseed, a drop of spike oil and a few pieces of soaked bread. This bait slowly disintegrates on the bottom and the gudgeon, always very sensitive to scents, come from a great distance. One word of advice when fishing for gudgeon—do not overfeed them. The bait should be quite small and ground-baiting must be less frequent when bites become fewer.

common bleak

The bleak abounds in most quiet waters. It is a small fish well known to all summer fishermen. With the roach, the gudgeon, the chub and the minnow, the bleak is one of the most numerous fish caught in the summer season.

The scientific name of the bleak is *Alburnus alburnus*, but its common name varies according to the region. It measures on average between 4 and 6 in. (10–15 cm) and rarely weighs more than an ounce (30 g). It has a greyish back with greenish or bluish tints and very bright silvery flanks and belly. In the old days lace-makers

the cyprinids and other fish

bitterling
chub
barbel
bream
ruffe
bleak
eel
gudgeon
hotu or nase

made a good living from fashioning spangles out of the scales.

The bleak usually spawns in late spring between April and July when large shoals of several thousand bleak gather to mill around incessantly in the eddies and on the edges of the currents. The females deposit their eggs on weedbeds or submerged stones while the males fertilise them. This crowded spawning scene used to attract the poachers who slaughtered the bleak with fine-meshed nets.

able or small river bleak

(Leucaspius delineatus (Heckel))

This is a small fish (*Leucaspius delineatus* (Heckel)) about the size of a bleak and often confused with it. However, it is less common, being found only in about twenty areas. In order not to mistake it for the bleak, count the three straight and thirteen branching rays on its anal fin, which is much smaller than the bleak's. Another distinctive sign is the incomplete marking of its lateral line which is only visible for a third of the length of its body, starting from the head. Its body is tapered, its mouth oblique, with the lower jaw slightly more prominent than the upper. It has a green back, very light flanks with brilliant silvery flecks, and a white belly.

spirlin

This fish, known as *moderlieschen*, is not found in Britain.

The spirlin bleak is particularly fond of fast, oxygenated water. In different regions it is also known as smelt, sparling, Seine sparling, grey bleak, etc. Its scientific name is *Spirlinus bipunctatus* (Bloch), and it cannot be confused with the common bleak as their shape and coloration make them easily recognisable. The spirlin's body is broader and its back is slightly humped between the head and the dorsal fin. The pelvics are very close to the anal fin and the dorsal is slightly set back. The jaws are equal in size but the mouth is slightly tilted upwards. *Spirlinus* has between 44 and 52 scales on the lateral line. The back is dark grey or dark blue and sometimes greenish. The silvery flanks and belly have a double line with triangular black spots level with the lateral line near the head, and this curves down level with the pelvics and then returns to the lateral line as far as the tail. Another distinguishing mark of this fish is the orange base to the fins.

On average the spirlin (sparling) is between 2 and 3 in. (6–8 cm) long but some grow to nearly 5 in. (12 cm). It never reaches the maximum size of the bleak which has been known to measure 8 in. (20 cm) long, particularly the Paladru bleak, which takes its name from a lake in Isère.

The spirlin is found in most European rivers, but it is more particular than the common bleak about the purity of the water. It is a gregarious fish, living on shoals on the sandy bottom or gravel beds, particularly in swifter currents. It is not found in Britain.

Finally, this fish, typical of small fry, makes a good live-bait for zander and pike and it is said to be more robust than the common bleak. However, the zander is rarely concerned about the liveliness of the bait, its main preoccupation being with the taste and not with its physical state.

bitterling

The bitterling (*Rhodeus amarus*) is mostly found in the same areas in the north and east of France. This little fish weighs about a quarter of an ounce (5–7 g) and is never more than 3 in. (8 cm) long, and it possesses among other peculiarities a distinctive method of spawning. At the time of egg-laying, a long tube emerges from the uro-genital papilla (the oviduct leading to the ovary) through which it deposits its eggs in the cleft in the valves of a freshwater mussel. These eggs, fertilised by the male, develop on the gills of the mollusc, and after hatching the young remain for some time in this shelter before venturing out.

The flesh of this fish is far too bitter for it to be of value for eating. It was introduced into lakes in north-west England where it is thought some survive.

gudgeon

Nowadays a good bag of gudgeon is harder to come by than a good bag of trout, although less than twenty years ago this fish abounded in most rivers and streams with clear, limpid water. The author can still remember the first time he fished for gudgeon in the holes of the Senouire which had been almost dried up by long periods of sultry heat. They were resting on the large stones in a few feet of water and the slightest ground-baiting brought them on the feed and they rarely refused such a tasty morsel as a water shrimp.

Gobio gobio, the gudgeon, rarely measures more than 7 in. (18 cm) and although it looks like a little barbel, it possesses distinctive characteristics. Its head is large, almost massive, with a rounded nose and a barbel on each side of the prominent upper lips. Its coloration may vary according to its environment, but it often has a dark-brown back with lighter, almost golden flanks and a grey-white belly. The back and the flanks have black spots and a few darker, vertical bars. The shape of its underslung mouth shows that, unlike the bleak, it is a scavenger. It lives on the bottom, where it searches out all sorts of grubs and small prey.

miller's thumb or bull-head

This fish is seldom caught on rod and line, so it will not be discussed in detail. It is a member of the Cottidae family of the genus *Cottus*. Its large head is huge in proportion to the rest of its body and gives it the impression of a tadpole from above. Among its characteristics are the spines protruding from each side and at the front of the gill-cover and its spiny dorsal fins with the second higher than the first. Its back is dark grey or brown with regular brown spots and the flanks and belly are lighter. The bull-head likes darkness and lives under stones and in dark corners of trout streams. Lively and strong, the bull-head is also one of the trout's favourite foods. However, its capture for live-bait poses problems although some fishermen defy a ban and leave tiny lines out at night on the bottom, baited with earthworms.

spined loach

Another "tiddler" (a relative of the cyprinids) which is difficult to catch. The spined loach (*Cobitis taenia*) lives in small streams and rivers with pebbly beds where it eats aquatic worms and insects. It sports six barbels on the upper lip, and above each eye there is a retractable spur which comes out of a cavity. Its general coloration is yellowish, the back is darker, the belly is bright yellow and the flanks have two bars of black spots. It is rarely longer than 4 in. (10 cm). Having observed the loach in its environment some fishermen have noticed that it uses its upper-lip barbels as bait to attract the young fry which it easily captures. The saying "as fat as a loach" suggests that this little fish has an appetite.

minnow

The smallest of the freshwater fish may be caught for amusement or as live-bait. The minnow is the favourite fish of children and beginners who are happy to stay at a baited swim where they soon have shoals of minnows.

Linnaeus provided the scientific name of the minnow, *Phoxinus phoxinus*, but in popular language it has many names. This cyprinid cannot be confused with the bleak (different shape and coloration), or with the chub. Its back is a grey-olive colour, its flanks lighter with silvery tints, its belly is metallic grey and the back flanks are covered with darker spots and patches.

The spawning livery of the minnow is distinctive as the male is dressed in iridescent colours of bluish tints with light spots on the flanks and gill-cover and bright red on the fins.

Food for the trout and many other predators, the minnow loves the swift currents of small streams, but it is also found in more sluggish rivers if the purity of the water suits it.

carp family
physical characteristics

carp

The carp (*Cyprinus carpio*) is a deep fish, only four times as long as it is deep. It has prominent yellow, leathery, prehensile lips and it carries two pairs of barbels on the upper jaw. The common carp has fine, broad, golden scales, sometimes deeply set with between 35 and 40 scales on the lateral line. Its most usual colouring is a brown or greenish back, coppery-tinted flanks, a light yellowish belly with the lower fins sometimes shading to red. Intensive breeding down the centuries has modified the carp, and the so-called king carp is much deeper than the common carp. This fish can thrive in low-oxygen water and is particularly useful for rearing. Thus in the Far East, the East and the West it has become domesticated and is appreciated for its relatively rapid growth and its nutritional value.

There are five varieties of carp including the common carp with its body entirely covered with scales; the mirror carp with a few large, golden scales; the leather carp, as its name indicates, entirely devoid of scales; the Chinese or grass carp, covered in scales but longer than the common carp, and looking rather like a chub; and the crucian carp, which has no barbules and bears the scientific name *Carassius carassius*. Crucian carp, rarely exceeding 4 lb (1·80 kg), may be taken on roach-type tackle and favour small still waters. Recently introduced into Western Europe, the Chinese carp is essentially herbivorous, and several attempts have been made at establishing it in France.

chub

Leuciscus cephalus or *squalius*, the chub has more than fifty names in various dialects, the best known being: loggerhead, chevin and chavender.

Very common in most European rivers, the chub also live in the calm water of lakes and ponds. This cyprinid invader is anathema to game fishermen, for it often invades trout waters and chases the salmonids away. However, it is important to recognise that in these waters the chub can be a worthy adversary for the sporting fishermen.

It has a thick-set, powerful-looking body and a wide, rounded mouth. Its broad, silvery scales are fringed with a darker colour and there are between 44 and 46 on the lateral line. The back is dark grey and it has bronze flanks and a white belly. The pectoral fins are yellowy orange, the lower fins redder and the caudal and dorsal fins are dark grey, almost black. The chub can reach exciting weights for the fisherman and a record chub of more than 16 lb (7·50 kg) was caught in the Rhône. The average size, however, is between 1 and 2 lb (450–900 g).

tench

From the cyprinid family, the tench (*Tinca tinca*) is one of the most delightful of the freshwater fish. Its taste depends on the nature of the water in which it lives. Tench from the slower rivers are always better than the tench from ponds and static waters as the latter have a tendency to keep to the mud and feed on plant material, thus giving their flesh a distinctive taste. Pond tench, when caught, are often kept alive in baskets and then left for a few days in clear water to "clear" their systems of the muddy flavour.

In favour of the tench it must be added that, apart from its taste, it has surprising fighting qualities and stamina. Unlike its neighbour the bream, it often surprises the fisherman by its repertoire of tricks, finishing up by suddenly parting company with him.

Like the carp, the tench is a robust fish and its shape reveals its strength. Its thick-set body, broad fins, the wide base of its caudal fin and its rounded form prevent it from being a streamlined fish. However, if it is not an elegant mover it lacks nothing in strength and effectiveness.

The tench has between 95 and 110 scales on the lateral line and it has a particularly slimy covering of mucus. Its prehensile mouth is upturned and has a small barbel on each side.

It has a dark-green back with lighter flanks turning to yellow, and a bright-yellow belly tinged with gold. The average tench in France measures between 8 and 12 in. (20–30 cm) long and weighs from 8 oz (250 g) to just over 1 lb (500 g), though specimens have been taken up to 16 in. (40 cm) long and weighing over 4 lb (2 kg). In Britain 4 lb (1·8 kg) tench are not uncommon and the average is about 2 lb (900 g). This fish lives on the bottom and is almost inactive during the winter, although with the return of the finer weather it recovers its appetite.

roach

The roach (*Rutilus rutilus*) has a streamlined body which is slightly compressed and flat. Its mouth slants slightly and the scales are quite large, with between 42 and 45 on the lateral line. Its colour may vary according to the environment but it usually has a greeny grey-blue back with gold tints; the belly is invariably a silvery white; the eyes are red ringed with gold; the dorsal and caudal fins are reddish and the lower fins are red or orange-red. The roach may measure 12 in. (30 cm) or more but generally averages between 6 and 9 in. (15–22 cm). A 2 lb (900 g) roach is a fine fish.

Not a very particular fish it gets used to most waters and is even found in some badly polluted rivers. It has a fancy for gently running water with a sandy bottom as well as calmer waters littered with weedbeds. Spawning takes place in April, May or June in shallow water. Its fecundity (a female may lay 100,000 eggs) explains its presence and abundance throughout Western Europe.

The roach may hybridise with the rudd, which is almost its double, or with the bleak or the bream.

bream

The bream (*Abramis brama*) is one of the commonest fresh-water cyprinids. The body is deep-bellied, hump-backed and thin in section and the depth of the body is a third of the length. Its mouth is protractile and it possesses between 50 and 55 scales on the lateral line. Its anal fin is particularly long, and on the caudal fin of some bream there is an elongation of the lower lobe. Its colouring consists of a green or brown back with silvery-grey flanks. The underside is buff with pink tints and the fins are more or less dark grey. The bream usually measures between 10 and 14 in. (25–35 cm) long and weighs between 7 oz and 1 lb (200–500 g). Larger bream are caught, however, and fish of over 10 lb (4·5 kg) have also been taken. A 6 lb (3 kg) fish is a good one.

There is a smaller species of bream, the silver bream, measuring between 4 and 8 in. (10–20 cm). It differs from the common bream in that it is longer in relation to its depth, its eyes are larger and its anal fin is smaller. Its scientific name is *Blicca bjoerkna*.

The common bream spawns from the age of three, and this prolific fish can lay up to 150,000 eggs, which explains its invasion of certain lakes where it is considered vermin. The bream may hybridise with the roach, the rudd, and also with its close relative, the silver bream.

rudd

The rudd (*Scardinius erythrophthalmus*) is also called red-eye, blue roach, etc.

This cyprinid has between 40 and 45 scales on the lateral line, its body is compressed laterally and its back humped. The mouth is strongly oblique with the lower jaw projecting upwards. The dorsal fin is set well behind the pelvics, thus making it easily distinguishable from the roach.

Its eye is bright red, and the fins range from orange on the dorsal to red on the others. The greenish back is darker at the top, paling towards the lateral line, while the belly is white. Like the chub, the rudd is almost omnivorous and it is caught on most baits used for the other cyprinids. It is fond of rising to the surface for food, and it can be taken on natural insects and sometimes on the fly.

The rudd spawns between May and July, according to the temperature of the water. The rudd may hybridise with the roach, the bleak and the bream.

dace

The dace (*Leuciscus leuciscus*) is distinguished from the chub by its different shape. It is a slimmer fish, its head is smaller and it has an underslung mouth and a rounded lip. The fins are also different, particularly the anal fin with its concave edge. Its coloration is almost identical to the chub, although its back is slightly lighter and the lower fins not so red. Finally this energetic fish, which hybridises with the bleak, is smaller than the chub.

The dace is more fussy about the quality of the water than the chub. It likes cool, swifter currents. It is just as wary as the chub, perhaps more so, therefore in order to fish for it successfully the same rules of silence and keeping out of sight must be observed.

barbel

The barbel is one of the largest freshwater fish and attains 20 lb (9 kg).

Anyone hearing the scientific name of the barbel (*Barbus barbus*) might think that this fish ought to have a beard. However, the name refers to four small barbels, two on each side, placed near the mouth right on the upper lip. The nose is pointed and the mouth is distinctly underslung, with thick, rounded, leathery lips. Its body is almost cylindrical, ending in a very forked caudal fin. Its pectorals are strangely spade-shaped and there are between 56 and 62 scales on the lateral line.

The barbel has a green-brown back with golden flanks, a cream or buff belly, and reddish fins which turn bright red during spawning. In the rivers the barbel frequents some of the haunts of the bream or other cyprinids, but particularly favours the slower regions of the grayling zone, otherwise known as the barbel zone.

Certain ichthyologists have written that the barbel migrates before spawning. These statements have been checked in rivers where marked barbel had moved several hundred miles a month. However, in certain sectors of mountain rivers the barbel seem to be more localised and migration is confined to a journey of a few miles. Spawning generally takes place in May and June.

*Anglers in a stout punt, moored by anchors in bows and st
across the current, trot their floats down the clear waters o
the Hampshire Avon for roach, chub and dace*

other fish

eel

the great migrator

Far back in history the most improbable legends circulated about the eel. The *Halieutica* of Oppian of Cilicia maintains that the eel is the result of the unnatural mating of the moray and the snake, while Aristotle writes that the eel is produced spontaneously from warm mud. The eel was supposed to have many strange habits owing to its peculiar birth, and most people were uncertain whether it was more fish or snake. Great naturalists such as Linnaeus and Lacépède mistook the eel for a viviparous fish. The veil of mystery was lifted much later when, in this century, the Danish scholar Schmidt discovered thc ccl's spawning grounds in the Sargasso Sea.

A great migrator, the eel journeys to lay its eggs at sea. Unlike the salmon, which returns to spawn in the river after a period of growth at sea, the eel grows in the rivers and lakes and then returns to the Atlantic depths where it was born. The eggs hatch into tens of millions of transparent larvae called leptocephali. These larvae are carried far by the Gulf Stream to the coasts of Europe where they arrive in about their third year. Then metamorphosis takes place and the larvae become tiny eels or elvers, only a few inches long.

At this second stage of their life, the eels ascend the waterways again guided by the currents and the salinity of the estuaries or river mouths. For the run the elvers enter the river in dense strings and during the journey they grow and settle in rivers and streams. Some, taking the tiny tributaries, reach even the most isolated ponds. After a few years' growth in fresh water, the eel undergoes a new metamorphosis. Now it has reached sexual maturity and, with the spawning urge operating, it sets off on its long journey to the Sargasso Sea. This transformation sees a change in the livery; the yellow eel turns silvery, its belly becomes very bright, almost white with silvery flecks, while the back darkens to black. Numerous taggings, notably in the Baltic, have enabled naturalists to establish that during migration the eel, although it is slower than the salmon, nevertheless manages to cover between 15 and 30 miles (25 and 50 km) a day, or rather night, since the eel is essentially nocturnal. It arrives at its spawning ground, and after the completion of spawning it disappears. Professor Bertin, an eminent specialist, writes: "When they reach the Atlantic they disappear. One may assume that their organic deterioration does not enable them to survive their first spawning."

There are two types of eel in Europe. One has a broad head and is sometimes called *platbec* (flat nose), while the other has a pointed nose and thus is named *longbec* (long nose). The first is said to be more predatory, but there is no scientific evidence to corroborate this.

eel fishing

Although the eel does not lend itself to eminently sporting methods, the best known and most effective will be mentioned. A nocturnal fish, the eel is often caught at night in any type of water where night fishing is either legal or tolerated. Otherwise use a *cordeau*, a practice requiring a special licence in France. This is a rudimentary method. Several large, round-bend,

A good specimen of flat-nose eel. ▶

The Loiret, a calm river full of fish, contains some huge eels. ▼

standard eyed-type hooks or special "eel hooks", are mounted on droppers on thick nylon of 19–35 lb b.s. (8·60–15·80 kg) which are tied to the main line, which is merely strong flax, hemp, or even thick braided-nylon line. A heavy weight is attached to the end of the main line, and each hook is baited with a large earthworm, piece of fish or even a live fish. The line is stretched out either at the edge of a pool, in deep water, or simply on a sandy or shingle bank in a few inches of water. The eel, with its highly developed sense of smell, quickly finds the baited hook.

Legering dead-bait is a more normal method, which requires a fairly heavy, stiff spinning-rod, a fixed-spool reel, a 9–12 lb b.s. (4–5·40 kg) nylon line, a 9 lb b.s. (4 kg) leader, a ½–1 oz (15–25 g) running lead, which can be either a round bullet or a pear lead. An eyed or spade-end hook can be attached to the line, and should be baited with a bunch of earthworms, a live or dead fish, or a piece of fish. Bits of bleak are particularly effective after a storm, in very muddy water, or in between times while fishing for pike with live-bait. Early in the morning, at midday or at dusk the eels often become active. The take is signalled by a quiver of the rod-top, then by repeated tugs. One must strike and retrieve as quickly as possible, otherwise the eel will reach its lair in a cleft in the rocks or under a stump, where it becomes extremely difficult to dislodge.

Babbing is a special method in which no hook is used; large lob-worms are threaded with a big needle on to darning thread, cotton, or some other worsted material, provided it is not monofilament. They are then rolled into a big ball which is tied to a nylon line and this is tied directly to the tip of a very stiff rod or an ordinary piece of wood. The eel comes upon the bait and begins to nibble the worms, little suspecting the presence of the thread. It is not until it partially swallows one that it realises that something is wrong, it begins to panic and tries to break free. Too late—the cotton thread has caught round its teeth. The eel struggles in an attempt to free itself. This is the moment when the fisherman must show his skill because the take is violent. The idea is to raise the rod and throw the eel on to the bank. It usually unhooks itself before landing, sometimes falling back into the water. A favourite trick is to place an upturned umbrella nearby to catch the eel, before it manages to get back to the water.

Having dealt briefly with the methods of fishing for eels, some observations about it and its role as a predator *par excellence*, might be of interest. The eel plays a useful part in the types of water which provide sufficient food for most fish and encourage an abundance of fry some of which, perhaps injured by zander or pike, will be taken by eels, which will eat them even when they are in a state of advanced decomposition. On the other hand the presence of the eel in salmon waters is more controversial. It qualifies as vermin in trout streams. Here the natural conditions are poorer, the number of fish generally fewer, and food scarcer. The eel harries the small trout, eats its fry and certainly its eggs, and also large numbers of minnows which constitute the trout's basic diet in many waters. In private waters, the owners have no hesitation in laying thick lines armed with big eel hooks, to destroy the eels and thus protect the trout. A more efficient method is electric fishing, which is used under the supervision of bailiffs.

burbot

Although this fish is not particularly interesting to the sporting fisherman, it is worth mentioning the methods of catching it. In shallow meres or lakes, the burbot feeds mainly at night, but it can be caught during the day, in very muddy water, after a storm.

Like the eel, the burbot takes all types of live-bait, dead fish on the bottom, pieces of fish, earthworm, etc. The best results are obtained at night with bottom-fishing.

The author discovered the burbot when, as a young man, he was collecting worms in a back water of the Allier at a place called Bac de Fontannes. Every two or three stones he turned over revealed a dark fish which slipped away to another hiding place; occasionally, blinded by the light, the burbot froze in front of him, but when the author attempted to grasp it, it slipped through his fingers, for its skin is extremely slimy. The presence of a burbot may be a sign of abundant food in a river but the fishermen do not like it, because this nocturnal ravager is a super-predator which attacks eggs and fry. So one can say that bottom-fishing for burbot at night is beneficial to the other species.

Burbot are rare in England and found only in a few rivers in the east Midlands.

The burbot, the only fresh-water fish of the cod family.

miscellaneous

The catfish takes everything. One was caught by the author on a potato while fishing for carp, others while live-baiting for perch and worming for chub. So there is no point in specifying any particular method for catching catfish. If there is one in a swim it will soon make its presence felt. It is voracious and greedy, and it will take a bait right down. For the fisherman it takes its place among other vermin like the rainbow perch, the ruffe and many others.

The proliferation of the catfish has ruined many attempts at restocking rivers and ponds. It can stand up to all sorts of ill-treatment, including being left out of water for several hours. Its destruction and eradication are difficult, well-nigh impossible, in waters which it has invaded. A massive overpopulation of predators is the only way to re-establish a relative balance.

The rainbow perch and the ruffe are also vermin which take all usual baits (see characteristics of these two fish).

The huchen and *Siluris glanis* (the scavenging sheat-fish) are interesting fish but confined to Central Europe. The huchen (*Hucho hucho*), called the Danube salmon, lives mainly in this river basin (attempts to acclimatise it in Morocco and the Savoyard river Des Usses have been partially successful).

A localised salmonid, the huchen is like the salmon. It can measure up to 4 ft and weigh 50 lb. This predator loves nase and spawns in spring (April). It is caught at the end of autumn and in winter on spinning lures and dead bait.

Siluris glanis could be the Loch Ness monster of certain Swiss or Czechoslovak lakes, where it can weigh up to 400 lb (180 kg). Half conger, half catfish, it is bottom-fished with enormous meat-baited hooks certainly not suitable for catching tiddlers. The catch of a 183 lb (83 kg) monster in Lake Morat (Switzerland) has been recorded, also one of over 600 lb (270 kg) from the river Dnieper.

The coregonids (gwyniads), excellent lake salmonids, are caught from a boat by unsporting methods. They are found in Central and Eastern Europe and in Britain.

Feet in the water, catching fish for the pan. ▶

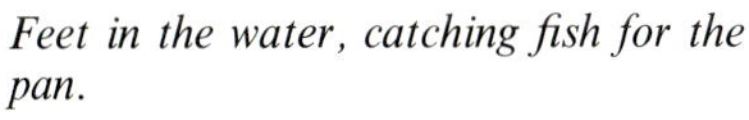

◀ *Looking for bait.*

Coarse fishing in autumn.
▼

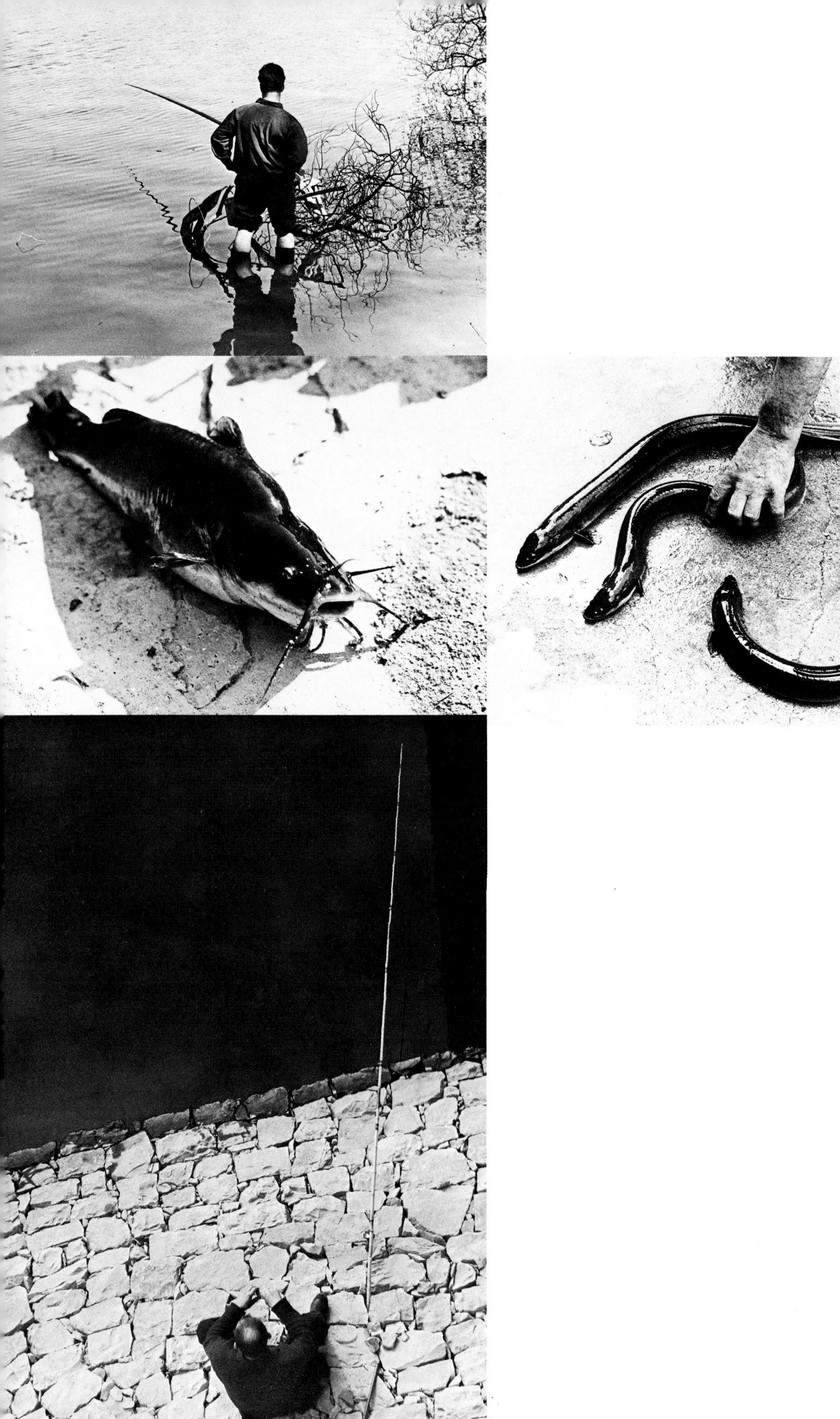

other fish

physical characteristics

eel

The eel (*Anguilla anguilla*) belongs to the Apodan order (most snake-like fish, devoid of pelvics). The Anguillidae have one genus: *Anguilla*.

Its long, almost cylindrical body is not truly snake-like, for the extremity is compressed sideways.

The eel's head is marked by particularly narrow, branchial gill-slits and by the insertion of the pectoral fins. It has a single median fin made up of 500 rays which extends for a third of the length as far as the vent, passing round the end of the tail and continuing underneath. In other words, it is a dorsal, caudal and anal fin, all in one.

The head is worthy of detailed mention. First, it has a very long mouth which stretches almost to the eye, and rear-set nostrils which are simple cavities. The front nostrils are small tubes situated at the end of the nose and there are several mucus pores at different points on the head. Notice also the prominent lower lip. The eel's mouth is armed with numerous teeth which enables experts to distinguish several species of eel in the *Anguilla* genus. Scales are tiny and embedded in the skin.

burbot

The burbot (*Lota lota*) is the only freshwater representative of the Gadidae family, of which other members are the cod and the pout-whiting. The Gadidae can be recognised by the single barbel under the jaw.

The burbot has a curious shape. Its body is not snake-like, yet its long dorsal and anal fins sometimes make it look like an eel, at other times like the wels. It has two dorsal fins; the first is situated a third of the way along its body and is relatively small, with a few rays. Some inches behind there is a second, very long dorsal fin which reaches to the base of the caudal. The latter is very unusual, triangular or oval and rounded at the end; the long anal fin is symmetrical with the bigger dorsal. The pelvics are set slightly forward and below the pectorals. The huge mouth is armed with sharp teeth and it has prominent nostrils set in the head in front of the eyes.

Its colour varies according to the environment. However, the top of the body is always marbled with dark brown or green and lighter spots and the belly is uniformly yellow.

This extremely prolific fish is believed to lay up to a million eggs.

catfish

Closely related to *Siluris glanis*, the catfish (*Ameiurus nebulosus*) was introduced into Europe at the beginning of the century. The catfish has above all a massive, flat head, out of all proportion to the rest of its body, and sporting several barbels, giving it a faint resemblance to a cat. There are eight barbels, four long ones on the upper lip and four smaller ones on the lower. It has a huge mouth and tiny eyes. Its first dorsal fin is armed with a sharp, venomous spine, as are the pectorals.

Its usual colour consists of a black or very dark-green back with lighter flanks below the lateral line and a dirty-white or very yellow belly. The average catfish is no more than 12 in. (30 cm) long but in some lakes a few specimens up to 27 in. (70 cm) long have been found weighing up to 4 lb. (2 kg)

Spawning is in May or June according to the temperature, and sometimes as late as July. The catfish spawns in weedy, shallow water and the prolific female lays between 4,000 and 6,000 eggs, which she deposits in a nest. After the eggs are hatched, the young remain stuck together in a kind of very dark ball which provides a fine titbit for other predators.

rainbow or sun-perch

The rainbow or sun-perch (*Lepomis gibbosus*) belongs to the Centrarchidae family, whose principal representative in Europe is the black bass. It is also called pumpkin seed.

In spite of its shape and iridescent colours which are worthy of the finest tropical species, the rainbow perch is regarded by fishermen as vermin. Its delightful coloration is very difficult to describe. The dorsal fin is divided into two parts; the first has short, spiny rays and the second has soft rays. The fish has a deep and narrow body, a small mouth and 40–50 scales on the lateral line.

The introduction of this fish was catastrophic for fish-rearing in ponds. Shortly after its importation at the beginning of the century, it was noticed that this perch, although not as big as the common variety, was far more voracious. This exogenous predator consumes vast quantities of the eggs and fry of other fish in the waters where it has proliferated. So stocks of other fish are considerably depleted. Rainbow perch are caught mainly while fishing for, say, the roach, with bloodworm, maggots, red worm, etc.

pope or ruffe

Gymnocephalus cernua is not the offspring of the perch and gudgeon, although it is called gudgeon-perch by many fishermen. It does, however, have some features of both; it moves like a perch and has the colour of a gudgeon. The gill-cover is armed with short spines, the dorsal fin has about 15 spiny rays followed by as many soft rays.

The ruffe or pope is a small, voracious fish of no great interest to the angler, for it is never longer than 6 in. (15 cm). It lives on bloodworms, the fry of other fish and larvae.

It spawns in April and May and the female may lay up to 200,000 eggs, which stick to stones after fertilisation. It has a varied habitat, but it is generally found in backwaters and inlets or wherever the current is slack or non-existent.

There is no special way of catching ruffe, which sometimes arrive inopportunely in a swim; and the peaceful roach fisherman is surprised when he lands one. It is acceptable enough, but if a shoal of ruffe arrives, the fisherman may as well pack up fishing for roach as the ruffe will monopolise the swim. It is always hungry, so the fisherman can land one after another, if he wants to.

Its favourite baits are earthworms, bloodworms and maggots.

tackle

Modern fishing tackle is superb; rods, reels, lines, lures, floats, landing gear, etc. are available to cover every task and fulfil just about every whim and fancy of the world's anglers.

Hollow fibreglass is used for most rods today. It is very light, strong and flexible; it makes rods nearly half the weight of the older cane, greenheart and whole tonkin cane and bamboo combinations. It makes long, light and quick-actioned rods so beloved of Continental anglers with their reel-less techniques; it makes fine fly rods for salmon and trout; accurate spinning and baitcasting rods and slender light Avon rods and carp rods for the British school.

Glass takes much more punishment than wooden rods; it does not become warped after fighting many big fish, nor does it take much harm from being left wet. And with modern designs involving mathematically calculated tapers and wall thicknesses glass closely approaches fine split-cane rods for that almost indefinable "feel" demanded by many fly-fishers.

Hollow glass has also made the old heavy and rigid metal ferrules obsolete. Now glass rod sections are joined by spigots, a tapered projection on the lower joint(s) fitting smoothly into the upper joint(s), thus avoiding weight and giving almost unbroken curves.

Yet good split-cane rods, made from, normally, six triangular sections of selected bamboo cane glued together, are still in great demand. And with some rods impregnated with resins so that the whole job is bonded as a whole and does not need varnishing since it becomes impervious to water, it is likely cane will remain for as long as bamboo grows and anglers cast flies.

Modern aluminium alloys and other metals make light, strong, smooth-working reels: fixed-spool reels for long casting and spinning, baitcasting multipliers for spinning for big salmon and pike, narrow-spooled centrepin reels for the English style of trotting float tackle downstream. There are lightweight fly reels with multiplying actions to retrieve loose line quickly when playing a lively fish, others that recover the line at the depressing of a lever that activates a rewind spring.

Nylon and Terylene for lines have many advantages over the old silk and linen lines that were thicker for their breaking strain and, if you wanted them to last, needed drying. And if you wanted them to float they needed greasing.

Nylon as an extruded single filament is used for most coarse fishing and spinning, also for fly-fishing leaders. It is fine for its test, tough, blends with the background in water and lasts a long time. It deteriorates in sunlight and to a minor extent from wet oxidation, but it is so cheap that no angler need use a line long enough to risk those actions. Nylon can also be made in a continuous tapered length for fly leaders, without knots which had to be tied in the old silkworm gut leaders to get a taper from line to fly.

Braided lines of nylon and Terylene are used for heavy pike and salmon spinning, but in truth monofilament nylon does everything asked of it in test up to 20 lb (9 kg), which is usually more than adequate for freshwater use.

Braided nylon forms the core of modern floating fly lines, the core covered with plastic enclosing air bubbles for flotation. Terylene, because it is heavier than water, forms the core of the plastic-covered sinking fly line.

Man's inventive mind uses many materials and designs for lures: floating plastic self-coloured plugs, sinking plugs, soft plastic plugs and devon minnows. And in the dressing of flies he now uses plastic filaments, fluorescent materials, animal hairs and furs, dyed in many colours, to replace the exotic plumage of birds once used but now protected by conservation measures. And the hair flies catch even more trout and salmon, etc.

Because modern tackle is technically so good, reels especially, they need careful maintenance. A little oil in the right place is worth lots in the wrong place. Sand and dust must be cleaned from the works and the whole reel sprayed with a volatile oil that protects it from corrosion.

On rods, the rings need constant inspection for grooves worn by the line, since they can wear an expensive fly line or cut nylon. Rings with hard chrome coating are best. Tungsten carbide is even harder, but it is brittle and can be cracked by a sharp blow.

The only thing that is still lacking is that which is so symbolic of angling: the hook. It is often said that modern mass-produced hooks are not so good as those made by backyard craftsmen a century ago. And having compared some, one can see the truth of that statement, so far as freshwater and fly hooks are concerned, at least.

rods

Spinning rods (from left to right)

Luxor Wading (cane)

Telebolic BB1 (cane)

Shakespeare (glass)

Seyler (glass)

Mitchell special (glass)

Mitchell expert (glass)

Luxor 400 (cane)

Seyler (glass)

Telebolic 7 (cane)

Japanese Telescopic (on the show-case).

Fly rods. (from left to right)

Seyler combination 7–8½ ft (2–2·50 m) (glass)

Parabolic Normal 8½ ft (2·50 m) (cane)

Parabolic P.P.P. Bretonvilliers 7½ ft (2·20 m) (cane)

Impregnated Sharpes' Featherweight 8 ft (2·40 m) (cane)

Mitchell Expert 8½ ft (2·50 m) (glass)

Ritz 7 ft (2·10 m) (glass)

Ritz (8 ft (2·40 m) (glass)

reels

ALCEDO MICRON
Reel for ultra light-weight casting, and one of the smallest fixed-spool reels, made in Italy. Weight: 6·7 oz. (190 g). Recovers 23·6 in. (60 cm) per revolution crank. 2 spools, capacities 787 ft (240 m) of 14/100 mm and 328 ft (100 m) of 14/100 mm.

CRACK 100
French reel for light-weight casting. Weight: 9·18 oz. (260 g). Recovers 27·5 in. (70 cm) per revolution crank. 2 spools, capacities 492 ft (150 m) of 28/100 mm and 246 ft (75 m) of 22/100 mm.

BRETTON 104 S "Judoka"
French reel for ultra light-weight casting. Weight: 10·5 oz. (300 g). Recovers 27·5 in. (70 cm) per revolution crank. 1 spool, capacity 492 ft (150 m) of 20/100 mm and, with plastic packing, 246 ft (75 m) of 18/100 mm.

MITCHELL 410
Reel for medium-weight casting, made in France. Weight: 10·5 oz. (300 g). Recovers 29·5 in. (75 cm) per revolution crank. 2 spools, capacities 492 ft (150 m) 24/100 mm and 492 ft (150 m) 30/100 mm.

MITCHELL 408
Reel for ultra light-weight casting. Weight: 7 oz. (200 g). Recovers 27·5 in. (70 cm) per revolution crank. 2 spools, capacities 492 ft (150 m) of 24/100 mm and 246 ft (75 m) of 20/100 mm.

LUXOR No. 1
French reel for light-weight casting. Weight: 8·1 oz. (230 g). Recovers 27·5 in. (70 cm) per revolution crank. 2 spools, capacities 492 ft (150 m) of 28/100 mm and 328 ft (100 m) of 18/100 mm.

ABU CARDINAL 77
Reel for medium heavy-weight casting, Swedish make. Weight: 13·94 oz. (395 g). Recovers 22·8 in. (58 cm) per revolution crank. 1 spool, capacity 656 ft (200 m) of 40/100 mm.

ABEILLE AUTOMATIQUE
Fly reel for trout fishing, with automatic winder with spring. French make. Weight: 8·4 oz. (240 g). Can hold all lines for trout fishing, but little backing.

ABU DELTA
Fly reel for trout fishing, sea trout, small salmon. Weight: 8·3 oz. (235 g). Conventional single-action reel—lateral check system with graduated brake. Holds all fly lines up to No. 8 plus more than 147·6 ft (45 m) of 30 lb Dacron.

PRIDEX
Single-action salmon fly reel, made in England. Weight: 12·4 oz. (350 g) approx. Can hold all salmon lines plus adequate backing.

INTREPID GEARFLY REGULAR
Multiplying fly reel for trout fishing, with 2·5:1 gear ratio. English make. Weight: 5·12 oz. (145 g). Can hold trout lines and up to 60 yards 20 lb Dacron backing.

the future of angling in Europe

the dangers

It is no more possible to dissociate the art of fishing from the fish than it is to dissociate the fish from its surroundings: water and its domain; rivers, lakes and ponds.

By championing his sport, the angler can protect these surroundings against the many incursions to which they fall victim. These incursions, whether transient or continuous, form the real threat to the sport of angling.

The transient incursions are some of the less serious of the temporary harms. Firstly, there are the intermittent or accidental pollutions, often in the form of very localised contamination due to the discharging of toxic products. Flora, fauna and micro-fauna disappear for several hundred yards or several miles, often along the length of an entire river (e.g. poisoning of the Rhine). In other words, apart from the animal life, the river-bed is virtually sterilised by toxic matter.

All the same, the waterway dies with some hopes of regeneration; indeed, Mother Nature manages to regain her rights. Pure water comes back, driving out the pollution and bringing back all the living organisms. Vegetation gradually shoots up again and helps to oxygenate the water. Phytoplankton, zooplankton and all the micro-organisms reappear, as do the fish which feed off them, and as do the carnivores.

This regeneration continues until the initial habitat is re-established, and with it relative biological equilibrium. Thus this contamination, classified as a temporary harm, will merely have been a bad interval for the stricken area, followed by a long period of revival.

Some non-biodegradable heavy chemicals are deposited on the river-bed and hold up the process of natural purification. Then, only a heavy growth will stamp out this resistant magma.

Not all of the accidental incursions are caused by man. Natural disasters remain uncontrollable phenomena which must be added to this chapter.

Ice can harm fauna, especially in confined waters. (In 1956, there were forty consecutive days of ice, with local records showing temperatures of -20 °F (-30 °C).)

Drought reduces the space which is essential for fish and brings about the destruction of young fish.

Floods unsettle the river-beds, destroying the spawning grounds and carrying off the spawn, even more so in deforested regions. Storms displace enormous quantities of arable land, which choke up the beds of the least disturbed stretches of river.

Poaching is another incursion which can be classed as transient if it is carried out by amateurs. Small, very localised poaching includes fishing by hand, with a sweep-net or gill-net in streams, fishing for trout by night with a line or a selvagee and fishing in the spawning grounds during the closed season.

We will continue this heading of dangers by talking about inadequate, or rather, unbalanced re-stocking, which is more dangerous in inland waters than in rivers. No young fish or adult fish should be poured into a river without a preliminary assessment of the existing stock, in order to avoid overpopulation with certain species, as this can generate much harm.

Too many white fish, and there will be epidemics to worry about; too many predators, and the stock of foraging fish will dangerously diminish, and cannibalism will increase amongst the carnivores.

The dwarfing of the perch and the disappearance of the pike are, lamentably, often due to human intervention, which has proved catastrophic in the introduction of new species.

The catfish and the rainbow perch, introduced into Europe almost a century ago, have rapidly become an invading plague. Extremely prolific, very resistant, voracious and insatiable, these exogenous fish have implanted themselves to the detriment of the native species, and can be considered positively harmful.

The nase, about and over which disputes still rage, has managed to leave its home in Central Europe and turn up at several French drainage basins. Although quite acceptable in small quantities, it becomes harmful when it moves about in shoals, large tightly packed shoals of 1,000–2,000 fish or more.

The author remembers fishing to destroy in the river Allier between 1954 and 1957. Several dozen tons of nase had been caught in all sorts of ways, but the more one took out, the more the shoals kept on arriving. The nase plague overcame all obstacles; the invasion continued relentlessly. Since that not-so-distant time, it has been impossible to keep them back from busy river courses. Springtime insurgences still occur, yet there can be no comparison with the great invasions of the fifties.

Continuous incursions with serious and lasting consequences remain the prime danger. This section could be developed more widely, but let it suffice to comment briefly on each harm, at the same time trying to indicate what measures could be taken to suppress or minimise their disastrous effects.

Firstly, there is chronic pollution from dirty water discharged after factory or household use. There is pollution due to spraying cultivated land with chemicals (pesticides and fertilisers), which infiltrate through the subterranean layers down to the ground water, trickling from the surface into the streams.

Then there is mechanical pollution, generated by dredgers, mechanical scoops and other machines for quarrying building materials (destroying the natural habitat). Another irritant verging on pollution is the heating of the water used in heat exchangers in nuclear and steam generating stations.

After the publication of a report by the Club of Rome, dealing with the gloomy future of mankind and nature unless we take a step backwards to arrive at "zero growth", we could succumb to pessimism, thinking pollution will increase relentlessly —and that will be the end of fishing!

But all is not lost as the next section indicates.

fishing tomorrow

Still on the subject of long-lasting harmful effects, we should mention dams, whose principal evils are: obstacles to migrating fish, involving their disappearance in the medium term (following their cyclic patterns) through blocking access to their zones of life and reproduction; the extensive destruction of all species of young fish for several dozen miles downstream from the dam walls; occasions when the dams cause the river-bed to almost dry up. In a contrary way, the spawning grounds are laid waste and the spawn carried off by the current of untimely floods. Moreover, especially in summer, the water which remains over the scorching stones of a dried-up river-bed becomes considerably heated.

The only available means of alleviating the heinous effects of dams and hydro-electric plants—installing improved fish ladders or building regulating dams to maintain a constant level and flow—are very costly.

Finally, there is fishing with snares, a repetitious if not continual incursion against the aquatic fauna. It is hard to believe that there are some thousands of professional net fishermen who pillage streams and some rivers, protected by the privileges granted by Colbert, which contradict the events of "1789" and other glorious periods in history.

More than thirty large net barriers set up along the river Loire draw the fish to the meshes—thus salmon, shad and trout meet premature and not very sporting deaths.

Trail-nets, drag-nets, seine-nets, sweep-nets; so many names which conjure up particularly lethal types of poaching tackle. Unfortunately, these methods are legal when practised by the professional fisherman using this tackle—an anachronism surviving from an age which cared little about tomorrow.

There is no longer any room for commercial exploitation of freshwater fauna. A handful of privileges should not be able to impinge upon the common good. The doctrine of *res nullius* bring about efforts in cultivation, gamekeeping and husbandry from sporting anglers. "You re-stock! . . . We will do the rest!" This could be the regal command of the kings of the net to the knights of the rod, who are shocked by such iniquity.

There are two kinds of fishermen: the "catchers" (match anglers) and the essentially sporting "purists". The former continuously make fun of the others for being "unable to catch as many fish as them and more concerned with the beauty of the act than with the hamper".

The purists do not hold the "flesh-mongers" in high respect, as their only preoccupations are the "score-board"—the number and weight of the catch. This dispute is encountered in the writings of several specialists of the past, and the author will take care not to be impartial by expressing a mild opinion, coming round to the point of view that "let each one fish in his own way . . . it is the most cunning who catches the most".

Tomorrow's fisherman (*Homo halieuticus*, if M. du Boistouvray will excuse the plagiarism) should be a different type altogether, combining the respective qualities of the catchers and the purists. Above all of a sporting temperament, he will be concerned with all the problems, both direct and indirect, posed by his sport.

As an ecologist, tomorrow's fisherman will make reasonable demands on the existing stock of fish that he finds in open or confined waters, in the public or private sector. Adhering strictly to the rules and regulations, he will acknowledge there are ways of fishing different from his own, and he will be a worthy instructor to beginners.

The fisherman must not be an anti-social egoist, although some forms of his sport oblige him to seek solitude. The religion of tomorrow's fishermen will necessarily involve the protection of nature. Being a lover of wide-open spaces, lost valleys and pure rivers, what will he do when faced with the great danger of the population explosion and all that it directly entails?

The answer lies with the futurists, the dread prophets of the "Destroyers of Nature".[1]

[1] *Open Letters to the Destroyers of Nature*, Pierre Pellerin, Stock.

gadgets

Having looked into the future as it concerns the angler, and given the options open to him in order to safeguard the sport of fishing, we turn now to fishing equipment and its world-wide development, appreciably greater in America than in Europe.

The American manufacturers of fishing tackle employ all their resources to endow the angler with modern "up-to-date" equipment.

But what can all the mechanics, electronics and chemistry which are at the fisherman's service provide when confronted with a European tradition, notably from the British, the true creators of our sport? The author, having benefited moderately from technological developments, prefers the methods of our ancestors; however, for the huge federation of American states and their 30 million fishermen, "progress" often outstrips itself, and the halieutic sport risks losing its main attractions.

In our old continent, progress is more restrained. The strength of fishing lines is being progressively increased, so that a nylon line which fifteen years ago had a test rating of 15·4 lb (7 kg) for a diameter of 50/100 mm has today a test of more than 22 lb (10 kg) for the same diameter—a considerable improvement. In the same way, materials used for making fishing rods are also improving: for example the practically unbreakable fibreglass. Baits have been made more practical, so one can find in the trade freeze-dried baits, notably of worms and maggots. There are baits in soluble packaging that can be thrown in the water without dirtying one's hands.

The following are fairly typical of this new generation of gadgets; perhaps these could give some inspiration to European manufacturers.

fish-brush

This is a sort of unsinkable raft in moulded plastic on which the fisherman lies. The means of propulsion is very economical since it involves the occupant using the flat of his hands or feet underwater, so that the apparatus can be propelled with the legs, whilst keeping the arms free to devote to fishing (the fish-brush weighs only 20 lb (9 kg)).

buzz-ray

"With the 'Buzz-Ray', the fish will come to you", claims the manufacturer of this strange machine, which is an ultrasonic vibrator as well as producing intermittent flashes of light. When lowered to the depths of the water, this little barrel makes a buzzing noise and copies the glow of fire-flies. The fish, ever curious, draw close, and all that remains is to get them to bite which is a bit more difficult.

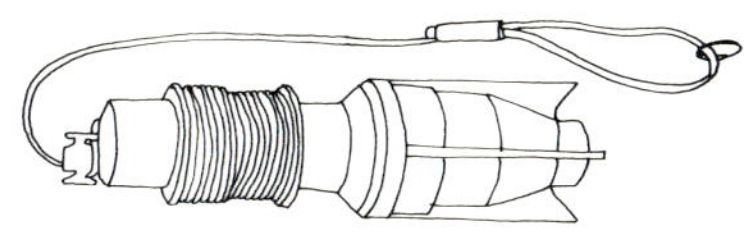

fish-flasher

When used on a boat, this precision-built sonar detects fish both around and below one's boat, and indicates their exact location, size and number. In addition, it operates to a depth of about 90 yards (80 m). This extraordinary instrument, which is not altogether a piece of fishing equipment, functions just as well in fresh water as in salt water, in muddy water, and even through ice.

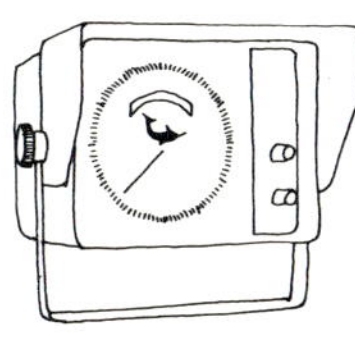

terra-tiger

This boat, supported on cushions of air, threads its way through woodlands, climbs hill slopes and easily takes to water, since it remains suspended. Propelled by an 18 h.p. motor, it can do 30 m.p.h. (50 km) on land, and 3 m.p.h. (5 km) on water. It remains to be seen if it will be too noisy to be used for pike fishing.

red-eye

This particularly tempting lure is in fact a corrugated spoon, the twirlings of which cannot fail to attract even the most apathetic of carnivores. This lure is fitted with two eye-like red protuberances.

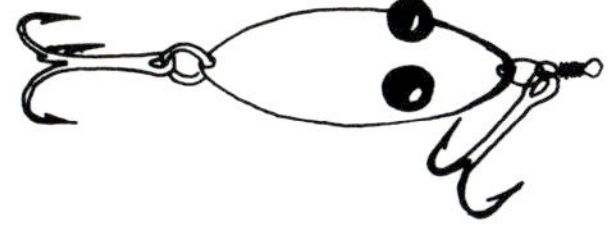

the future of angling in Great Britain

The last Thames salmon was taken in the 1820s or 1830s, according to two historians with slightly different views. The exact date is of little importance: what is important is that both salmon and shad, another migratory species, were unable to live in the river roughly 100 years after the start of the Industrial Revolution. The story of the Thames is the story of the Rhine, the Moselle, the Seine and many others.

Britain's environmental problem is the world's problem: overpopulation. Every ill that besets wild animals, including fish, can be traced back to the fact that mankind has ruined the environment, the habitat of animals and fish. Too many people demand too many houses; too many houses take up too much precious land; people need transport, so steel and other metals are made, polluting the air and the waters with their waste; cars need fuel, so refineries add to the problem. Cars need roads, so more valuable land is swallowed up; ribbons of concrete and tarmac criss-cross the land.

So much land under concrete. The water cannot drain down to fill underground reservoirs and watercourses. People need more water to drink, to produce consumer products. Farmers take more water from the rivers to irrigate crops, and do so because they have demanded, and got, land drainage works done at great expense in the vain belief that they will be able to grow more crops more cheaply on the drained land.

To drain the land, channels are cut to get the water to sea as quickly as possible. The courses of rivers, beautiful and winding, tree-girt and lined with the gravels so important to game-fish breeding, and weeds so important to coarse-fish breeding, are dredged into featureless straight canals—again to get the water to sea as fast as possible, especially when heavy rain swells the stream.

Fast shallows become muddy sluggish deeps. The natural succession of deep slow pools and fast shallows is changed into one straight level canal. The flow is constantly abstracted for use on farmland and homes and factories, or for storage in reservoirs or for generating electricity. In this case dams cause the flow to back-up, prevent the river from cleansing itself from the increasing number of pollutants the farmers, the houses and the factories pour in; some with, some without the permission of government officials whose responsibility it is to maintain, nay improve even, our rivers as a natural heritage, for proper use and as fisheries.

We have already discussed overfishing for salmon and sea trout. While fewer rivers become capable of holding these valuable migratory species, so the commercial netsmen rape and pillage the few that still try to maintain their strength by running the rivers that are left—a dwindling number. Coarse fish are seldom eaten in Britain and so the Continental problem in that respect does not apply. But rivers are so polluted and so abstracted that even coarse-fish stocks are dwindling. Often still waters, less liable to pollution than rivers, and where valuable coarse fisheries can be sustained, are filled in to make way for . . . yes, more houses, more factories, more roads.

The fertilisers and insecticides the farmers apply to the land to try to make it unnaturally produce more crops wash off in times of heavy rain (due to that drainage already mentioned) and poison the rivers and lakes. Too much of a good thing in the form of mineral salts cause waters to become over-enriched with nutrients and heavy algal blooms occur. When the algae die its breakdown by bacteria demands oxygen, and fish need oxygen to thrive. They die. The water is discoloured by the algae. Weeds which need sunlight to thrive also die. Even if fish do survive their food supply is cut. Stunting takes place. This is the modern evil known as eutrophication. Even in Ireland, a less densely populated and less industrialised land than England, Wales or Scotland, a recent report draws attention to eutrophication in some of the finest trout loughs of the midland plain. Apart from nutrients from agriculture, it is abetted by the run-off from intensive animal-rearing units and useless sewage works, even raw sewage.

Against this background of more and more people having to be housed, needing more food, more cars, washing machines, oil, electricity, this bulldozer of environmental decay, the increasing army of anglers tries to pursue its sport—too often the small voice warning against decline of the quality of life, for it has been anglers who live so close to the world of nature who have in the past been the early warning system of the country's ills. For the most part their voice has been drowned by the clamour of the public for more material wealth and creature comforts.

It is a fact that, no matter what some government spokesmen repeat, parrot fashion, to the contrary, Britain's inland waters are continuing to decline at an alarming rate and that no matter how much may be done (an unlikely event) to try to right the wrongs, the growth of population and its demands will eventually cause every river to become a poisonous canal or disappear entirely. In fact, due to abstraction at source from their underground springs by boreholes, some rivers (for instance several in Hertfordshire, just north of London, which a few years ago formed important trout and coarse fisheries) have disappeared for ever!

Life cannot exist without clean water: it is to all life the elixir. One day, not only in Britain but throughout the world, all life will cease to exist. That is not a fanatical angler making a wild statement: world-famous environmentalists have said as much.

However, humans, besides being the wreckers of their own world, are also optimists. We cannot allow even truths like that mentioned to kill optimism. We try to brake the decline; we must fish, and we try to ensure that our children fish in the future.

Against this miserable background angling bodies try to slow the decline of fisheries. Two of the most effective are the Anglers' Co-operative Association, formed in 1947 by a lawyer, John Eastwood, and the Salmon and Trout Association. The A.C.A., poorly supported by the anglers whose interests it is trying to promote, has had numerous successes against polluters of all kinds, its legal actions based on the common-law premise, that a riparian owner is entitled to water undiminished in flow and unchanged in content flowing through his property. It is academic that few riparian owners enjoy such rights, but then many do not know their rights, nor seem to care about the water.

The Salmon and Trout Association seeks to maintain and improve stocks of salmon, trout and sea trout, monitoring the national situation. It, too, is not well supported.

The British Government has for several years been saying it will talk turkey to only one body that is representative of all anglers—in the same way that the British Lawn Tennis Association and the Football Association represents those two ball games. However, the organisation, which was formed in the late sixties to represent the coarse, game and sea anglers of Britain, is also poorly supported and (in 1973) lost money. The National Anglers' Council has enjoyed some successes, however, but it will not really succeed until it gets more support, especially finance.

Many of Britain's alleged 3 million anglers belong to angling associations; some of them, such as the London Anglers' Association, the Birmingham Anglers' Association and others in the North and Midlands in particular, have many thousands of members. However, anglers do not appear to want to pay much for protecting their sport, and so many richer sports tend to push angling further and further into the background.

Angling is a quiet pursuit and anglers tend to be individualists, which to some extent weakens their bargaining powers against the more organised national bodies. For example, sailing gets large government grants, yet angling not only gets less money handed out, but anglers and the sport are heavily taxed.

Indirectly, anglers are participating in the national effort to build more roads to cater for the growing number of cars, because as the waters decline, so anglers tend to chase further and further afield for their sport. At week-ends many travel to fisheries 150 or more miles away from their homes to try to improve their results.

Some people feel that if a stream is dammed to form a lake, or if a depression is otherwise flooded to create a pool, then stocked with fish, this is the answer to the shortage of fisheries. It is not. Helpful though such ventures are, it would be a terrible end-product if all fishing had to take place on man-made still waters, for fish bred in fish-farms. Fishing in rivers has a special charm, and to acknowledge that rivers can be allowed to fall into the hands of those whose sole interest it is to canalise, abstract and pollute, is to acknowledge defeat and the earlier-than-doomsday end of naturally bred fish in purely natural surroundings.

Although there are many fish-farms in Britain producing trout, mainly rainbows, little breeding of coarse fish goes on. There is a move by the N.A.C. to set up a national coarse fish-farm, but this will need a great deal of public investment to succeed.

And such moves tend to obscure the basic truth, which is that if the rivers and lakes were kept clean and flowing strongly, with natural beds, and waterside and in-the-water vegetation, then the fish would thrive and reproduce themselves. There is more fun in catching truly wild fish than those reared in farms and put in the water. That is why catching stew-fed rainbow trout of 3 lb (1 kg) or so (fish that might have been put into the river or lake at that weight the previous day, week or month) can quickly pall. And such fish often bear the marks of the stew-pond: frayed or non-existent tails and fins, a generally dark coloration, and, even more important to the thinking angler, a cupidity that makes them grab any old fly, however badly fished, because they are not used to fending for themselves, having no fear of man since man has been feeding them pellets for two or three years!

When compared with the casting of a fly to a small wild brown trout in a babbling stream, where the water is clear and the fish can see and recognise man the enemy, fishing for stew-pond trout is an apology for the spirit of angling. As similarly, many coarse fishers mourn the reduction in the number of lakes where true wild carp breed naturally, lean fish of up to 10 lb (4·50 kg) or so that fight by swimming fast over long distances. What has happened is that carp from Holland and Italy, the big, fat, fast-growing type bred for Continental tables, have been stocked, to replace or breed with the true wild fish. The fight of a 10 lb (4·50 kg) wild carp is said to be much better than that of a domesticated carp three times its weight.

The one type of angling that has proved a popular development in Britain involves the stocking of water supply reservoirs with brown and rainbow trout. Although this is a form of put-and-take angling, the vast expanses of water in which the stocked fish roam and feed helps not only to produce superbly fit, fat fighting fish but to make them quite a difficult and nearly wild proposition for the fly-rod men. Reservoir trout fishing has brought trout within the reach of most anglers and the tackle trade has been quick to see the opportunities and much specialised gear has been channelled into this quarter.

Nevertheless, it must never be forgotten that for every reservoir built that dams a river or stream or takes water pumped from them, the running waters suffer badly, no matter how hard the engineers and politicians argue to the contrary.

Until April 1974, the welfare of the inland fisheries of England and Wales lay in the hands of twenty-eight River Authorities, but from April 1974 the system changed, the River Authorities being replaced by eight Regional Water Authorities with complete control of all water resources. There are some hopes that the many ills that befell freshwater fisheries while the River Authorities were in power will not be repeated by the Regional Water Authorities. Many anglers feel, however, that the vast pressures imposed by the population will make the new system as fallible as the old.

In Scotland the fishing is administered in a different way, by district boards interested in game fishing only, in general. In Scotland there is no close season for coarse fish.

In the Irish Republic inland fisheries are the responsibility of the Department of Agriculture and Fisheries, and there are seventeen Fishery Districts, each under direct control of a Board of Conservators. Again, as in Scotland, the protection of salmon and trout are the main theme, there being no close season for coarse fish.

Northern Ireland has two fishery districts, but overall responsibility lies with the Ministry of Agriculture. Again the interest for preservation lies mainly with trout and salmon, there being no coarse-fish close season.

So, England and Wales alone have coarse fish protected during the alleged spawning period, which usually runs between March 14 and June 15, though in truth many coarse fish spawn throughout the summer.

Many of the fishery laws can be varied by local bye-laws.

One of the major problems in the management of Britain's inland fisheries, in general, has been the limited Government financial backing channelled into the fisheries. The result has been too few people adequately trained in the field to do the work properly. Anglers have often stood by, enraged but powerless to do anything, while fishery officials, obviously knowing very little about their jobs, have allowed great damage to be done or have actually done the damage themselves.

What can you think about a fishery officer in charge of a vast area who maintains that a certain fish is not found in a certain area, when anglers who are trying to prove a point are catching that very fish as the man makes his ignorant statement?

Under the new system of Regional Water Authorities in England and Wales the intention is that anglers will be able to have far more say in the administration of fisheries through consultative bodies to fishery committees. At the time of writing (four months after the Regional Water Authorities came to power) it is too early to judge whether this is the case. At least one of Britain's leading anglers feels that the new system will make no difference.

Above: Fishery Authority workers and anglers net the unwanted carp from a famous English trout reservoir—Weir Wood, near East Grinstead, Sussex.

Left: A big fish for a little boy; nine-year-old Stuart Harris with a $20\frac{1}{4}$ lb (9·25 kg) Hampshire Avon salmon which he hooked and played himself while spinning.

Above right: A brown trout suffering from ulcerative dermal necrosis (UDN), a disease which has hit salmon, sea trout and trout stocks on many British rivers.

Right: This sad scene at a lock on a river in southern England shows dead fish—killed by pollution upstream—piling up near the gates.

Above: A good bag of tench from an English Midland lake.

Left: Flooded gravel-workings on the Earl of Aylsford's Packington Estate in Warwickshire are a good example of put-and-take trout fisheries—these photographs were taken in March.

Right: Fine English roach. Fish like these are most often caught in autumn and winter.

glossary

a

Abeille French fishing-tackle maker; Abeille automatic fly reel.
A.B.U. Swedish manufacturers of fishing tackle.
A.B.U. Optic-Salmo A salmon fly with metal eyes, made by the Swedish A.B.U. tackle company.
Action (or Technique) of Fishing Used to define various ways of fishing. The action (technique) of fly-fishing is different from the action of float fishing.
Adam Brand of fishing tackle, lures, Adam's spinners.
A.F.T.M.A. The Association of American Fishing Tackle Manufacturers.
Alarm Audible and/or visual electric apparatus for signalling a bite, especially at night. Used by carp and pike anglers more than by others.
Alcedo Italian make of reel, known for its ultra-light reel "Micron".
Alpine Charr The European term for the non-migratory arctic charr, *Salvelinus alpinus.*
Alto-Minno A spinning lure.
Amadou A spongy fungus used for drying the artificial fly after a catch, or when wet it sinks and needs re-oiling.
Anglers' Co-operative Association British national anti-pollution organisation.
ASSOCIATIONS (French)
A.N.D.R.S. National Association for the Protection of River Salmon.
A.P.P. Chartered Association of Fishing and Fisheries.
A.P.P.S.B. Association for the Protection and Exhibition of Brittany and Lower Normandy Salmon.
A.P.S. Association for the Protection of Salmon (Allier).
C.F.P.M. French Club of Fly-Fishers.
T.O.S. Association of Sporting Anglers founded by M. Gagniard ((*Pleasures of Fishing*), presided over by M. Richard, who is also President of the A.N.D.R.S.
U.D.P.A. Union for the Protection of Amateur Anglers.
C.S.P. Upper Chamber for Fishing.
Atlantic Salmon The salmon species of Britain and Europe, as opposed to the Pacific salmon species and others.
Automatic Retrieve Reel A reel, usually for fly-fishing, which is wound up so that the drum retrieves line quickly when a lever is depressed.

b

Babbing Method of catching eels; worms are threaded on worsted yarn and formed into a bunch; eels' teeth entangle with the yarn and they may be lifted out of the water.
Backing A secondary line attached to a casting line, to fill a spool and to use when playing a fish that runs a long way.
Bait Food placed on a hook in order to lure fish.
verb—to bait: to fix: thread or stick on a hook.
Bamboo A reed-like wood from whose tough outer skin built-cane rods are made. Most come from Red China.
Barb The slice made inside the point of a hook, then lifted to prevent the hook coming out once it has penetrated the jaw of a fish.
Barbel Species of freshwater fish, *Barbus barbus*; also the appendages dependant from the mouths of some fish.
Barbellion A writer on trout fly-fishing.
Bass, black Species of American origin which has been introduced in a few European waters; two species, largemouth and smallmouth.
Beaked Carp Of the Cyprinidae family (nase).
Beats The area of waterside bank into which fisheries, especially game fisheries, are divided.
Bertin (Léon) French scientist (eels).
Bertin (Pierre) An expert on salmon fishing.
Biological Balance A desirable situation in which forms of water life thrive in harmony.
Biological Equilibrium—of a river—relative equilibrium between organisms living in a particular environment.
Biotope The smallest subdivision of a habitat, characterised by a high degree of uniformity in its environmental conditions and in its plant and animal life.
Bite Indicator See Alarm.
Bitterling Small fish which lays its eggs in the shell of a living freshwater mussel.
Bleak Small silvery freshwater fish.
Blood-knot Used to join nylon monofilament lines.
Bloodworm Wriggling red larva of chironomid (midge).
Boisset, Louis de French fly-fishing writer.
Bonnenfant, Lucien Expert French salmon angler.
Boyer, H. French salmon-fishing author.
Braid Textiled plaits, uncoated.
Brake On a reel, method of slowing down the drum or the spool, generally by clamping and friction, not to be confused with the lock.
Bream Freshwater species of the Cyprinidae family; the bronze or common bream, *Abramis brama.*
Bream (Bordelière) Small species of bream, not exceeding 12 in. (45 cm) in length.
Bream, Silver Smaller species than the common bream.
Bridge Rings Rings on a rod, the centres of which are supported by wire to form bridges.
Brook Trout The American charr, *Salvelinius fontinalis.*
Bucknall, Geoffrey British writer on freshwater angling, especially on trout and pike.
Bucktail A kind of streamer-fly made of hair.
Buldo Trademark of weighted transparent "bubble" floats, shaped like a sphere.
Bullet Ball of lead with a hole through it, for legering.
Bull-head Small ugly fish living under stones; Miller's thumb.
Burbot Also called "eel-pout", the only freshwater member of the cod family in Europe.
Burnand, Tony French writer on angling, widely renowned. Founder of magazine *Au Bord de l'Eau.*

c

Caddis Grub Larva of the sedge fly.
Calderwood, W. L. British salmon expert and author.
Carnivores Fish which are predatory on other fish and fauna.
Carp The biggest of the cyprinids.
Carp, Common Fully scaled carp.
Chinese or Grass: species which eats vast amounts of vegetation, being used experimentally in Britain.
Crucian: smallest carp, has no barbels.
Leather: carp with no scales in its skin.
Mirror: carp with a few large scales embedded at random in the skin.
Carrière, Louis French angling writer.
Casting The act of projecting the bait, lure or fly line onto or into the water.
Category 1st category: waterways dominated by the Salmonidae family. 2nd category: other waterways and stretches of water.
Catfish Bottom fish of scavenging nature with long barbels, several species.
Caudal Tail (fin).
Celta A French bar-spoon.
Centrepin Reel A single-action reel whose drum revolves freely on a pivot, used mainly in Britain for trotting.
Chamberet (de) Manufacturer of artificial flies (famous Gallica range).
Charpy General Officer of Forests and Water.
Chavender, Chevin Old names for the chub.
Chromex Chromex rings—hard chromium-plated rings which are not worn into grooves by the friction of the line.
Chub Common cyprinid fish in rivers; exists in some still waters.
Clubs See Associations.
C.N.E.X.O. French National Centre for the Study and Exploration of Oceans.
Coarse Fish Species such as carp, bream, chub, pike, as opposed to game fish (salmon and trout).
Coiling Down To unreel a line in the shape of a double circle on the ground. Also used in talking about manually recovering a line (coil fishing).
Colorado Obsolete spoon-shaped spinner with propeller mounted on a weighted axis. Used mainly for pike.
Continental Bar-spoon Spoon-shaped spin-

ner mounted to revolve from one end on a bar; has surplanted colorado spoon.
Coregonids The white fish, such as houting, powan, etc.
Crack Make of French reel.
Crayfish Looks like a small freshwater lobster; edible, and good bait for chub, trout.
Creusevaut, Pierre French angler, rod designer and tournament caster of world-wide repute.
Cristivomer Namaycush trout of American origin, introduced into some mountain lakes.
Cyprinids The carp family.

d

Dace Small cyprinid favouring swift streams.
Damper Originating in the town of Roubaix, rubber yarn (usually fixed on to the tip of the rod) which is attached to the line.
Dap, Dapping The technique of using a long rod and thick air-resistant light line to permit the wind to blow the natural or artificial fly lightly on the water. Mainly used on vast lakes. Also to lower a bait under bushes to surface-feeding fish.
Devaux Manufacturer of artificial flies "à champagnole".
Devon Minnow Fusiform spinning lure, wood, plastic or metal, used mainly for salmon or trout.
Dottrens, Professor Swiss fish scientist.
Downstream See Upstream.
Dragnet A net used by a team of anglers to catch unwanted fish.
Drop Minnow Either a metal heavy lure or a dead minnow with a lead in its mouth, both fished sink-and-draw or jigged.
Dropper A link standing off from the main line or leader carrying bait or fly.
Dry Fly A fly that floats on the water's surface.
Duborgel, Michel French angling writer.
Dubos Fishing expert from Paris, founder of schools of fly-fishing and dressing flies.
Dust Shot Very tiny split lead weight for fine fishing.
Dwarfism Degeneration due to overcrowding (especially in enclosed waters).

e

Eastwood, John The founder of the Anglers' Co-operative Association.
Eel The European eel, *Anguilla anguilla*.
Ephemera Insect (flies) whose life is short.

f

Farlow British tackle company, now merged with Sharpes of Aberdeen.
Ferrule Metal or fibreglass tube used for assembling the sections of the rod.
Fibreglass Woven cloth of glass fibres bonded with various resins to make fishing rods, tubular and solid.
Fins The fish's organs of propulsion and balance:
Dorsal: on the back.
Caudal: at the end of the tail.
Anal: near the anus.
Pectoral: connected to the skull.
Pelvic: abdominal or jugular.
Adipose: peculiar to Salmonidae, situated between the dorsal and the caudal fin.
Fishing Club of France Group of anglers for the protection of fish and waters (*Fishing Illustrated*).
Fixed Leger Bottom rig on which a lead is fixed above the hook, not sliding on the line.
Fixed-spool Reel Casting reel on which the line flows off the side (front edge) of a transversely mounted spool.
Flies Both dry and wet.
Floating Line Opposite to sinking line.
Float-leger Rig on which the lead lies on the bottom and just cocks the float for sensitive bite registration.
Flopy Soft Plug French rubber plug-bait, good for pike, salmon, trout and perch in particular.
Flounder A saltwater flat fish that often runs into rivers—to pure fresh water.
Fly-fishing Using a lissom rod, heavy casting line and artificial flies.
Fly Line The heavy line, floating or sinking, used to present artificial flies to fish.
Free-spool Multiplier Casting reel mounted on top of the rod on which the revolving spool is free of gears during the cast.
Freshwater Shrimps Freshwater version of sea crustaceans (see Gammarid).
Friture Generally referring to little fish cooked in oil or fried.
Fry Term to describe small fish.

g

Game Fishing Opposite to coarse fishing—for salmon, trout and sea trout; all members of the salmon family.
Gammarid Small freshwater crustacean, excellent as bait.
Gill Net Suspended from floats, it catches by their gills fish that swim into it.
Grayling A "maverick" salmonid that spawns in spring with coarse fish.
Grease Hydrophobic grease is used to make dry flies and non-floating lines float.
Greaser Little lubricating device for silk lines used for fly-fishing.
Greenheart Rod A rod made from a dense but flexible wood—seldom used today.
Grilse A salmon that returns to the river after one winter at sea.
Ground-bait Bait thrown into the water to attract fish to the angler's baited hook, or to get fish feeding on a pre-selected hook-bait.
Gudgeon Small bottom-feeding fish used for live-bait and esteemed at table in France.
Gudgeon-perch Colloquial name for pope or ruffe.

h

Hackle English term describing a feather used to put together an artificial fly. Most hackles are feathers taken from cocks' necks. The feather at the throat or behind the head of an artificial fly.
Halford, Frederic Maurice An English exponent on exact imitation fly-fishing for trout, and author of books on fly-fishing.
Hardy Famous tackle company in Alnwick, England.
Hatching "Fly" hatching—appearance on the water's surface of "flies", having finished their stages as larvae or nymphs.
Hatching of Young Fish (Alevins) Birth of the alevin in its first stage of life outside the egg.
Hollow-glass Rod Fibreglass rod made in tubular form.
Hook Link The nylon or wire link between reel-line and hook.
Hotu (Nase) Bottom-feeding European fish.
Huchen Of the Salmonidae family.
Hundredth Part The hundredth of a millimetre, a measurement of the diameter of monofilament fishing lines.

i

Ide A cyprinid imported into the north of France.
Imago Definitive stage in the formation of the perfect insect.
Incubation Period between the laying of the eggs and the hatching of the alevins.
Inland Rainbow Trout Non-migratory form of rainbow trout.
Ivens, T. C. A famous British fly-fisher, best known for original book on still-water fly-fishing for trout.

j

Jack Pike Small pike, usually under 6 lb (3 kg).
J.B. Brand of fishing tackle (Jean Barrault): famous for its swivels.
Jet Brand-name of Hardy fibreglass fly rods.
Johnsons, K. M. A Redditch-based firm of rod makers, especially built cane.

k

Keepnet Long net with wire frame in which fish are kept alive before being put back in the water after a fishing session.
Kelt A spawned salmon.
Kite, Oliver A British authority on fly-fishing, especially nymph fishing; author of books.
Kroic French brand of polyamide (nylon) line.
Kype The hooked lower jaw of a cock salmon or trout.

l

Lamprey An eel-like parasitic fish that sucks body fluids from other fish, particularly

salmon, by attaching its suckered mouth to the fish.
Larva Insect state coming after the egg.
Lateral Line Perceptive organ (certainly involving hearing) sited as a line on the fish's side.
Lead Weight made of lead to take the tackle to the prescribed depth or to hold it on the bottom.
Leader, Nylon Similar meaning to hook-link, usually used in fly-fishing to connect fly to line.
Leger The lead weight used to anchor a bait on the bottom; also the technique of doing so.
Leger
Fixed: see under F.
Roving: leaded tackle that rolls along the bottom of a river, often used for barbel and chub.
Lerc French brand of tackle, famous for glass-fibre rods.
Light Rod Rod with flexible action for use with fine lines.
Line Made from nylon, Dacron, silk, for all types of angling.
Live-bait Any bait of animal nature, used alive, but usually small fish for pike, perch, zander, etc.
Loach Small fishes with barbules.
There are three sorts of loach:
2 in.–4 in. (8–15 cm) long—the most common; found in rivers.
2 in.–4 in. (8–15 cm) long—slightly different morphology; found in ponds.
8 in.–12 in. (30–45 cm) long—living in stagnant waters.
Loggerhead Colloquial name for chub; see Chavender, Chevin.
Looping Looping occurs when the hook locks on to the line during casting (especially when fly-fishing), making it inoperative.
Low-water Flies Salmon flies with sparse dressings and fine-wire hooks for salmon in low clear rivers.
L.P. Brand of light fishing tackle (Louis Perrot).
Lure Any artificial used to catch fish, but in Britain a long fly used for still-water trout fishing.

Mars-Vallet French angling writer and conservationist, General Secretary of France's Union for the Protection of Amateur Anglers.
Martin (reel) American make of fly reel, automatic.
Match Fishing Coarse fishing in competition.
Mauborgne French firm of reel makers.
M.E.P.P.S. French manufacturer of fishing tackle, internationally famous for their Mepps lures.
Mepps Bar-spoon Brand of French spinner; see Continental Bar-spoon.
Mepps-Minnow Similar to above but with rubber fish behind spinning spoon.
Mepps Tandem Spoon Two bar-spoons, one behind the other.
Milt Sperm-containing fluid of male fish.
Mimesis (Mimicry) Facility of the fish to adapt its skin colour to the colour of its surroundings.
Mimicri Brand of very strong nylon monofilament line.
Minnow Of the Cyprinidae family. See "little fish".
Minnow A lure shaped like a fish, propelled by fins which make it spin round when recovered (devon minnow, quill minnow, etc.).
Mitchell French reel-making company.
M.P. Brand of spoons (Marcel Plantin of Brioude).
Mullet Saltwater fish that runs into rivers; thick-lipped variety into brackish water, thin-lipped into pure fresh water.
Multiplying Casting Reel Reel fished on top of the rod, with light revolving spool, usually with quadruple gears for fast line retrieve.
Muskellunge Large pike-like fish of North American continent; reaches 65 lb (30 kg).

N.A.C. British anglers' body, the National Anglers' Council.
Nase See Hotu.
National Union National Union of A.P.P. Federations, connecting almost all the departmental (French) federations, presided over by Mme Bouchard.
Natural Bait Any bait dug from soil, collected from water, etc.; usually worms, insects, crustacea.
Netboy, Anthony American author of *The Atlantic Salmon*, a concise book on the decline of the species.
Nylon (line) Man-made fibre, used for lines (monofilament and braided) and for leaders (monofilament).
Nymph Sub-aquatic immature stage of many flies, especially ephemerid flies, also anglers' imitation.

Olfacto-gustatory Separate senses of smell and taste.
Ondex Bar-spoon French bar-spoon with unweighted bar.
Operculata Bony lateral parts of the head covering the gills.
Orfi A particularly strong brand of nylon line (Rhodia).

Parabolic (series) Term to describe rods that bend into the handle in a smooth curve; also brand name of Pezon et Michel rods.
Parr (marking) "Thumb-print" marks on young salmon and trout.
Paternoster Bottom tackle with lead at the end of the line; hook on dropper above.
Peal English West Country term for sea trout.
Pectoral The fins behind the gills of a fish.
Perch Spike-finned predatory fish; good eating.
Perch-trout Colloquial term for black bass.
Perlon German brand of fishing lines.
Pethe Specialist in fly dressing, author of a very full treatise on fly dressing.
Pezon et Michel French tackle company.
pH The coefficient of the acidity or alkalinity of water.
Pike Large predatory fish, *Esox lucius*; in North America, the Northern pike.
Pike Culture Rearing pike in fish-farms.
Pikeperch The zander.
Platil German fishing line. The "Strong" Platil is famous for its toughness.
Plucky Soft Plug Similar to Flopy plug—soft rubber, made in France.
Plug Wriggling spinning lure, wood or plastic, for pike, salmon, big trout, etc.
Point Fine tip of nylon leader; also term to describe a fish pulling the rod down until it is on a level with the line—often breaks the line.
Polaroid Glasses Glasses with special lenses which eliminate surface reflection; useful for spotting fish.
Pool Stillest and deepest part of the river following the current.
Pope Small perch-like fish, also called ruffe.
Pores Orifices connected to certain sensory organs (sensorial pores).
Profile The shape of a fly line, looked at from above when laid out on the ground.
Pumping When fighting a fish this consists of raising the rod, then winding to recover the line as the rod is smoothly lowered again and tension is released.

Quill, Cocked Float made from bird quill, standing upright in water, ballasted by lead.

Ragot Manufacturer of artificial flies at Loudeac, Côtes-du-Nord. Creator of numerous lines, of which the "Bretonnes" and 'Allier" type are used for salmon.
Rainbow Perch Of the Centrarchidae family (also called pumpkin seed).
Rainbow Trout Imported to Europe from North America, raised in fish-farms, for food and for stocking fisheries, *Salmo gairdneri*.
Rat-tail Tapered line with a fine point, a larger part (the belly) and a second fine end (see "lines for fly fishing").
Rays Spokes of fins (soft, or flexible and hard, sometimes prickly).
Redd Trough dug in river-bed by hen salmon and trout in which eggs are shed.
Red Eye Colloquial name for rudd; also used for other species.
Reel Several types—fly, fixed-spool, multiplier for storing line, casting from and for playing fish.
Release Method of handling the line intended to make the snagged bait jerk free (slacking off) by pulling the line in the opposite direction to the current.
Righyni, R. V. A famous British game angler, author of important books on the subject.
Ripple Made on water by fish breaking surface, or by a breeze.
Ritz, Charles Famous Swiss-born angler, rod designer and fly-fishing expert, author.
Roach Common European cyprinid fish, *Rutilus rutilus*.
Roach Rod Long, stiff, tip-action rod for fine fishing for roach.
Rod The angler's "buffer" between fish and line.
Rod Rings Hard wire rings whipped to rod shaft, through which line runs to the reel.

Romani Trade-mark of a manufacturer of flies from Langogne (Lozère).
Rublex Factory for the manufacture of fishing lures. Founded by R. Bocchino, who with others launched the famous Rublex rubber minnow.
Rublex Rubber Devon Minnow French-made devon-type spinning lure—good for salmon.
Rudd Cyprinid fish common on still waters and sluggish rivers.
Ruffe See Pope.
Run Movement of migratory fish, i.e. salmon, into rivers; also the fast swimming of a hooked fish; and a bite which takes line from the reel.
Running-leger Rig Bottom tackle on which the lead runs freely on the line, stopped above the hook.

s

Saint-Marc, Philippe Senior official, author of *The Socialisation of Nature*, a very forthright work in the fight against harmful effects, notably water pollution.
Salmon
Atlantic: *Salmo salar*, the European salmon.
Pacific: five oncorhynchus types, chinook, coho, sockeye, pink, chum.
Trout: colloquial name for sea trout.
Salmon and Trout Association British national game anglers' organisation.
Salmonids Fish of the salmon family, distinguished by adipose fins.
Sawyer, Frank Famous English river-keeper on the Avon, also fly-fisher and inventor of nymph techniques, author of fly-fishing books.
Sea-run Rainbow Trout Migratory form of rainbow trout, *Salmo irideus*, the Pacific steelhead.
Sea Trout Migratory form of brown trout, *Salmo trutta*.
Seine A net which is cast or dropped and is pulled in to encircle a shoal.
Sewin Welsh name for sea trout.
Shad Saltwater fish that runs into rivers; good fighting fish.
Shank Straight part of the hook between the bend and the end part (eye or spade) to which the line is attached.
Sharpes British tackle company, based in Aberdeen, now merged with Farlow.
Sheatfish The Danubian catfish or wels.
Shock-absorber Originating in Roubaix (Damper).
Shoot Final action in the movement of casting a fly.
Siluridae The siluris family (catfish, sheatfish or wels).
Siluris See Catfish or sheatfish.
Single-action Reel Reel on which one turn of the handle produces one revolution of the spool—without gears.
Sinking Line Opposite to floating line.
Sinking Tip Found on some floating fly lines, to sink the fly while retaining line control.
Skues, George Edward Mackenzie A famous British writer and fly-fisher.
Slob Trout Brown trout that live in estuaries and brackish water.
Smelt Small saltwater fish, often runs into estuaries, good eating, smells of cucumber.
Smolt Stage of salmonid fish after parr markings have disappeared; salmon and sea trout when they first go to sea.
Snake Rings Wire rings found on fly rods.
Snares Various nets, pots and other devices used by professional fishermen.
Snood Link on a fishing line, such as a paternoster, which makes hooks stand out away from the main line.
Sparling Small European fish, bleak-like.
Spawn Eggs of fish (ova).
Spawning time Reproductive period.
Spinner, spinning A spinning lure; the technique of casting and retrieving a spinning or wobbling lure for predatory fish.
Split-cane Rod Rod made from, usually, six sections of bamboo cane, glued into a hexagonal shape, excellent for fly rods.
Split Shot Balls of lead, split, to be squeezed on the line to sink the bait or cock a float.
Spoon Flies Small spoons with a fly attached, used usually for trout or perch.
Springer Salmon that runs the river in the February to May period; large fish.
Stalking Quiet approach to previously seen fish.
Steelhead See sea-run rainbow trout.
Streamer Flies Flies on long-shank hooks with elongated profiles—long wings.
Strike Action of pulling hook into a fish's mouth.
Subimago Stage of transformation of the insect to the almost perfect state (dun).
Sun-perch Member of the Centrarchidae.
Swallow The action of a fish taking the hook (and bait) past the mouth.
Swedish Wobbling Spoon Non-spinning lure for salmon, pike, etc.
Sweep Net Net used actively to encompass fish, pulled through water from bank or boat.
Swim Place where anglers fish successfully.
Swimfeeder Tube of transparent plastic on line above hook in which ground-bait is put.
Swimmer Hinged lure made of wood or plastic (plug).
Swivel Small article of fishing tackle intended to avoid excessive twisting of the line, especially when using spinning lures.
Swivel, Three-way Swivel with an eye at a right angle from which a dropper is tied, as in paternoster fishing.

t

Take The action of a fish grabbing a lure or bait.
Tangled Line Ravelled line.
Tench Cyprinid fish of still and sluggish waters; *Tinca tinca*.
Terminal Line The end part of the line on which the hook is attached.
Test Word to describe breaking point or a line or leader.
Timing A pause during the motions of fly casting (back-cast), also used to indicate rhythm.
Tonkin Cane Bamboo for rods from Tonkin area of China.
Toric Ring (of a ferrule) Supple synthetic ring placed on a male ferrule, producing a perfect joint without any play between the two units.
Toulouse-style Float Slim French-style float.
Trace Link from swivel to lure, often of wire for pike and zander, to resist teeth.
Trailing Action of pulling a lure behind a boat—see also Trolling.
Treble Hook Three hooks brazed together, usually used on lures or tube-flies.
Trimmer A device involving a large float and baited hooks, often used by professional fishermen to catch pike and other large predatory fish.
Trolling Currently used in preference to trailing; originally described casting a dead leaded fish and using sink and draw retrieve for pike.
Trout *Salmo trutta*, the native European brown trout.
Tru-Art American make of reel, for fly-fishing.
Tube-fly Fly dressed in metal or plastic tube with treble hook on leader, for salmon and sea trout.

u

Ulcerative Dermal Necrosis Salmon and trout disease.
Upstream Towards the upper waters (casting upstream). Opposite to downstream.

v

Vario-Power Name of Pezon et Michel composite glass and cane fly rod.
Vavon, Colonel Specialist on fly-fishing.
Veltic Bar-spoon French weighted bar-spoon.
Veniards English company supplying fly-dressing materials.
Versailles Float French competition float.
Vesicle The vitelline vesicle (or yolk-sac) of an alevin containing a nutrient liquid.
Vibert Official of Waters and Forestry Commission. Inventor of incubation boxes —the Vibert Boxes.
Vibert Box Container in which eyed ova of game fish are reared in natural conditions.
Virex French spinning lure.
Vivier Honorary Custodian of Waters and Forests.
Voblex Headed Spoon French bar-spoon with rubber-covered lead head.

w

Waders Trouser boots coming up to the chest.
Wading Fishing while walking in the water.
Walker, Richard Famous British angler and author, holder of carp record at 44 lb (20 kg).
Walleye American pike-perch.
Walton, Izaak Famous English angler and author of *The Compleat Angler*.
Wandering Style of fishing whereby the fisherman frequently changes position; also called roving.
Water-sense Gifts which certain anglers possess, enabling them to find easily where the fish are gathering, depending on the circumstances, and to foresee their reactions. Water-sense can also be acquired with experience.
White Trout Irish name for sea trout.

z

Zander European pike-perch.

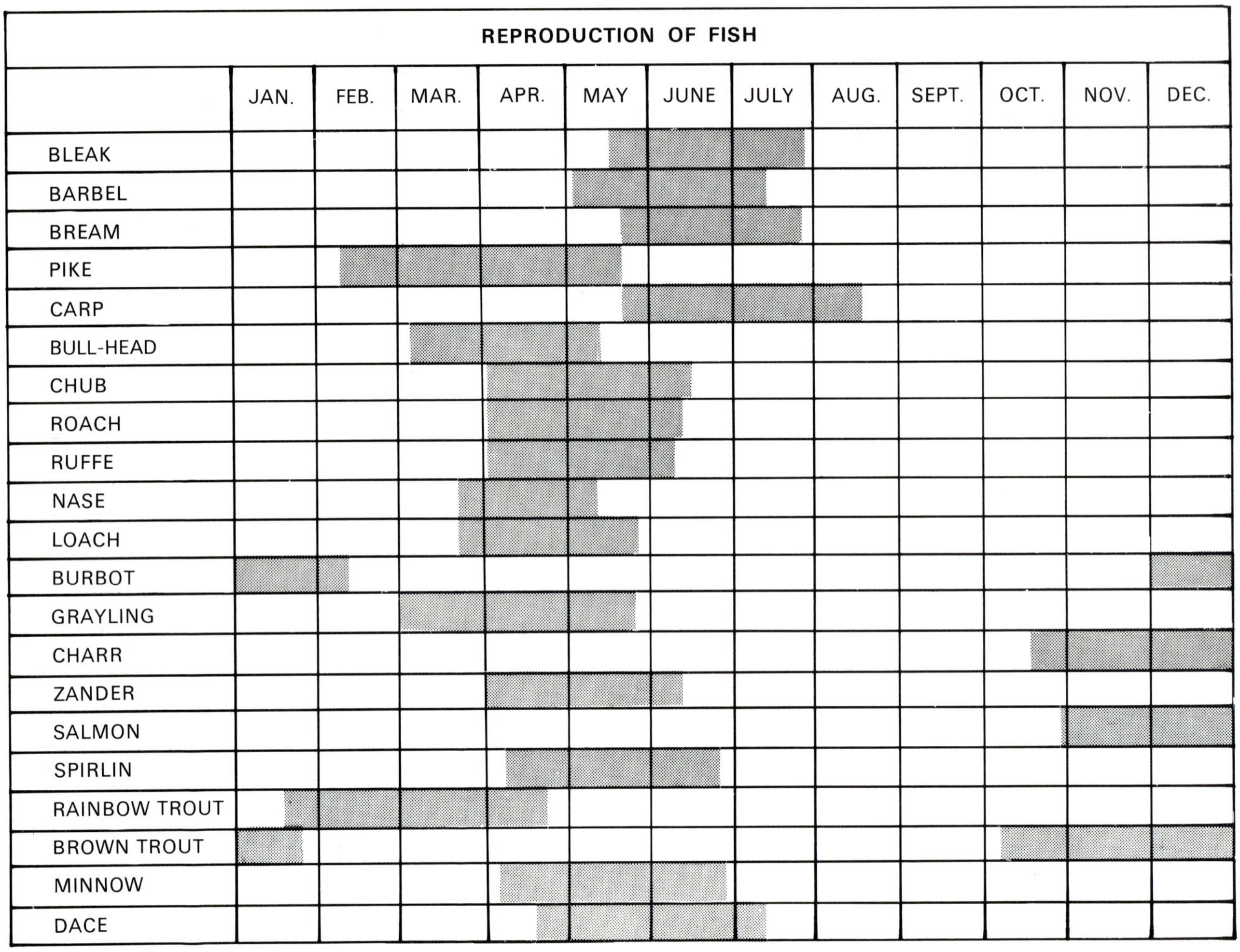

REPRODUCTION OF FISH												
	JAN.	FEB.	MAR.	APR.	MAY	JUNE	JULY	AUG.	SEPT.	OCT.	NOV.	DEC.
BLEAK												
BARBEL												
BREAM												
PIKE												
CARP												
BULL-HEAD												
CHUB												
ROACH												
RUFFE												
NASE												
LOACH												
BURBOT												
GRAYLING												
CHARR												
ZANDER												
SALMON												
SPIRLIN												
RAINBOW TROUT												
BROWN TROUT												
MINNOW												
DACE												

PRINCIPAL FLIES			MAR.	APR.	MAY	JUNE	JULY	AUG.	SEPT.	OCT.
ALDER	dry	*			●	●	●			
BLACK AND SILVER	wet				●	●	●	●	●	
BLACK AND RED SPIDER	wet	*			●	●	●	●	●	
BLACK GNAT	dry	*			●	●	●	●	●	
BLACK ANT	dry						●	●		
BLACK PALMER	dry or wet	*	●	●	●	●	●	●	●	●
BLUE DUN	dry	**	●	●	●	●	●	●	●	
BROWN PALMER	dry	***	●	●	●	●	●	●	●	●
BROWN ANT	dry				●	●	●	●		
BROWN ANT RED PARTRIDGE	wet				●	●	●	●		
COACHMAN	dry	*	●	●	●	●	●	●	●	●
COQ D'AUVERGNE	wet		●	●	●	●	●	●	●	
COCH-Y-BONDHU	dry		●	●	●	●	●	●	●	●
COW DUNG	dry or wet	**	●	●	●	●				
GREENWELL'S GLORY	dry or wet	*		●	●	●	●		●	
GREY AND YELLOW PARTRIDGE	wet				●	●	●			
GOVERNOR	dry	***	●	●		●	●		●	●
GREY QUILL	dry	***						●	●	●
HARE'S EAR	dry					●	●	●		
HOFLAND'S FANCY	dry		●	●						
IRON BLUE DUN	dry	*	●	●	●	●			●	
MARCH BROWN	dry	**	●	●	●	●				
MARCH BROWN SPIDER	wet		●	●	●	●	●			
MOLE FLY	dry	*	●	●	●	●	●			
OLIVE DUN	dry	***	●	●	●	●	●	●	●	
OLIVE SPINNER	dry	**	●	●	●	●	●	●	●	
OAK FLY	dry				●	●				
ORANGE DUN	dry					●	●	●	●	
PALE WATERY DUN	dry					●	●			
PALE WATERY SPINNER	dry					●	●			
PANAMA	dry	*	●	●	●	●	●	●	●	
PHALÈNE	dry	*	●	●	●	●	●	●	●	
RED QUILL	dry	***	●	●	●	●	●	●	●	
RED PALMER	dry or wet	***	●	●	●	●	●	●		
RED ANT	dry	*					●	●	●	
SAND FLY	dry	*		●	●	●	●	●	●	
SHERRY SPINNER	dry	**					●	●	●	
SPECIAL FANCY	dry		●	●	●	●	●	●	●	
TUPS INDISPENSABLE	dry	***		●	●	●	●	●	●	
WATER CRICKET	dry or wet	*	●	●	●					
WICKHAM'S FANCY	dry			●	●	●	●	●	●	
WHITE MOTH	dry					●	●			
WILLOW	dry	*							●	●
YELLOW DUN	dry	***		●	●	●				
ZULU	dry or wet				●	●	●	●		

good general pattern *
very good **
extremely good ***

Artificials to be used during corresponding insect hatching time ●

acknowledgements

Photographs: Bichiceanu M., 8, 9, 14, 19, 26, 70, 71, 102, 103. Boyer P., 16, 17, 23, 29, 33, 34, 35, 38, 45, 54, 55, 60, 61, 66, 67, 68, 82, 83, 84, 86, 88, 92, 93, 99, 100, 101, 103, 108, 109, 112, 113, 122, 123, 125, 126, 144, 156, 157, 158, 159, 173, 178, 181, 215, 219, 220, 221, 226, 234, 255, 256. Chayito D., 79, 95, 120, 121, 137, 196, 197, 222, 223, 256. Chevallier S., 6, 14, 85, 86, 87, 92, 99, 112. Cooper J., 172, 173. Deuil H., 4, 5, 37, 88, 89, 98, 112, 125, 148, 151, 152, 153, 154, 162, 163, 172, 173, 176, 177, 182, 183, 184, 213, 214, 235, 256. Gaillard J.-F., 66, 88. Gruhl H., 84, 104, 105. Horsfall Turner E., 22. Jagusch H., 86, 98, 99, 107, 108, 109, 118, 119, 125, 127, 132, 133, 134, 135, 138, 139, 140, 141, 145, 149, 152, 153, 154, 155, 159, 165, 166, 167, 171, 174, 175, 178, 180, 181, 189, 195, 200, 206, 207, 209, 210, 211, 214, 215. Keal S., 23, 49, 130, 179, 206, 231. Linsell K., 75 (top), 239. Meurou P., 13. Nevison A., 99, 228, 229, 230, 239. Niermans E., 66, 67. Rebouleau B., 172, 174, 209, 212, 213. Steuart D., 49. Steuart K., 228. Studio Jean-Pierre, 222, 223. Van den Brande H., 155, 170, 178, 179, 185, 201, 256.

Original translation :
George Attenborough
Michael Hopf

Second impression, 1975

Published in Great Britain by
Guinness Superlatives Limited, 2 Cecil Court,
London Road, Enfield, Middlesex, England

ISBN 0 900424 16 8

Filmset in Great Britain by
Jarrold and Sons Limited, Norwich

Printed by Maury Imprimeur S.A., 45 Malesherbes, France.
Binding by Brun, 45 Malesherbes, France.

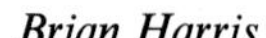

Brian Harris

Paul Boyer

Henri Deuil

Brian Harris